Independent Contractor vs. Employee Quagmire

A Tax Guide

Robert L. Sommers

SOMMERS-TAXAPEDIA.COM

ISBN-10: 0983791902
ISBN-13: 978-0-9837919-0-4

Cover art and layout by Crawshaw Design

Sommers-Taxapedia.com

Prnted in the United States of America

About the Author

Robert L. Sommers provides sophisticated legal advice concerning complex tax, business and estate planning issues.

As an acknowledged expert in the field of tax law, Bob has written hundreds of articles, columns, and action guides and spoken at dozens of events.

Bob Sommers is The Tax Prophet. He has created and written The Tax Prophet website, a vital resource to those seeking solid U.S. tax information, issue spotting and analysis.

As a full-time practicing attorney in the heart of San Francisco's Financial District, Bob owns and operates a general tax law firm.

He focuses on U.S. and foreign individuals and small companies in the areas of

- Estate planning (wills, trusts and family-based entities)
- Foreign tax
- Business start-ups and funding
- Employee stock options
- Probate and trust administration
- Federal and California tax controversies (audits, appeals and litigation)

Certified as a Tax Specialist by the California Board of Legal Specialization of the State Bar of California (a distinction earned by less than .05% of all attorneys licensed to practice law in California,) Bob also received a postgraduate legal degree (LL.M.) in taxation from New York University School of Law in 1985, the premier graduate tax program in the U.S.

Bob has testified before the US Senate's Finance Committee regarding tax scams on the Internet. He is in demand as an expert witness in both criminal and civil cases involving Tax and Trust Law, Tax Fraud, Busted Tax Shelters, and Bogus Trust Arrangements.

The Wall Street Journal, New York Times, Forbes, CNN to Money magazine and the Best of the Web have all reviewed Bob's work and his contributions to legal education. Reviews online.

You can sign up to receive his Free Newsletter, a monthly update on current tax issues.

CONTENTS

1. KEY EXECUTIVE DECISIONS.. 3

2. INTRODUCTION 4

3. TRADITIONAL ANALYSIS... 5

4. COMMON-LAW TESTS... 6

    4.1. Federal 20 Common-Law Questions 6

    4.2. Additional State Law Factors 7

5. SECTION 530 - THE FEDERAL EXCEPTION 9

    5.1. Safe Havens.. 10

    5.2. Safe Havens Are Note Exclusive 10

    5.3. Court Decisions:.. 11

6. FEDERAL LAW CHANGES... 14

7. SECTION 530 SAFE HAVENS... 15

    7.1. Judicial Precedent... 15

    7.2. Reliance on a Prior Audit 15

    7.3. Long-Standing Recognized Practice.................... 16

    7.4. Burden of Proof Shifts to IRS 17

    7.5. Later Reclassification Allowed 18

8. SPECIAL CIRCUMSTANCES 19

    8.1. Section 530 Does Not Apply to Certain Consultant Companies.. 19

    8.2. Sec. 3508: Direct Sellers of Consumer Products are Independent Contractors. 19

    8.3. Sec. 3508 Applies to Real Estate Agents 21

    8.4. Domestic Workers... 21

9. STATE LAW CONCERNS 24

    8.1. "Form Over Substance" Analysis........................ 24

8.2.   Presumption of Independence for Professionals . 26

8.3.   Regulations Involving Language Interpreters 26

8.4.   Real Estate Agents Are Not Employees 27

9.   DEALING WITH AN ENTITY 28

9.1.   IRS Position 28

9.2.   Case Law 29

9.3.   Right to Direct and Control Performance 30

9.4.   Worker's Choice of Entity 32

9.5.   Avoiding Employee Status 32

10. CONCLUSION 34

1. KEY EXECUTIVE DECISIONS

As you read through this Guide, bear in mind the following key issues and decisions that must be made with respect to the classification of a worker as an employee or independent contractor:

1. Whether to treat a worker as an independent contractor?

   a. Potential claims by the worker;

   b. Potential claims by the state's taxing or labor authorities.

   c. Potential third party claims against the business.

2. Whether the worker falls within the traditional concepts of an independent contractor?

3. Whether the worker falls within the "good faith" misclassification exception?

4. Whether IRS or state authorities have specific industry tests for independent contractor status.

5. Penalties for misclassification of a worker as an independent contractor.

   a. Mitigation of penalties if the worker filed and paid taxes on compensation as an independent contractor.

   b. Mitigation of penalties under IRS employment classification procedures.

6. Protection of the company by obtaining a Form W-9 and reporting payments on Form 1099 when required and having a written independent contractor agreement.

2. INTRODUCTION

When an employer-employee relationship exists, the tax consequences (payroll, unemployment taxes, retirement and fringe benefits) can be staggering to the employer. To avoid these extra costs, many companies seek to hire independent contractors in lieu of employees. However, the classification of a worker as either an independent contractor or employee often turns on the facts and circumstances in each particular case, and which law applies to the determination.

For example, just because a worker meets the definition of independent contractor under federal tax law does not mean the state taxing or labor authorities will consider a worker an independent contractor under their often contradictory and narrowly-interpreted set of rules. As many companies discover, the anti-business mindset of these bureaucrats causes a built-in prejudice in favor of finding a worker was an employee, even when both the worker and company insist the person was an independent contractor.

In California for instance, workers' compensation laws relating to employee versus contractor status are different from the laws applied to this status question by other state and federal agencies, further increasing the complexities in making an accurate determination.

Nevertheless, companies that need to treat workers as independent contractors should thoroughly understand the rules and, with proper advice, stand a good chance of surviving federal and state scrutiny.

3. TRADITIONAL ANALYSIS

The traditional tests (developed by the courts and referred to as "common-law" tests) to determine whether a worker is an employee or independent contractor involve the concept of control: Are the services of the worker subject to the taxpayer's (company's) will and control over what must be done and how it must be accomplished? In <u>Revenue Ruling 87-41</u>, 1987-1 CB 296, IRS developed 20 factors used to determine whether a worker is an independent contractor under the traditional common-law analysis. In general, at least 11 of these factors must show independent contractor status.

Although there are numerous safe-harbors and carve-outs for various industries, if none of those apply, the analysis falls back to the 20 common-law factors used to determine whether the employer has the requisite control over the worker to classify him or her as an employee.

4. COMMON-LAW TESTS

4.1. Federal 20 Common-Law Questions

The following questions analyze the relationship between the company and worker under the traditional 20 common law factors used by the Internal Revenue Service and should be used by the reader as a checklist:

1. Does the principal provide instructions to the worker about when, where, and how he or she is to perform the work?

2. Does the principal provide training to the worker?

3. Are the services provided by the worker integrated into the principal's business operations?

4. Must the services be rendered personally by the worker?

5. Does the principal hire, supervise and pay assistants to aid the worker?

6. Is there a continuing relationship between the principal and the worker?

7. Does the principal set the work hours and schedule?

8. Does the worker devote substantially full time to the business of the principal?

9. Is the work performed on the principal's premises?

10. Is the worker required to perform the services in an order or sequence set by the principal?

11. Is the worker required to submit oral or written reports to the principal?

COMMON-LAW TESTS

12. Is the worker paid by the hour, week, or month?

13. Does the principal pay the business or traveling expenses of the worker?

14. Does the principal furnish significant tools, materials and equipment?

15. Does the worker have a significant investment in facilities?

16. Can the worker realize a profit or loss as a result of his or her services?

17. Does the worker provide services for more than one firm at a time?

18. Does the worker make his or her services available to the general public?

19. Does the principal have the right to discharge the worker at will?

20. Can the worker terminate the relationship with the principal any time he or she wishes without incurring liability to the principal?

4.2. Additional State Law Factors

The following questions involve the additional factors used in California and possibly other states:

1. Is the worker engaged in a separately established occupation   or   business?

COMMON-LAW TESTS

2. In this locality, is the work usually done under the direction of the principal without supervision?

3. Is skill required in performing the services and accomplishing the desired results?

4. Do the parties believe they are creating an employer/employee relationship?

5. SECTION 530 - THE FEDERAL EXCEPTION

In 1978, Congress mandated that IRS stop reclassifying workers as employees, provided the company had "any reasonable basis" for treating the worker as an independent contractor. Section 530 of the Revenue Act of 1978. Since it was intended to be a temporary measure, Sec. 530 was never codified as part of the Internal Revenue Code, but it has continued in effect since enactment. Because it was not part of the Internal Revenue Code, Section 530 does not apply to independent contractor status disputes with California and the other states that incorporate the Internal Revenue Code into their tax laws.

As part of the Small Business Act, Section 1122, Congress clarified and expanded the scope of Sec. 530 (described below). Section 530 is available to companies that treated workers as independent contractors, if –

1 The company always treated the particular worker as an independent contractor and the general class of workers performing similar work as independent contractors;

2. After 1978, the company filed all returns (including information returns –- Form 1099) required for the worker and all such returns were consistent with independent contractor status; and

3. The company had a "reasonable basis" for treating the worker as an independent contractor.

A company goes a long way to meeting the Section 530 requirements by obtaining a Form W-9, timely reporting payments of more than $400 on Form 1099, when necessary, and having a written independent contractor agreement with the worker

SECTION 530

5.1. Safe Havens

There are three express safe harbors associated with the reasonable basis standard –

1. A judicial precedent, published rulings or technical advice or letter ruling to the employer;

2. A prior IRS audit in which no assessment was made on account of improper treatment of the worker; or

3. A long-standing recognized practice of a significant segment of the industry in which the individual worked.

These safe havens are described in detail in Chapter 6.

5.2. Safe Havens Are Note Exclusive

These safe havens are not exclusive; a taxpayer may demonstrate a reasonable basis in some other manner. Congress directed that the reasonable basis standard should be "construed liberally in favor of the taxpayer." General Investment Corporation, 823 F. 2d 337 (CA-9, 1987). As the following cases demonstrate, the courts have liberally construed Section 530 in favor of taxpayers; in fact, taxpayers have won most cases under Section 530 in which a legitimate controversy existed!

In Smokey Mountain Secrets, Inc., 910 F. Supp 1316, the court discussed Section 530 in relation to receiving professional advice whether workers were independent contractors or employees and ruled in favor of the taxpayer stating:

> SMS [Taxpayer] claims that its reliance on the advice of two professional tax advisors is sufficient to demonstrate a reasonable basis under §530 for

SECTION 530

> not treating its telemarketers and delivery persons as employees. I agree. Under the circumstances of this case, reliance upon the professional advice rendered by two CPAs constitutes a reasonable basis for SMS having treated its [workers] as independent contractors.

Thus, Smokey Mountain confirms that reliance on a tax professional's advice that workers are independent contractors satisfies the reasonable basis requirements of Section 530.

5.3. Court Decisions:

In Queensgate Dental Family Practice v. U.S., 91-2 USTC 50,536 (DC-PA, 1991), a corporation relied on a Pennsylvania Dental Board decision that the company could not legally treat its licensed dentists as employees. When later challenged by IRS regarding the classification of the dentists as independent contractors, the court found that reliance on the Dental board's decision was reasonable under Section 530. The court stated that the inquiry was simply whether the taxpayer's beliefs and decisions regarding his treatment of individuals as either employees or independent contractors were reasonable and made in good faith.

The Queensgate court also stated that Section 530 was enacted explicitly to eliminate the need for courts to engage in the traditional common-law practice of balancing complex factual issues in deciding whether an individual is an independent contractor or employee. The threshold inquiry is whether the taxpayer is entitled to relief under Section 530. If Section 530 applies, then the court need not apply the 20-factor test set forth in Revenue Ruling 87-41, supra, to determine worker control under

SECTION 530

the common law. If Section 530 is unavailable -- because the taxpayer either: (1) failed to consistently treat the worker as an independent contractor; (2) had no reasonable basis for treating the worker as an independent contractor; or (3) failed to file all necessary tax returns -- then the taxpayer must prove its case under the common law approach taken by IRS.

Similarly, in Darrell Harris, Inc., 770 F. Supp 1492 (DC-Okla, 1991), the court stated that the "any reasonable basis" test under Section 530 was met by a taxpayer's good faith showing in determining whether its workers were independent contractors.

In Critical Care Registered Nursing Inc. v. U.S., 91-2 USTC 50,481 (DC-PA, 1991), the taxpayer supplied specialist registered nurses to hospitals for temporary additional staffing and treated the nurses as independent contractors. The court held that the Section 530 taxpayer could apply the traditional worker control tests to establish that it had a reasonable basis for treating the workers as independent contractors. The taxpayer did not have to prove by a preponderance of the evidence (more than 50% of the evidence must favor the taxpayer) that its workers were independent contractors; it only needed to show that it had a "reasonable basis" for treating the workers as independent contractors under the traditional common law tests for worker control. This decision greatly expanded the application of Section 530 and severely undercut IRS's ability to prevail in independent contractor controversies.

In REAG, Inc., 801 F. Supp 494 (DC-Okla, 1992) the court held that under Section 530, the taxpayer need only show a "substantial rational basis" to meet its burden of proof for its

SECTION 530

decision to treat a worker as an independent contractor. This new standard fell somewhere between the usual taxpayer standard necessary to prevail under the preponderance of the evidence burden of proof and the usual IRS burden of proof of a prima facie showing of correctness. <u>REAG, Inc</u>. has been followed in another Tax Court decision, <u>J & J Cab Service, Inc. v U.S.</u>, 98-1 USTC Paragraph 50,360, however, in <u>Boles Trucking, Inc.</u>, 77 F. 3d. 236 (8th Circuit), the court decided that the taxpayer's burden of proof remains the standard preponderance of the evidence. This issue usually arises when surveys or other circumstantial evidence is introduced to show the long-standing practice of a significant segment of the industry (discussed below).

The string of pro-taxpayer decisions has continued. In <u>Apollo Drywall, Inc. v U.S.</u>, 96 USTC Para 50,196, the court ruled that IRS's interpretation of Section 530 was not "substantially justified" and awarded attorney fees and costs to the taxpayer under 26 U.S.C. Section 7430.

The federal courts expanded the reach of Section 530 and, recently, Congress followed suit. Unfortunately, California never adopted Section 530 and so the treatment of the same worker by IRS and California could be inconsistent. It is California, rather than IRS, that causes most of the tax problems for small companies in this difficult area. **Note:** This could be the situation with other states as well.

6. FEDERAL LAW CHANGES

As discussed above, as part of the Small Business Act, Section 1122, Congress clarified and expanded the scope of Sec. 530. In general, these changes benefit companies who classify their workers as independent contractors. Section 530 states that the "any reasonable basis" standard may be satisfied by meeting any of three statutory "safe havens." These safe havens are, in general:

1. Judicial precedent and published IRS rulings, whether or not they relate to the particular industry or business in which the taxpayer is engaged;

2. A past IRS audit of the taxpayer where no assessment was made regarding employment taxes of workers holding positions substantially similar to the position held by the worker whose status is at issue; and

3. A long-standing recognized practice of a significant segment of the industry in which the worker was engaged -- although the practice need not be uniform throughout the entire industry.

In fact, taxpayers with full-time household workers may obtain relief under the second or third safe haven above. In Rev. Ruling 77-279, 1977-2 IRB 12, held that even an individual providing full-time child-care services was engaged in an independent trade or business.

This constitutes a published ruling under the "judicial precedent and published IRS ruling" safe haven described above, and thus it may be applicable to full-time or part-time child care. Although the worker in <u>Rev. Ruling 77-279</u> provided child care in the worker's own home, this was not a factor in the IRS ruling.

7. SECTION 530 SAFE HAVENS

As discussed above, as part of the Small Business Act, Section 1122, Congress clarified and expanded the scope of Sec. 530. In general, these changes benefit companies who classify their workers as independent contractors.

7.1. Judicial Precedent

Court cases, including those contained in the research section of this Guide, as well as published IRS pronouncements and rulings, are considered judicial precedent. As discussed above, the holding in the Smokey Mountain case that taxpayers may rely on advice from their tax professionals on the issue constitutes reliance on judicial precedent.

7.2. Reliance on a Prior Audit

Under the original law, any audit, whether or not it involved employment tax issues, came within the prior audit safe harbor exception. The new law limits this exception to prior employment tax audits involving the particular worker, or workers performing similar jobs. Companies may rely on audits that began prior to 1977 under the old rules. **Note:** Taxpayers should retain documents from the prior audit to successfully invoke this exception.

SECTION 530 SAFE HAVENS

7.3. Long-Standing Recognized Practice

In addition, Section 530 contains a safe-harbor exceptions for a long-standing industry practice of a significant segment of the industry. Evidence and documents supplied by the Company may demonstrate that it is industry practice to treat workers as independent contractors. A showing of 25% or more of the companies in an industry, excluding the taxpayer's company, meets the significant portion of the industry standard. Often, a trade publication that polls its members as to practices in the industry may be used as evidence of the practice in a significant segment of the industry.

IRS incorrectly maintained that a long-standing recognized practice safe harbor exception required a 10-year period or that the practice was in existence prior to 1979, thus preventing emerging industries from using the exception. Congress stated that there is no fixed percentage needed to show reliance on the significant segment of the industry exception. This change benefits new industries.

The Tax Court in <u>Western Neuro Residential Centers, Inc. v US</u>, 2002-1 USTC ¶50,368, allowed the employer's established practices to show long-standing practices within the industry. Industry custom can also be demonstrated at trial through the employer's own personal experiences with competitors and testimony of workers whose experiences with other similar employers were in the capacity of independent contractors. <u>KM Systems, Inc. v. U.S.</u>, 360 F. Supp.2d 641 (D. N.J. 2005).

SECTION 530 SAFE HAVENS

7.4. Burden of Proof Shifts to IRS

Companies who rely on one of the three safe harbor exceptions will have to make a prima facie showing only; however, the company must cooperate with an IRS investigation in order to shift the burden of proof to IRS.

IRS must request information that is related to the taxpayer's position regarding reasonable basis, and compliance with IRS must not be impractical given the particular circumstances and relative costs involved. Once the burden of proof shifts to IRS, it applies to all aspects under Section 530, including the consistency and filing requirements.

With respect to the consistency requirement (workers in substantially similar positions were treated as independent contractors), consideration of the relationship between a taxpayer and a worker includes the degree of supervision and control by the taxpayer. This will permit separate treatment for the same general class of worker if the degree of supervision and control is different. The IRS Training Guide, issued in July 1996, evidently provides several pro-independent contractor interpretations that IRS is supposed to use in an audit, including –

1. The intent of the parties is considered important in cases of professional workers and in close cases.

2. The designation of a worker as an independent contractor in a contract is persuasive.

Also, exclusion of a worker from employee benefit plans is

relevant.

7.5. Later Reclassification Allowed

A company may classify a former independent contractor as an employee without jeopardizing the past classification under the consistency requirement of Section 530. Current classification of a worker as an employee will not be used as evidence of an improper classification for any year prior to the reclassification.

8. SPECIAL CIRCUMSTANCES

8.1. Section 530 Does Not Apply to Certain Consultant Companies

Under IRC 530 (d), workers who, through their separate consulting company, obtained jobs as an engineer, designer, drafter, computer programmer, systems analyst, or other similar skilled worker engaged in a similar line of work are not entitled to relief under Section 530. Prior to this change in the law, professionals who formed single-owner consulting businesses considered themselves independent contractors, but Congress then singled out high-tech programmers, engineers and analysts and reclassified them as employees of the companies receiving their services. Thereafter, many large and mid-sized high-tech firms stopped hiring professionals operating as independent companies and forced them to join the payroll as employees.

8.2. Sec. 3508: Direct Sellers of Consumer Products are Independent Contractors.

Under IRC Sec. 3508, certain individuals who are common law employees are not treated as such for federal income and employment tax purposes. These individuals are referred to as statutory non-employees. They include qualified real estate agents and direct sellers. For purposes of §3508, a "direct seller" includes any person who meets the following conditions:

1. selling (or soliciting the sale of) consumer

2. products to the ultimate consumer or for resale to a buyer on a buy-sell basis, a deposit-commission basis, or any similar basis, provided the sale or resale of the product occurs in a place other than in a permanent retail establishment, or

SPECIAL CIRCUMSTANCES

3. the delivery or distribution of newspapers or shopping news (including any services that are directly related to such trade or business such as solicitation of customers or collection of receipts). Substantially all of the remuneration received by the seller must be directly related to sales or other output rather than to the number of hours worked.

4. Finally, the services of the seller must be performed pursuant to a written contract between the seller and the person for whom the services are performed that provides that the seller is not treated as an employee with respect to such services for federal employment tax purposes.

The TEFRA Conference Report (§3508 was added to the Internal Revenue Code under TEFRA in 1982) observed that a direct seller can include someone who attempts to increase direct sales activities of direct sellers and who realizes remuneration dependent on the productivity of those direct sellers. These activities include providing motivation or encouragement, imparting skill, knowledge or experience or recruiting activities. H.R. Rep. No. 760, 97th Cong., 2d Sess. 651 (1982).

The term "consumer products" includes intangible consumer services, such as cable television subscriptions. Cleveland Inst. & Elec. Inc. v. U.S., 787 F. Supp. 741 (N.D. Ohio 1992); The R Corp. v. U.S., 94-2 USTC ¶ 50,380 (M.D. Fla. 1994). Thus, direct sellers of cable television subscriptions are considered independent contractors under §3508.

SPECIAL CIRCUMSTANCES

8.3. Sec. 3508 Applies to Real Estate Agents

Under IRC Sec. 3508, qualified real estate agents meeting the following requirements are classified as independent contractors:

1. The individual is a licensed real estate agent;

2. Substantially all of the agent's compensation is directly related to sales or other output (including the performance of services) rather than to the number of hours worked; and

3. The individual's services are performed pursuant to a written contract which provides that the individual will not be treated as an employee with respect to such services for federal tax purposes.

Property management services and loan activities do not fall within IRC Sec. 3508.

8.4. Domestic Workers

Many taxpayers are concerned that by hiring a neighbor's teenager as a baby-sitter or by using a housekeeper on a part-time basis, they are required to file the federal information return (Form 942) and pay Social Security and Medicare taxes on their "employees." Contrary to the position taken by both IRS and numerous tax commentators, part-time domestic workers may qualify as independent contractors; and in such cases, taxpayers are under no obligation to file tax returns or pay taxes.

SPECIAL CIRCUMSTANCES

Although there are no reported cases involving household workers and Section 530, IRS in Rev Proc. 85-18, 1985-1 CB 518, has acknowledged the validity of Section 530 in general and, specifically, in its application to all taxes imposed on an employer -- including IRC Sec. 3111 Medicare and Social Security taxes involving household employees.

The decisions in Critical Care Registered Nursing, Inc. and REAG, Inc., which constitute judicial precedent under the first safe-harbor above, provide the legal justification for classifying most part-time baby-sitters, housekeepers, gardeners, and other household workers as independent contractors. Some common-law tests applicable to a part-time household worker may include whether the worker: (1) works part-time for any one person; (2) works for one or more unrelated persons at the same time; (3) negotiates dates, times and hours for the work; (4) is paid on a per-job basis; (5) is free to accept or decline assignments; (6) offers his or her services to the public (such as through advertising or classified ads); (7) works in teams, uses helpers or delegates the work to someone else; (8) uses his or her own tools and equipment; (9) is hired to produce a certain result (a clean house, a well-groomed garden) and is not given step-by-step instructions for accomplishing the task; (10) is not trained to perform the services in a particular manner by the person hiring the worker; and (11) does not have a continuing relationship with the person hiring the worker.

Also, according to some courts, the taxpayer's burden of proof has been substantially lowered -- if several of these factors demonstrate independent contractor status, that should be enough to satisfy the

SPECIAL CIRCUMSTANCES

"any reasonable basis test" under Section 530.

Remember, Section 530 contains a major hurdle: to qualify for relief, taxpayers must not have "treated" household workers as employees, something done by filing Form 942.

9. STATE LAW CONCERNS

8.1. "Form Over Substance" Analysis

Note: Although the following discussion involves California, it could apply to other states as well.

Unlike the federal government, which has been tilting toward finding an independent contractor relationship in close cases, the California's Employment Development Department (EDD) has maintained a traditional paternalistic attitude of invariably finding an employment relationship. California continues to apply the traditional common-law tests to determine independent contractor status.

EDD focuses on the "appearance of independence" shown by the worker, rather than engaging in an intellectually honest analysis of the "control" issue. Therefore, it is crucial that the worker hold himself or herself out to the public as being in business.

While one may question EDD's insistence on form and appearance as being irrelevant to the control issue — the true substance of the relationship — that governs the independent contractor status, compliance with EDD's cosmetic appearance requirements is not unduly difficult and can insulate both company and worker from adverse tax consequences arising from a reclassification of the worker as an employee.

State Law Concerns

Since the focus of most EDD auditors is on the independent business trappings of the worker, the following should be considered by companies concerned about this issue –

- The worker should conduct business under a fictitious business name. Auditors look for individual names on Form 1099's. Use of "John Smith and Associates" or "John Smith Consulting," rather than merely "John Smith" is evidence of an independent business relationship.

- The worker should have his or her own federal identification number, rather than using a social security number. An auditor reviewing Form 1099's will be less inclined to question a worker who uses a federal ID number.

- The worker should have a business license and have a listing or advertisement in the telephone directory under the company name. These steps are helpful in convincing an auditor that the worker is engaged in an independent business.

- The worker should have printed stationery, business cards and website or other on-line business presence. Resumes, promotional materials and email addresses should use the company's name. For a business located in the home, the answering machine and greetings should be in the company's name (EDD is known to call just to check on how the phone is answered).

State Law Concerns

- Invoices should be on the workers stationary and for services rendered. Avoid statements that look like time sheets. When possible, workers should bill on a flat rate per project, rather than on an hourly rate. The parties should have a written contract stating that the worker is responsible for completing the job, may hire sub-contractors or have employees work on the project, and is liable for contract damages for negligence in the performance of the contract.

- The company should have provisions requiring that the worker cooperate with the company in any employment tax audit, including presentation of the worker's Schedule C or other tax forms showing that income was reported as an independent business.

8.2. Presumption of Independence for Professionals

Under California Unemployment Insurance Code Section 656, there is a rebuttable presumption in favor of independent contractor status for those engaged in a professional practice, such as physicians, attorneys, accountants, engineers and architects. Scientists in the physical, chemical, biological and natural sciences also fall within this presumption. Those involved in the social sciences do not enjoy the benefit of this presumption. If the presumption applies, then the burden of proof shifts to the state to prove that an employment relationship existed.

8.3. Regulations Involving Language Interpreters

There is a new set of regulations and criteria for determining whether a "language interpreter" is an independent contractor.

State Law Concerns

See Regulation 4304-9 of Title 22, California Code of Regulations. Language interpreters include translators of text and interpreters of conversations. This set of new regulations was enacted after extensive hearings and is generally favorable toward the classification of such workers as independent contractors.

Although seminar presenters are not literally within the definition of language interpreters, the criteria for determining independence is similar and these new regulations can be argued, by analogy, to apply to professionals in the social sciences that are performing similar work.

8.4. Real Estate Agents Are Not Employees

In Grubb & Ellis Co. v. Spengler (1983) 143 Cal.App.3d 890, a California court of appeals held that IRC Sec. 3508 applied to an employment relationship between a California real estate agent and his company. The court stated that the minimum wage law excluded outside sales persons.

In an unpublished decision, Tolentino v Redhill Remax Realty, 2003 Cal. APP (Unpub) Lexis 11390, the court confirmed that a real estate salesperson is not the employee of his or her broker, citing Grubb & Ellis Co. and IRC Sec. 3508. In Ramirez v. Yosemite Water Co., 62 Cal. App. 4th 912 (1998), the court cited with approval the analysis in Grubb & Ellis Co. that outside salesperson are not covered by minimum wage and overtime pay rules because these employees control their own hours and are paid on a commission basis.

9. DEALING WITH AN ENTITY

Another approach which may avoid the question of classification altogether is the imposition of an entity between a company and a worker, such that the company contracts directly with the entity, thereby skirting the issue of worker classification entirely. The entity replaces the worker as the contracting vehicle, but - the worker owns the entity.

> **Note:** This approach does not work for those providing services as an engineer, designer, drafter, computer programmer, systems analyst, or other similar skilled worker engaged in a similar line of work (see the discussion above).

In most cases, if the company contracts with an entity which, in turn, enters into an employment agreement with an individual worker and, pursuant to the company-entity contract, the worker performs services for the company, there is no employer-employee relationship between the worker and the company.

> **Note:** The worker cannot be an independent contractor of his or her company. Officers of corporations are statutory employees under IRC 3401 (c). Also, employee leasing schemes where a worker is "hired" by a third party and "leased" back to his or her company also do not work.

9.1. IRS Position

IRS, in its training course for determining employee versus independent contractor relationships, concedes that if a company contracts directly with a corporation which, in turn, hires a worker to perform services for the company on behalf of the corporation, the relationship will be respected and the worker will not be an employee of the company. Rather, the worker will be an employee

DEALING WITH AN ENTITY

of the worker's corporation that entered into the contract with the company.

The following authorities should apply to a limited liability company to the same extent as a corporation since each is a separate entity under state law. In a Memorandum For All IRS Participants In Worker Classification Training, dated July 15, 1996 on page 38, IRS states the following:

> Questions sometimes arise concerning whether a worker, who creates a corporation through which to perform services, can be an employee of a business that engages the corporation. Provided that the corporate formalities are properly followed and at least one non-tax business purpose exists, the corporate form is generally recognized for both state law and federal law, including federal tax law, purposes.

Disregarding the corporate entity is generally an extraordinary remedy, applied by most courts only in cases of clear abuse. Thus, the worker will usually not be treated as an employee of the business, but as an employee of the corporation.

9.2. Case Law

In Sargent v. CM, 93 T.C. 572 (1989), reversed 929 F.2d 1252 (8th Cir. 1991), the 8th Circuit Court of Appeals reversed the Tax Court's finding that Gary Sargent and Steven Christoff, professional hockey players with the Minnesota Northstars hockey team, could not assign their player contracts to their respective personal service corporations. The 8th Circuit held that the personal service corporation must have the right to control the

DEALING WITH AN ENTITY

employment of the worker (an employment contract or understanding) and the personal service corporation and the entity receiving the services must have a contract for the services of the worker. The court stated:

> Accordingly, within Regulation section 31.3121(d)-(1)(c)(2), two necessary elements must be met before the corporation, rather than the service-recipient, in this case the North Stars Hockey Club, may be considered the true controller of the service-provider. First, the service-provider must be just that -- an employee of the corporation whom the corporation has the right to direct or control in some meaningful sense. [citation omitted] Second, there must exist between the corporation and the person or entity (Club) using the services a contract or similar indicium recognizing the corporation's controlling position. [citation omitted].

9.3. Right to Direct and Control Performance

The formation of a separate entity in itself is not a guarantee that the Courts will not scrutinize these relationships when called into question. A crucial factor in determining employment status, and one that must be considered, is the right to direct and control. If the employer has this right, whether or not that right is exercised, the courts have routinely decided that the "independent contractor" is actually an employee (even if the person is licensed).

When a company exercised near total control over the worker, the tax court disregarded the worker's corporation and held the worker to be an employee of the company. The following case, involving a basketball player who personally guaranteed his

DEALING WITH AN ENTITY

entity's contract with the Houston Rockets (the company), illustrates some of the issues that could cause a company to be considered the employer of a worker, despite the imposition of an entity between company and worker.

In <u>Leavell v. Cm</u>, 104 T.C. 140 (1995), the Tax Court found that because of the tightly controlled contractual terms and conditions imposed on a personal service corporation and because the employee of the personal service corporation had to personally guarantee the performance of the terms and conditions of the contract between the service-recipient and the personal service corporation, the individual was considered the owner of the funds paid to the personal service corporation. In other words, the personal service corporation was disregarded with respect to ownership of the funds received. The Tax Court was divided as to its reasoning, cognizant of its reversal in the <u>Sargent</u> case quoted above.

In <u>Leavell</u>, the Tax Court seized upon the language of the Uniform Player Contract, which was the standard contract in the National Basketball Association, as clearly indicating that the company contemplated binding a specific individual person to perform the services for, and under the specific supervision of, the basketball team. The Tax Court concluded the contract gave the service recipient a degree of control over an individual player "that transcends the control most employers have over their employees."

The situation in <u>Leavell</u> involved a basketball player for the Houston Rockets. A company, by steering clear of the extreme control exhibited by the Houston Rockets with respect to Leavell's

DEALING WITH AN ENTITY

contract, should be able to avoid employer-employee status with respect to its contracts with corporations formed by its workers.

9.4. Worker's Choice of Entity

If a worker decides to form an entity, the issue becomes which type of entity should be formed. While a company may prefer dealing with an S corporation (income and loss are reported by the shareholders and not the corporation), the worker may prefer forming an LLC (taxed similar to an S corporation) which is treated as a disregarded entity, thereby permitting the worker to report the business income and expenses as a sole practitioner (Form 1040, Schedule "C").

A corporation eliminates the company's obligation to file Form 1099 (corporations do not receive Form 1099's) and there is solid precedent supporting the legal position that a company contracting with a corporation falls outside the worker classification controversy. In contrast, a single member LLC eliminates the need for an additional tax return, but Form 1099s are required for payments to an LLC, a distinct drawback. In any event, forming a regular "C" corporation (a separate taxpaying entity) is usually not advantageous.

9.5. Avoiding Employee Status

To the largest extent possible, the company should not control how the worker performs the job. Allowing the personal service corporation to substitute a worker for a particular job, as long as the substitute worker has the requisite skills to do the job, should be permitted. Also, the corporation should strictly follow all corporate formalities regarding corporate minutes, resolutions and documents. The company should contract only with the corporation and all documents should reflect that the agreement is made between the company and the corporation.

10.   CONCLUSION

The rules involving classification of workers as independent contractors are complex and contradictory. It largely depends on whether the federal government or a state is investigating the situation. In both situations, however, it is important to document the worker's status and to the extent possible, the worker should have a separate and independent business with all the usual business trappings, such as a fictitious business name, stationery, business cards and yellow page or similar advertising announcing the business to the public.

If the company is dealing with an entity, rather than an individual, the case for independent contractor status is strengthened. The company should have on file a Form W-9, and should send a timely Form 1099 to the worker for payments exceeding $400 per year, unless the company has contracted with a corporation.

First, look for an exception under Section 530 and the specific exceptions for certain worker classifications. Then, analyze the worker relationship under the 20 common-law factor and state law factor tests. Remember, some of these factors may be shifted by a carefully worded contract between the worker and company. In a close case, consider obtaining a written opinion by a tax professional, as occurred in <u>Smokey Mountain</u>.

NOTE: THE FOLLOWING ARE EXAMPLES FOR ILLUSTRATION PURPOSES ONLY.

APPENDIX A

[Form Cover Letter]

Date

Name of Contractor
Name of Company
Address
City, State and ZIP

RE: AGREEMENT TO PERFORM SERVICES

Dear Contractor:

Enclosed is the Agreement to Perform Services for Anycompany, LLC. It is expressly understood and agreed that your company will be performing services as an independent contractor and that you or your company will not take any position with any government agency to the contrary.

This means that you will ***not list*** Anycompany, LLC as your "employer" on any tax form or with respect to any claim for benefits, such as unemployment benefits or worker's compensation. The correct response to any question regarding working with, or payments received from, Anycompany is that you were "self-employed."

Please sign the acknowledgement of this letter below, and return it along with a copy of the signed contract.

Very truly yours,
Anycompany, LLC

_____
George Twig, President

I have read and agree to be bound
by the terms of this letter and the
Agreement to Perform Services.

Dated: _____

Name of Company: _____

By: _____

print name: _____

APPENDIX B

MEMORANDUM

To: Client
From: Professional
Re: Independent Contractor vs. Employee status

Enclosed is a standard contract that should be used in connection with hiring an independent contractor. Also, a cover letter should be sent and signed by the worker.

To avoid a reclassification by California's EDD of a worker from an independent contractor to an employee, the following steps should be taken:

- The worker should conduct business under a fictitious business name. Auditors look for individual names on Form 1099's. Use of "John Smith and Associates" or "John Smith Consulting," rather than merely "John Smith" is evidence of an independent business relationship.

  NOTE: it is preferable (some companies make it mandatory) that the worker form an LLC or corporation and that all Company payments be made to the entity.

  NOTE: If the worker's company is a Corporation, there is no Form 1099 requirement.

- The worker should have his or her own federal

identification number, rather than using a social security number. An auditor reviewing Form 1099's will be less inclined to question a worker who uses a federal ID number.

- The worker should have a business license and have a listing or advertisement in the telephone directory under the company name. These steps are helpful in convincing an auditor that the worker is engaged in an independent business. The worker should work for more than one company.

- The worker should have printed stationery and business cards. Resumes and promotional materials should use the company's name. For a business located in the home, the answering machine and greetings should be in the company's name.

- Invoices should be on the workers stationary and list services rendered. Avoid statements that look like time sheets. When possible, workers should bill on a flat rate per project, rather than on an hourly rate.

- The parties should have a written contract stating that the worker is responsible for completing the job, may hire sub-contractors or have employees work on the project, and is liable for contract damages for negligence in the performance of the contract.

- The company should have provisions requiring the worker to cooperate with the company in any employment tax audit, including presentation of the worker's Schedule C or other tax forms showing that the income was reported as an independent business.

· The worker should never file an unemployment claim listing the Company as an employer. The worker should signify in writing that he/she understands that the worker must mark down "self-employed" with respect to any sums received from the Company.

APPENDIX C
CONTRACT FOR SERVICES

Contractor

Company Name:_____

Address:_____

Telephone:_____

EMAIL:_____

EIN: _____

Services to be performed ("Services"):

_____

_____

The following are the terms and conditions covering the hiring of the above independent contractor (hereafter "Contractor") by *Anycompany, LLC, a California LLC* (hereafter "Company").

1. **Services.** Company hereby hires Contractor to perform the services above-described.

2. **Compensation.** Contractor shall be paid *[DESCRIBE PAYMENT, e.g. the rate per hour with time determined in 1/10 hour increments. Contractor shall also be reimbursed for long-distance telephone charges.]* Contractor shall not be entitled to any other compensation or benefits. All other costs will be the responsibility

of Contractor. Contractor shall submit invoices for services rendered on Contractor's letterhead.

3. **Performance of Services**. Contractor is solely responsible for performing the Services in a competent and professional manner and will take no actions that could reflect negatively on Company. Contractor warrants and represents that Contractor is an independent contractor engaged in the business of providing said Services, and is duly qualified to provide the Services. Contractor will be held legally responsible and liable for any and all breaches of this Agreement by Contractor that cause damage or loss to Company. Contractor agrees to make good faith efforts to comply with the Company's written policies pertaining to all workers.

Contractor will use its own business equipment and materials in connection with the work to be performed under this Agreement. Any and all costs incurred by Contractor in connection with the work performed under this Agreement shall be the exclusive responsibility of Contractor, unless there is an explicit agreement to the contrary with respect to a specific project. Contractor and Company acknowledge that Contractor may work for other companies, (but not at the same time), provided Contractor is not in violation of this Agreement or Company's agreement or other entities. Nothing in this Agreement shall limit Contractor's right to work for other companies or to obtain direct business in Contractor's areas of expertise. Contractor will set his or her own hours and work schedule, and will be responsible for performing his or her services without any training, supervision or control by Company. Contractor is not required to perform the services personally, but may hire other competent people or companies to provide those services, provided Contractor and those individuals or companies are in full compliance with this Agreement.

4. **Contractor as Independent Contractor.** Contractor is an independent contractor and shall be solely responsible and liable for the payment of any and all taxes, levies, licenses and fees, whether federal, state or local, of every type and description, arising from, or pertaining to, any and all consideration or compensation paid to Contractor under this Agreement or for any services performed hereunder. Contractor shall not : (1) make any claims; (2) take any position or make any representations to any government agency or instrumentality; or (3) apply for any benefits with any government agency or instrumentality (or in any court or other tribunal), which may violate, be inconsistent with, or be contrary to, its status as an independent contractor. It is expressly understood and agreed that Company will not: (a) withhold FICA (Social Security) from Contractor's payments; (b) make state or federal unemployment insurance contributions on Contractor's behalf; (c) withhold state or federal income tax from payments to Contractor; (d) make disability contributions on behalf of Contractor; or (e) obtain worker's compensation, employer's liability or disability insurance on behalf of Contractor.

5. **Cooperation with Company.** Contractor agrees to cooperate and complete any written surveys, questionnaires or statements provided by Company in connection with Contractor's independent contractor status. Contractor will promptly notify Company of any inquiries by any third party, including, but not limited to, federal, state or local employment, payroll or taxing authorities, or any other company or person (hereafter collectively "Third Party") inquiring about or investigating the working relationship between the parties hereto. Contractor and Company hereby warrant, covenant, promise and agree not to sign any written document or make any oral statement to any Third Party which is inconsistent

with, or contrary to, this Agreement. Contractor will not list Company as an "employer" on any government forms or documents or in any communication with any government officials, whether oral or in writing. Contractor acknowledges that Contractor is "self-employed" for purposes of Unemployment Insurance or other similar benefits and will mark any forms or documentation relating to such claims accordingly.

6. **Contractor's Indemnification Regarding Payment of Taxes.** Contractor shall indemnify, defend and hold harmless Company from any and all fees, costs, payments, fines, losses, liabilities, penalties and expenses (including reasonable attorney's fees and costs), and any interest paid thereon, or incurred by Company, as a result of any violations of paragraph 5 above. Contractor further agrees to maintain and furnish the Company with sufficient evidence of all appropriate business licenses, workers' compensation insurance and employer's liability insurance coverage for Contractor and all persons employed or utilized by Contractor, as well as sufficient general liability coverage and auto insurance coverage in such amounts as determined by Company.

Contractor will provide all documentation and will comply with all requests for information by Company with respect to any services performed under this Agreement. If the Company is audited, Contractor agrees to cooperate with all requests to provide evidence concerning Contractor's work relationship with Company, including the furnishing of Contractor's Schedule C to IRS Form 1040 (or other appropriate schedule(s)) filed with the Internal Revenue Service, the Franchise Tax Board, and/or any other state or local taxing authorities for the tax years under audit.

7. **Contractor's Indemnification Regarding Injury**. Contractor

shall indemnify, defend and hold harmless Company from and against any and all claims, causes of action, losses, liabilities, expenses and damages (including, but not limited to, court costs and reasonable attorney's fees), for any loss, injury, disability or death to any person, or loss, damage, destruction or injury to any property, arising or resulting from, or in connection with this Agreement, Contractor's performance or non-performance under this Agreement, or any breach of this Agreement by Contractor.

8. **Confidentiality.** As a material inducement to Company to retain Contractor and to pay Contractor compensation for services under this Agreement, Contractor covenants and agrees that Contractor shall not, at any time, during or after the term of this Agreement, directly or indirectly, disclose, use or transfer, by or through any medium of expression for any purpose, any confidential or privileged information (including, but not limited to, the identities, needs and requirements of venders, clients, present and potential projects, financial or accounting information) which has been discovered, disclosed or made available to Contractor by Company, or its agents, in connection with this Agreement.

9. **Warranties As to Contractual Capacity**. Each party warrants and represents to the other party that they: (1) have the requisite legal authority and ability to enter into this Agreement and perform according to its terms; (2) have no legal, contractual or other restrictions preventing them from entering into this Agreement and performing according to its terms; (3) are ready, willing and able to perform under this Agreement; and (4) are not party to any other Agreement or understanding, and do not have any obligations which conflict, or may conflict, with the terms, conditions and purposes of this Agreement. Contractor further warrants and represents that the owner and any person working for Contractor

is a United States citizen or has a valid permit to work in the United States.

Contractor further warrants that it will maintain the level of competence required by each state in which the services will be performed and will notify Company at any time that Contractor becomes unqualified under the applicable state or federal law. The deadlines, if any, for the services performed under this Agreement are determined by the Company's customers and clientele and not by Company.

The work performed by Contractor shall be subject to Company's general right of inspection and supervision to secure the satisfactory completion of the assignments given in accordance with this Agreement, any agreements between Company and its customers or clients and under the applicable state and federal law. The standards of performance are set forth in the Company's various materials and memoranda, as amended from time to time, and are available to Contractor.

10. **General Conditions Regarding the Performance of Services**. All services will be contracted for on a per-assignment basis. Contractor has the right to decline any assignment offered under this Agreement and Company is not obligated to offer any assignments to Contractor, or use its services under this Agreement. It is understood that Contractor has other clients and may, from time to time, need to modify its work schedule to satisfy other business obligations. Contractor may terminate any assignment under this Agreement due to conflicting business obligations, upon reasonable notice to Company.

Contractor and Company agree that all future work

performed by Contractor will be subject to the terms and conditions of this Agreement, whether or not there is a specific reference to this Agreement. Contractor and Company further agree that this Agreement will supersede any subsequent agreement or understanding, unless that subsequent agreement or understanding expressly states in writing that it is to supersede this Agreement. Except as otherwise provided in this Agreement, this Agreement may be terminated by either party by giving written notice to the other party and stating the termination date, at least 15 days prior to the date stated for termination.

11. **Expiration Of Agreement**. Subject to the right of termination under paragraph 10 above and the right of immediate termination under this paragraph, this agreement shall remain in full force and effect until _____. Company may terminate Contractor immediately if Contractor breaches his obligations under this Agreement with respect to the requirements imposed by Comcast and other entities. At the expiration of this Agreement, Contractor agrees to return any and all keys to Company's premises and files, and any and all documents, price lists, catalogues or brochures, files (paper or computer), books, or any copy of any such document or material received or made during the term of this Agreement which belong to Company.

12. **Arbitration.** Any controversy or claim arising out of, or relating to this Agreement, or the breach thereof, shall be settled by arbitration in the County of _____, State of *[State]* in accordance with the rules then obtaining of the American Arbitration Association ("AAA") with one arbitrator, and judgment upon the award rendered may be entered and enforced in any court having jurisdiction thereof. The parties in good faith shall agree to the selection of an arbitrator. If the parties cannot agree

or if a party fails to cooperate in the selection process, then the AAA shall select the arbitrator.

13. **Notices.** Any notice required or desired to be given under this Agreement shall be deemed given if in writing and sent certified mail to its address stated above in the case of Contractor, or to its principal office in the case of Company.

14. **Waiver of Breach.** The waiver by Company of a breach of any provision of this Agreement by Contractor shall not operate or be construed as a waiver of any subsequent breach by Contractor. No waiver shall be valid unless in writing and signed by Company.

15. **Assignment.** Contractor may assign any of its rights or delegate any of its duties or obligations under this Agreement; provided however, the Contractor will remain primarily liable for the services rendered by such assignee. Company, in Company's reasonable discretion, may either consent or refuse to consent to such assignment. As a condition to consent, Company may require the assignee to sign a new independent contractor's contract (which may contain terms and conditions different from this Agreement); however, the signing of such a contract shall not relieve the Contractor of any liability under this Agreement. The rights and obligations of Company under this Agreement shall inure to the benefit of and shall be binding upon the successors and assigns of Company. Company may assign this contract to a corporation, partnership or other entity, without the consent of Contractor and Contractor hereby agrees to look solely to such assignee for performance under this Agreement, including the payment of sums due to Contractor, from and after the date of such assignment.

16. *[State]* **Law Controlling**. This Agreement shall be interpreted and construed in accordance with the laws of the state of *[State]*.

17. **Attorney's Fees And Costs**. If either party breaches this Agreement and a lawsuit or arbitration is brought hereon, the prevailing party shall recover as additional damages, the costs of such action, including reasonable attorney's fees provided that: (i) such party is clearly the prevailing party; and (ii) the amount of the fees and costs awarded are reasonable as measured against the amount actually awarded or defended against, as the case may be.

18. **Paragraph Headings**. The paragraph headings are for convenience only and do not alter, modify or interpret this Agreement.

19. **Severability**. If a court of competent jurisdiction or an arbitrator declares any portion of this Agreement invalid, illegal or unenforceable, the remaining portions of this Agreement will nevertheless be carried into full force and effect.

20. **Number and Gender**. Throughout this Agreement, the masculine, feminine and neuter genders shall be deemed to include the others and the singular, the plural, and vice-versa.

21. **Priority of this Agreement**. This Agreement has priority and supersedes any other agreement made between the parties, whether written or oral, in case such other agreement conflicts with or is inconsistent with this Agreement.

21. **Amendments**. This Agreement cannot be altered, modified or amended orally, but only in writing signed by both parties by a

document which specifically refers to this Agreement. Any other agreements between the parties which do not specifically reference this agreement, will constitute separate and independent agreements.

22. **Entire Agreement.** This agreement represents the entire understanding of the parties; there are no other warranties or representations, whether written or oral, affecting this agreement.

23. **Definition of Contractor**. Under this Agreement, the term "Contractor" shall include the person above named as the Contractor and his or her partners, members, shareholders, independent contractors, agents, servants, employees, sub-contractors, other contractors, representatives, employers, assignees, acquaintances and any and all persons directly or indirectly acting for or with the person named above as the Contractor.

24. **Future Cooperation, No Inconsistent Positions.** Each party agrees to cooperate and execute any and all documents, filings and instructions necessary or appropriate to carry the objectives of this agreement into effect. The parties hereto shall not make any statements or take any positions, whether written or oral, with any third party, government agency or government instrumentality which are inconsistent with, or contrary to, this agreement.

25. **Retroactive Effect of This Agreement**. Both parties acknowledge and agree that this Agreement documents in writing and accurately reflects the ongoing relationship between Contractor and Company, effective to the first time Contractor performed services for Company. Each party warrants and

represents that there have been no breaches of this Agreement and that all covenants and conditions contained in this Agreement have been fully performed by the appropriate party, from the first time Contractor performed services for Company to the date this Agreement was signed.

26. **No Public Comment; Non-Disparagement**. Worker and Company agree that the terms of this Agreement are strictly confidential. Neither party will make any private or public Comments with respect to the other party, any vendor, customer or owner, office or employee of Company, or about the terms and conditions of the Agreement. Following termination of this Agreement for any reason, neither party shall make any negative oral or written Comments or statements to or with any third party about the other party hereto in connection with this Agreement.
As used in this paragraph, the term, "Comments," includes written and oral communications of all types, including all electronic, internet and web-based communications, messages, texts, voice mails, emails, and postings to bulletin boards and social media sites.

IN WITNESS WHEREOF, the parties hereto have signed this Agreement on the day and year first above written.

Dated: *[City]*, *[State]*: _____, 201_____

[SIGNATURES]

12. RESOURCE MATERIAL

TABLE OF AUTHORITIES AND RESOURCES

Item   **Description**   **Page**

1   Revenue Ruling 87-41, 1987-1 CB 296 53

2   General Investment Corporation v U.S.,
823 F. 2d. 337 (CA-9, 1987) 65

3   Section 530 of the Revenue Act of 1978
(as Amended by Small Business Act of 1122) 69

4   Smokey Mountain Secrets v U.S.,
910 F Supp 1316 77

5   Queensgate Dental Family Practice v U.S.,
91-2 USTC 50,536 (CD-PA, 1991) 91

6   Darrell Harris, Inc. v U.S., 770 F. Supp 1492
(CD-Okla, 1991) 97

7   Critical Care Registered Nursing Inc. v U.S.,
91-2 USTC 50,481 (DC-PA, 1991) 107

8   REAG, Inc. v U.S. , 801 F. Supp 494 (DC-Okla, 1992) 114

9   J and J Cab Service v U.S., 98-1 USTC 50,360 128

10 Boles Trucking, Inc., v U.S. 96-1 USTC 50,112 142

11 Apollo Drywall, Inc. v U.S. 1993 US – Dist
(Lexis 5611 (April 6, 1993) 151

12 Revenue Ruling 77-279, 1977-2 IRB 12 162

RESOURCE MATERIAL

TABLE OF AUTHORITIES AND RESOURCES (cont.)

Item   Description   **Page**

13   Western Neuro v U.S., 2002-1 USTC, 50,368 167

14   KM Systems v U.S., 360 F Supp 2d 641 175

15   California Unemployment Insurance
     Code Section 656 182

16   Grubb & Ellis Co. v Spengler (1983)
     143 Cal App 3d 890 183

17   Ramirez v Yosemite Water Co., 62 Cal App 4th 912 190

18   Section 1706 of the Reform Act 207

19   Internal Revenue Code Section 3508 209

20   Cleveland Institute v U.S., 787 F Supp 741 211

21   The R Corp. v U.S., 94-2 USTC 50,380 225

22   Revenue Procedure 85-18, 1985-1 CB 518 231

23   Sargent v CM 929 F 2d 1252 (1989) 237

24   Leavell v CM, 104 TC 140 (1995) 252

On-Line Resources

The IRS Training Guide, issued in July, 1996 (160 pages)

http://www.irs.gov/pub/irs-utl/emporind.pdf

1: REVENUE RULING 87-41

SUMMARY:

The employment status of technical service specialists was determined under generally applicable common law standard definitions for the obligation for the Federal Insurance Contributions Act, the Federal Unemployment Tax Act, the Collection of Income Tax at the source of Wages, and a determination of the affect of § 530 (d) of the Revenue Act of 1978, as added by § 1706 of the Tax Reform Act of 1986. Employment Tax Regulations: §§ 31.3121 (d)-1 (c); 31.3306 (i)-1; and 31.3401 (c)-1 provided guidelines for the determination. A specialist, who was provided by a firm to a client for a project was an employee of the providing firm because the firm regularly reviewed the programmer's work, could replace or terminate the programmer, and restricted the client's ability to hire the specialist outright. Specialists, who did not report to the firm after the initial placement, were not paid by the firm, were free to work for unrelated individuals, was not controlled by the firm, and was paid by the firm only if the client remitted funds for such payment were not employees.

APPLICABLE SECTIONS:
Section 3121.-Definitions
26 CFR 31.3121 (d)-1: Who are employees. (Also Sections 3306, 3401
31.3306 (i)-1, 31.3401 (c)-1.)

TEXT:

Employment status under section 530 (d) of the Revenue Act of 1978. Guidelines are set forth for determining the employment status of a taxpayer (technical service specialist) affected by section 530 (d) of the Revenue Act of 1978, as added by section 1706 of the Tax Reform Act of 1986. The specialists are to be classified as employees under generally applicable common law standards.

ISSUE

In the situations described below, are the individuals employees under the common law rules for purposes of the Federal Insurance Contributions Act (FICA), the Federal Unemployment Tax Act (FUTA), and the Collection of Income Tax at Source on Wages (chapters 21, 23, and 24 respectively, subtitle C, Internal Revenue Code)? These situations illustrate the application of section 530 (d) of the Revenue Act of 1978, 1978-3 (Vol. 1) C.B. 119 (the 1978 Act), which was added by section 1706 (a) of the Tax Reform Act of 1986, 1986-3 (Vol. 1) C.B. 698 (the 1986 Act) (generally effective for services performed and remuneration paid after December 31, 1986).

1: REVENUE RULING 87-41

FACTS

In each factual situation, [*2] an individual worker (Individual), pursuant to an arrangement between one person (Firm) and another person (Client), provides services for the Client as an engineer, designer, drafter, computer programmer, systems analyst, or other similarly skilled worker engaged in a similar line of work.

Situation 1

The Firm is engaged in the business of providing temporary technical services to its clients. The Firm maintains a roster of workers who are available to provide technical services to prospective clients. The Firm does not train the workers but determines the services that the workers are qualified to perform based on information submitted by the workers.

The Firm has entered into a contract with the Client. The contract states that the Firm is to provide the Client with workers to perform computer programming services meeting specified qualifications for a particular project. The Individual, a computer programmer, enters into a contract with the Firm to perform services as a computer programmer for the Client's project, which is expected to last less than one year. The Individual is one of several programmers provided by the Firm to the Client. The Individual has not been an employee of [*3] or performed services for the Client (or any predecessor or affiliated corporation of the Client) at any time preceding the time at which the Individual begins performing services for the Client. Also, the Individual has not been an employee of or performed services for or on behalf of the Firm at any time preceding the time at which the Individual begins performing services for the Client.

The Individual's contract with the Firm states that the Individual is an independent contractor with respect to services performed on behalf of the Firm for the Client. The Individual and the other programmers perform the services under the Firm's contract with the Client. During the time the Individual is performing services for the Client, even though the Individual retains the right to perform services for other persons, substantially all of the Individual's working time is devoted to performing services for the Client. A significant portion of the services are performed on the Client's premises. The Individual reports to the Firm by accounting for time worked and describing the progress of the work. The Firm pays the Individual and regularly charges the Client for the services performed by the [*4] Individual. The Firm generally does not pay individuals who perform services for the Client unless the Firm provided such individuals to the Client.

The work of the Individual and other programmers is regularly reviewed by the

1: REVENUE RULING 87-41

Firm. The review is based primarily on reports by the Client about the performance of these workers. Under the contract between the Individual and the Firm, the Firm may terminate its relationship with the Individual if the review shows that he or she is failing to perform the services contracted for by the Client. Also, the Firm will replace the Individual with another worker if the Individual's services are unacceptable to the Client. In such a case, however, the Individual will nevertheless receive his or her hourly pay for the work completed.

Finally, under the contract between the Individual and the Firm, the Individual is prohibited from performing services directly for the Client and, under the contract between the Firm and the Client, the Client is prohibited from receiving services from the Individual for a period of three months following the termination of services by the Individual for the Client on behalf of the Firm.

Situation 2

The Firm is a technical [*5] services firm that supplies clients with technical personnel. The Client requires the services of a systems analyst to complete a project and contacts the Firm to obtain such an analyst. The Firm maintains a roster of analysts and refers such an analyst, the Individual, to the Client. The Individual is not restricted by the Client or the Firm from providing services to the general public while performing services for the Client and in fact does perform substantial services for other persons during the period the Individual is working for the Client. Neither the Firm nor the Client has priority on the services of the Individual. The Individual does not report, directly or indirectly, to the Firm after the beginning of the assignment to the Client concerning (1) hours worked by the Individual, (2) progress on the job, or (3) expenses incurred by the Individual in performing services for the Client. No reports (including reports of time worked or progress on the job) made by the Individual to the Client are provided by the Client to the Firm.

If the Individual ceases providing services for the Client prior to completion of the project or if the Individual's work product is otherwise unsatisfactory, [*6] the Client may seek damages from the Individual. However, in such circumstances, the Client may not seek damages from the Firm, and the Firm is not required to replace the Individual. The Firm may not terminate the services of the Individual while he or she is performing services for the Client and may not otherwise affect the relationship between the Client and the Individual. Neither the Individual nor the Client is prohibited for any period after termination of the Individual's services on this job from contracting directly with the other. For referring the Individual to the Client, the Firm receives a flat fee that is fixed prior to the Individual's

1: REVENUE RULING 87-41

commencement of services for the Client and is unrelated to the number of hours and quality of work performed by the Individual. The Individual is not paid by the Firm either directly or indirectly. No payment made by the Client to the Individual reduces the amount of the fee that the Client is otherwise required to pay the Firm. The Individual is performing services that can be accomplished without the Individual's receiving direction or control as to hours, place of work, sequence, or details of work.

Situation 3

The Firm, a company [*7] engaged in furnishing client firms with technical personnel, is contacted by the Client,who is in need of the services of a drafter for a particular project, which is expected to last less than one year. The Firm recruits the Individual to perform the drafting services for the Client. The Individual performs substantially all of the services for the Client at the office of the Client, using materials and equipment of the Client. The services are performed under the supervision of employees of the Client. The Individual reports to the Client on a regular basis. The Individual is paid by the Firm based on the number of hours the Individual has worked for the Client, as reported to the Firm by the Client or as reported by the Individual and confirmed by the Client. The Firm has no obligation to pay the Individual if the Firm does not receive payment for the Individual's services from the Client. For recruiting the Individual for the Client, the Firm receives a flat fee that is fixed prior to the Individual's commencement of services for the Client and is unrelated to the number of hours and quality of work performed by the Individual. However, the Firm does receive a reasonable fee for [*8] performing the payroll function. The Firm may not direct the work of the Individual and has no responsibility for the work performed by the Individual. The Firm may not terminate the services of the Individual. The Client may terminate the services of the Individual without liability to either the Individual or the Firm. The Individual is permitted to work for another firm while performing services for the Client, but does in fact work for the Client on a substantially full-time basis.

LAW AND ANALYSIS

This ruling provides guidance concerning the factors that are used to determine whether an employment relationship exists between the Individual and the Firm for federal employment tax purposes and applies those factors to the given factual situations to determine whether the Individual is an employee of the Firm for such purposes. The ruling does not reach any conclusions concerning whether an employment relationship for federal employment tax purposes exists between the

1: REVENUE RULING 87-41

Individual and the Client in any of the factual situations. Analysis of the preceding three fact situations requires an examination of the common law rules for determining whether the Individual is an employee with respect [*9] to either the Firm or the Client, a determination of whether the Firm or the Client qualifies for employment tax relief under section 530 (a) of the 1978 Act, and a determination of whether any such relief is denied the Firm under section 530 (d) of the 1978 Act (added by section 1706 of the 1986 Act).

An individual is an employee for federal employment tax purposes if the individual has the status of an employee under the usual common law rules applicable in determining the employer-employee relationship. Guides for determining that status are found in the following three substantially similar sections of the Employment Tax Regulations: sections 31.3121 (d)-1 (c); 31.3306 (i)-1; and 31.3401 (c)-1.

These sections provide that generally the relationship of employer and employee exists when the person or persons for whom the services are performed have the right to control and direct the individual who performs the services, not only as to the result to be accomplished by the work but also as to the details and means by which that result is accomplished. That is, an employee is subject to the will and control of the employer not only as to what shall be done but as to how it shall be done. [*10] In this connection, it is not necessary that the employer actually direct or control the manner in which the services are performed; it is sufficient if the employer has the right to do so.

Conversely, these sections provide, in part, that individuals (such as physicians, lawyers, dentists, contractors, and subcontractors) who follow an independent trade, business, or profession, in which they offer their services to the public, generally are not employees.

Finally, if the relationship of employer and employee exists, the designation or description of the relationship by the parties as anything other than that of employer and employee is immaterial. Thus, if such a relationship exists, it is of no consequence that the employee is designated as a partner, coadventurer, agent, independent contractor, or the like.

As an aid to determining whether an individual is an employee under the common law rules, twenty factors or elements have been identified as indicating whether sufficient control is present to establish an employer-employee relationship. The twenty factors have been developed based on an examination of cases and rulings considering whether an individual is an employee. The degree [*11] of

1: REVENUE RULING 87-41

importance of each factor varies depending on the occupation and the factual context in which the services are performed. The twenty factors are designed only as guides for determining whether an individual is an employee; special scrutiny is required in applying the twenty factors to assure that formalistic aspects of an arrangement designed to achieve a particular status do not obscure the substance of the arrangement (that is, whether the person or persons for whom the services are performed exercise sufficient control over the individual for the individual to be classified as an employee). The twenty factors are described below:

1. Instructions. A worker who is required to comply with other persons' instructions about when, where, and how he or she is to work is ordinarily an employee. This control factor is present if the person or persons for whom the services are performed have the right to require compliance with instructions. See, for example, Rev. Rul. 68-598, 1968-2 C.B. 464, and Rev. Rul. 66-381, 1966-2 C.B. 449.

2. Training. Training a worker by requiring an experienced employee to work with the worker, by corresponding with the worker, by requiring the worker to attend [*12] meetings, or by using other methods, indicates that the person or persons for whom the services are performed want the services performed in a particular method or manner. See Rev. Rul. 70-630, 1970-2 C.B. 229.

3. Integration. Integration of the worker's services into the business operations generally shows that the worker is subject to direction and control. When the success or continuation of a business depends to an appreciable degree upon the performance of certain services, the workers who perform those services must necessarily be subject to a certain amount of control by the owner of the business. See United States v. Silk, 331 U.S. 704, 91 L. Ed. 1757, 67 S. Ct. 1463, 1947-2 C.B. 167 (1947), 1947-2 C.B. 167.

4. Services Rendered Personally. If the services must be rendered personally, presumably the person or persons for whom the services are performed are interested in the methods used to accomplish the work as well as in the results. See Rev. Rul. 55-695, 1955-2 C.B. 410.

5. Hiring, Supervising, and Paying Assistants. If the person or persons for whom the services are performed hire, supervise, and pay assistants, that factor generally shows control over the workers on the job. [*13] However, if one worker hires, supervises, and pays the other assistants pursuant to a contract under which the worker agrees to provide materials and labor and under which the worker is responsible only for the attainment of a result, this factor indicates an independent contractor status. Compare Rev. Rul. 63-115, 1963-1 C.B. 178, with Rev.

1: REVENUE RULING 87-41

Rul. 55-593, 1955-2 C.B. 610.

6. Continuing Relationship. A continuing relationship between the worker and the person or persons for whom the services are performed indicates that an employer-employee relationship exists. A continuing relationship may exist where work is performed at frequently recurring although irregular intervals. See United States v. Silk.

7. Set Hours of Work. The establishment of set hours of work by the person or persons for whom the services are performed is a factor indicating control. See Rev. Rul. 73-591, 1973-2 C.B. 337.

8. Full Time Required. If the worker must devote substantially full time to the business of the person or persons for whom the services are performed, such person or persons have control over the amount of time the worker spends working and impliedly restrict the worker from doing other gainful work. An independent [*14] contractor, on the other hand, is free to work when and for whom he or she chooses. See Rev. Rul. 56-694, 1956-2 C.B. 694.

9. Doing Work on Employer's Premises. If the work is performed on the premises of the person or persons for whom the services are performed, that factor suggests control over the worker, especially if the work could be done elsewhere. Rev. Rul. 56-660, 1956-2 C.B. 693. Work done off the premises of the person or persons receiving the services, such as at the office of the worker, indicates some freedom from control. However, this fact by itself does not mean that the worker is not an employee. The importance of this factor depends on the nature of the service involved and the extent to which an employer generally would require that employees perform such services on the employer's premises. Control over the place of work is indicated when the person or persons for whom the services are performed have the right to compel the worker to travel a designated route, to canvass a territory within a certain time, or to work at specific places as required. See Rev. Rul. 56-694.

10. Order or Sequence Set. If a worker must perform services in the order or sequence set by the [*15] person or persons for whom the services are performed, that factor shows that the worker is not free to follow the worker's own pattern of work but must follow the established routines and schedules of the person or persons for whom the services are performed. Often, because of the nature of an occupation, the person or persons for whom the services are performed do not set the order of the services or set the order infrequently. It is sufficient to show control, however, if such person or persons retain the right to do so. See Rev. Rul.

1: REVENUE RULING 87-41

56-694.

11. Oral or Written Reports. A requirement that the worker submit regular or written reports to the person or persons for whom the services are performed indicates a degree of control. See Rev. Rul. 70-309, 1970-1 C.B. 199, and Rev. Rul. 68-248, 1968-1 C.B. 431.

12. Payment by Hour, Week, Month. Payment by the hour, week, or month generally points to an employer-employee relationship, provided that this method of payment is not just a convenient way of paying a lump sum agreed upon as the cost of a job. Payment made by the job or on a straight commission generally indicates that the worker is an independent contractor. See Rev. Rul. 74-389, 1974-2 C.B. 330.

13. Payment [*16] of Business and/or Traveling Expenses. If the person or persons for whom the services are performed ordinarily pay the worker's business and/or traveling expenses, the worker is ordinarily an employee. An employer, to be able to control expenses, generally retains the right to regulate and direct the worker's business activities. See Rev. Rul. 55-144, 1955-1 C.B. 483.

14. Furnishing of Tools and Materials. The fact that the person or persons for whom the services are performed furnish significant tools, materials, and other equipment tends to show the existence of an employer-employee relationship. See Rev. Rul. 71-524, 1971-2 C.B. 346.

15. Significant Investment. If the worker invests in facilities that are used by the worker in performing services and are not typically maintained by employees (such as the maintenance of an office rented at fair value from an unrelated party), that factor tends to indicate that the worker is an independent contractor. On the other hand, lack of investment in facilities indicates dependence on the person or persons for whom the services are performed for such facilities and, accordingly, the existence of an employer-employee relationship. See Rev. Rul. 71-524. [*17] Special scrutiny is required with respect to certain types of facilities, such as home offices.

16. Realization of Profit or Loss. A worker who can realize a profit or suffer a loss as a result of the worker's services (in addition to the profit or loss ordinarily realized by employees) is generally an independent contractor, but the worker who cannot is an employee. See Rev. Rul. 70-309. For example, if the worker is subject to a real risk of economic loss due to significant investments or a bona fide liability for expenses, such as salary payments to unrelated employees, that factor indicates that the worker is an independent contractor. The risk that a

1: REVENUE RULING 87-41

worker will not receive payment for his or her services, however, is common to both independent contractors and employees and thus does not constitute a sufficient economic risk to support treatment as an independent contractor.

17. Working for More Than One Firm at a Time. If a worker performs more than de minimis services for amultiple of unrelated persons or firms at the same time, that factor generally indicates that the worker is an independent contractor. See Rev. Rul. 70-572, 1970-2 C.B. 221. However, a worker who performs services [*18] for more than one person may be an employee of each of the persons, especially where such persons are part of the same service arrangement.

18. Making Service Available to General Public. The fact that a worker makes his or her services available to the general public on a regular and consistent basis indicates an independent contractor relationship. See Rev. Rul. 56-660.

19. Right to Discharge. The right to discharge a worker is a factor indicating that the worker is an employee and the person possessing the right is an employer. An employer exercises control through the threat of dismissal, which causes the worker to obey the employer's instructions. An independent contractor, on the other hand, cannot be fired so long as the independent contractor produces a result that meets the contract specifications. Rev. Rul. 75-41, 1975-1 C.B. 323.

20. Right to Terminate. If the worker has the right to end his or her relationship with the person for whom the services are performed at any time he or she wishes without incurring liability, that factor indicates an employer-employee relationship. See Rev. Rul. 70-309.

Rev. Rul. 75-41 considers the employment tax status of individuals performing services [*19] for a physician's professional service corporation. The corporation is in the business of providing a variety of services to professional people and firms (subscribers), including the services of secretaries, nurses, dental hygienists, and other similarly trained personnel. The individuals who are to perform the services are recruited by the corporation, paid by the corporation, assigned to jobs, and provided with employee benefits by the corporation. Individuals who enter into contracts with the corporation agree they will not contract directly with any subscriber to which they are assigned for at least three months after cessation of their contracts with the corporation. The corporation assigns the individual to the subscriber to work on the subscriber's premises with the subscriber's equipment. Subscribers have the right to require that an individual furnished by the corporation cease providing services to them, and they have the further right to have such individual replaced by the corporation within a reasonable period of

1: REVENUE RULING 87-41

time, but the subscribers have no right to affect the contract between the individual and the corporation. The corporation retains the right to discharge the [*20] individuals at any time. Rev. Rul. 75-41 concludes that the individuals are employees of the corporation for federal employment tax purposes.

Rev. Rul. 70-309 considers the employment tax status of certain individuals who perform services as oil well pumpers for a corporation under contracts that characterize: such individuals as independent contractors. Even though the pumpers perform their services away from the headquarters of the corporation and are not given day-to-day directions and instructions, the ruling concludes that the pumpers are employees of the corporation because the pumpers perform their services pursuant to an arrangement that gives the corporation the right to exercise whatever control is necessary to assure proper performance of the services; the pumpers' services are both necessary and incident to the business conducted by the corporation; and the pumpers are not engaged in an independent enterprise in which they assume the usual business risks, but rather work in the course of the corporation's trade or business. See also Rev. Rul. 70-630, 1970-2 C.B. 229, which considers the employment tax status of salesclerks furnished by an employee service company to a retail [*21] store to perform temporary services for the store.

Section 530 (a) of the 1978 Act, as amended by section 269 (c) of the Tax Equity and Fiscal Responsibility Act of 1982, 1982-2 C.E. 462, 536, provides, for purposes of the employment taxes under subtitle C of the Code, that if a taxpayer did not treat an individual as an employee for any period, then the individual shall be deemed not to be an employee, unless the taxpayer had no reasonable basis for not treating the individual as an employee. For any period after December 31, 1978, this relief applies only if both of the following consistency rules are satisfied: (1) all federal tax returns (including information returns) required to be filed by the taxpayer with respect to the individual for the period are filed on a basis consistent with the taxpayer's treatment of the individual as not being an employee ("reporting consistency rule"), and (2) the taxpayer (and any predecessor) has not treated any individual holding a substantially similar position as an employee for purposes of the employment taxes for periods beginning after December 31, 1977 ("substantive consistency rule").

The determination of whether any individual who is treated [*22] as an employee holds a position substantially similar to the position held by an individual whom the taxpayer would otherwise be permitted to treat as other than an employee for employment tax purposes under section 530 (a) of the 1978 Act requires an examination of all the facts and circumstances, including particularly the activities

1: REVENUE RULING 87-41

and functions performed by the individuals. Differences in the positions held by the respective individuals that result from the taxpayer's treatment of one individual as an employee and the other individual as other than an employee (for example, that the former individual is a participant in the taxpayer's qualified pension plan or health plan and the latter individual is not a participant in either) are to be disregarded in determining whether the individuals hold substantially similar positions.

Section 1706 (a) of the 1986 Act added to section 530 of the 1978 Act a new subsection (d), which provides an exception with respect to the treatment of certain workers. Section 530 (d) provides that section 530 shall not apply in the case of an individual who, pursuant to an arrangement between the taxpayer and another person, provides services for such other [*23] person as an engineer, designer, drafter, computer programmer, systems analyst, or other similarly skilled worker engaged in a similar line of work. Section 530 (d) of the 1978 Act does not affect the determination of whether such workers are employees under the common law rules. Rather, it merely eliminates the employment tax relief under section 530 (a) of the 1978 Act that would otherwise be available to a taxpayer with respect to those workers who are determined to be employees of the taxpayer under the usual common law rules. Section 530 (d) applies to remuneration paid and services rendered after December 31, 1986.

The Conference Report on the 1986 Act discusses the effect of section 530 (d) as follows:

> The Senate amendment applies whether the services of [technical service workers] are provided by the firm to only one client during the year or to more than one client, and whether or not such individuals have been designated or treated by the technical services firm as independent contractors, sole proprietors, partners, or employees of a personal service corporation controlled by such individual. The effect of the provision cannot be avoided by claims that such technical service [*24] personnel are employees of personal service corporations controlled by such personnel. For example, an engineer retained by a technical services firm to provide services to a manufacturer cannot avoid the effect of this provision by organizing a corporation that he or she controls and then claiming to provide services as an employee of that corporation.
>
> ... [T]he provision does not apply with respect to individuals

1: REVENUE RULING 87-41

who are classified, under the generally applicable common law standards, as employees of a business that is a client of the technical services firm.

2 H.R. Rep. No. 99-841 (Conf. Rep.), 99th Cong., 2d Sess. II-834 to 835 (1986).

Under the facts of Situation 1, the legal relationship is between the Firm and the Individual, and the Firm retains the right of control to insure that the services are performed in a satisfactory fashion. The fact that the Client may also exercise some degree of control over the Individual does not indicate that the individual is not an employee. Therefore, in Situation 1, the Individual is an employee of the Firm under the common law rules. The facts in Situation 1 involve an arrangement among the Individual, Firm, and Client, and the services provided [*25] by the Individual are technical services. Accordingly, the Firm is denied section 530 relief under section 530 (d) of the 1978 Act (as added by section 1706 of the 1986 Act), and no relief is available with respect to any employment tax liability incurred in Situation 1. The analysis would not differ if the facts of Situation 1 were changed to state that the Individual provided the technical services through a personal service corporation owned by the Individual.

In Situation 2, the Firm does not retain any right to control the performance of the services by the Individual and, thus, no employment relationship exists between the Individual and the Firm.

In Situation 3, the Firm does not control the performance of the services of the Individual, and the Firm has no right to affect the relationship between the Client and the Individual. Consequently, no employment relationship exists between the Firm and the Individual.

HOLDINGS

Situation 1. The Individual is an employee of the Firm under the common law rules. Relief under section 530 of the 1978 Act is not available to the Firm because of the provisions of section 530 (d).

Situation 2. The Individual is not an employee of the Firm under [*26] the common law rules.

Situation 3. The Individual is not an employee of the Firm under the common law rules. Because of the application of section 530 (b) of the 1978 Act, no inference should be drawn with respect to whether the Individual in Situations 2 and 3 is an employee of the Client for federal employment tax purposes.

2: GENERAL INVESTMENT CORPORATION V U.S.

SECTION 530 OF THE REVENUE ACT OF 1978, AS AMENDED

Section 530 of the Revenue Act of 1978, 26 U.S.C.A. Sec. 3401 note, Pub. L. 95-600; as amended by Pub. L. 96-167, Sec. 9(d), Dec. 29, 1979, 93 Stat. 1278; Pub. L. 96-541, Sec. 1, Dec. 17, 1980, 94 Stat. 3204; Pub. L. 97-248 [Tax Equity and Fiscal Responsibility Act of 1982], title II, Sec. 269(c)(1), (2), 96 Stat. 552; Pub. L. 99-514, Sec. 2, title XVII, Sec. 1706(a), Oct. 22, 1986, 100 Stat. 2095, 2781; Pub. L. 104-188 [Small Business Job Protection Act of 1996] Sec. 1122, August 20, 1996, provides that:

(a) **Termination of Certain Employment Tax Liability.**

(1) In general.

If –

(A) for purposes of employment taxes, the taxpayer did not treat an individual as an employee for any period, and

(B) in the case of periods after December 31, 1978, all Federal tax returns (including information returns) required to be filed by the taxpayer with respect to such individual for such period are filed on a basis consistent with the taxpayer's treatment of such individual as not being an employee,

then, for purposes of applying such taxes for such period with respect to the taxpayer, the individual shall be deemed not to be an employee unless the taxpayer had no reasonable basis for not treating such individual as an employee.

(2) Statutory standards providing one method of satisfying the requirements of paragraph (1).

For purposes of paragraph (1), a taxpayer shall in any case be treated as having a reasonable basis for not treating an individual as an employee for a period if the taxpayer's treatment of such individual for such period was in reasonable reliance on any of the following:

(A) judicial precedent, published rulings, technical advice with respect to the taxpayer, or a letter ruling to the taxpayer;

(B) a past Internal Revenue Service audit of the taxpayer in which there was no assessment attributable to the treatment (for employment tax purposes) of the individuals holding positions substantially similar to the position held by this individual; or

2: GENERAL INVESTMENT CORPORATION V U.S.

(C) long-standing recognized practice of a significant segment of the industry in which such individual was engaged.

(3) Consistency required in the case of prior tax treatment.

Paragraph (1) shall not apply with respect to the treatment of any individual for employment tax purposes for any period ending after December 31, 1978, if the taxpayer (or a predecessor) has treated any individual holding a substantially similar position as an employee for purposes of the employment taxes for any period beginning after December 31, 1977.

(4) Refund or credit of overpayment.

If refund or credit of any overpayment of an employment tax resulting from the application of paragraph (1) is not barred on the date of the enactment of this Act (Nov. 6, 1978) by any law or rule of law, the period for filing a claim for refund or credit of such overpayment (to the extent attributable to the application of paragraph (1)) shall not expire before the date 1 year after the date of the enactment of this Act (Nov. 6, 1978).

(b) Prohibition Against Regulations and Rulings on Employment Status.
No regulation or Revenue Ruling shall be published on or after the date of the enactment of this Act (Nov. 6, 1978) and before the effective date of any law hereafter enacted clarifying the employment status of individuals for purposes of the employment taxes by the Department of the Treasury (including the Internal Revenue Service) with respect to the employment status of any individual for purposes of the employment taxes.

(c) Definitions.
For purposes of this section –

(1) Employment tax. - The term 'employment tax' means any tax imposed by subtitle C of the Internal Revenue Code of 1986 (formerly I.R.C. 1954, section 3101 et seq. of this title).

(2) Employment status. - The term 'employment status' means the status of an individual, under the usual common law rules applicable in determining the employeremployee relationship, as an employee or as an independent contractor (or other individual who is not an employee).

(d) Exception.
This section shall not apply in the case of an individual who, pursuant to an arrangement between the taxpayer and another person, provides services for such

2: GENERAL INVESTMENT CORPORATION V U.S.

other person as an engineer, designer, drafter, computer programmer, systems analyst, or other similarly skilled worker engaged in a similar line of work.

(e) Special Rules For Application of Section.

(1) NOTICE OF AVAILABILITY OF SECTION
An officer or employee of the Internal Revenue Service shall, before or at the commencement of any audit inquiry relating to the employment status of one or more individuals who perform services for the taxpayer, provide the taxpayer with a written notice of the provisions of this section.

(2) RULES RELATING TO STATUTORY STANDARDS
For purposes of subsection (a)(2) –

> (A) a taxpayer may not rely on an audit commenced after December 31, 1996, for purposes of subparagraph (B) thereof unless such audit included an examination for employment tax purposes of whether the individual involved (or any individual holding a position substantially similar to the position held by the individual involved) should be treated as an employee of the taxpayer,

> (B) in no event shall the significant segment requirement of subparagraph (C) thereof be construed to require a reasonable showing of the practice of more than 25 percent of the industry (determined by not taking into account the taxpayer), and

> (C) in applying the long-standing recognized practice requirement of subparagraph (C) thereof-

>> (i) such requirement shall not be construed as requiring the practice to have continued for more than 10 years, and

>> (ii) a practice shall not fail to be treated as long-standing merely because such practice began after 1978.

(3) AVAILABILITY OF SAFE HARBORS
Nothing in this section shall be construed to provide that subsection (a) only applies where the individual involved is otherwise an employee of the taxpayer.

(4) BURDEN OF PROOF-

(A) IN GENERAL

2: GENERAL INVESTMENT CORPORATION V U.S.

If-

(i) a taxpayer establishes a prima facie case that it was reasonable not to treat an individual as an employee for purposes of this section, and

(ii) the taxpayer has fully cooperated with reasonable requests from the Secretary of the Treasury or his delegate,

then the burden of proof with respect to such treatment shall be on the Secretary.

(B) EXCEPTION FOR OTHER REASONABLE BASIS

In the case of any issue involving whether the taxpayer had a reasonable basis not to treat an individual as an employee for purposes of this section, subparagraph (A) shall only apply for purposes of determining whether the taxpayer meets the requirements of subparagraph (A), (B), or (C) of subsection (a)(2).

(5) PRESERVATION OF PRIOR PERIOD SAFE HARBOR

- If -

(A) an individual would (but for the treatment referred to in subparagraph (B)) be deemed not to be an employee of the taxpayer under subsection (a) for any prior period, and

(B) such individual is treated by the taxpayer as an employee for employment tax purposes for any subsequent period,

then, for purposes of applying such taxes for such prior period with respect to the taxpayer, the individual shall be deemed not to be an employee.

(6) SUBSTANTIALLY SIMILAR POSITION

For purposes of this section, the determination as to whether an individual holds a position substantially similar to a position held by another individual shall include consideration of the relationship between the taxpayer and such individuals.

[End of Section 530, as amended]

3: SECTION 530 OF THE REVENUE ACT OF 1978 (AMENDED)

General Investment Corporation, Plaintiff-Appellee, v. United States Of America, Defendant-Appellant

Nos. 85-2604, 86-1652

UNITED STATES COURT OF APPEALS FOR THE NINTH CIRCUIT

823 F.2d 337; 1987 U.S. App. LEXIS 10044; 87-2 U.S. Tax Cas. (CCH) P9453; 60 A.F.T.R.2d (RIA) 5395; 23 Fed. R. Evid. Serv. (Callaghan) 623

January 15, 1987, Argued and Submitted
July 29, 1987, Filed

PRIOR HISTORY: [**1] Appeal from the United States District Court for the District of Arizona, D.C. No. 63-379 GLO-wdb, William D. Browning, District Judge, Presiding.

COUNSEL: James Benham, Esq., for the Appellee. Michael J. Roach, Esq., for the Appellant.

JUDGES: J. Blaine Anderson, Otto R. Skopil, Jr., and William C. Canby, Jr., Circuit Judges.

OPINION BY: CANBY

OPINION

[*338] CANBY, Circuit Judge: This appeal concerns a small mining company that, like others in its county, treated its workers as independent contractors for tax purposes. Two questions are before us. First, whether such treatment was justified under § 530(a)(2)(C) of the Revenue Act of 1978, 26 U.S.C. § 3401 note (1979), as undertaken in reliance on a "long-standing recognized practice of a significant segment of the industry." Second, for a later tax year to which § 530 cannot be applied, whether the workers in fact qualify as independent contractors under the common law. We conclude that the treatment was justified under the statute, but not under the common law.

BACKGROUND

The taxpayer-appellee, General Investment Corporation (GIC), is an Arizona corporation engaged in gold and silver mining in Gila County, Arizona. GIC took over operations at the Sunflower [**2] Mine site in 1973, following twenty-five years' operation by GIC's predecessor. GIC hired laborers to mine, transport ore,

3: SECTION 530 OF THE REVENUE ACT OF 1978 (AMENDED)

and to maintain the mine, the ore milling site, and mining equipment.

GIC provided the majority of tools, equipment, and supplies required for blasting, transporting, and milling of ore. Blasting and mining was done by a daily three-person crew, which would usually produce 20-25 tons of ore. Workers were treated as independent contractors for tax purposes, but they earned a daily flat-rate [*339] wage, which did not fluctuate according to productivity. GIC's president and principal officer, James Duncan, visited the mine daily to assure that mining practices complied with the federal Mine Safety and Health Act (MSHA).

Most of the workers were undocumented Mexican nationals, for whom GIC provided living quarters in its mining camp. While certain rules applied to conduct in the camp, it appears that GIC did not exercise detailed supervision over the daily work. Evidently, the miners themselves organized the taskwork required to extract and transport ore from the mine-tunnel rock face.

After a tax examination, the Internal Revenue Service (IRS) determined that the miners were employees. The IRS assessed a total of $ 82,950.67 for [**3] unpaid withholding, Federal Insurance Contribution Act (FICA), and Federal Unemployment Tax Act (FUTA) taxes for 1976-79, together with penalties for failure to file employment tax returns and failure to withhold. GIC paid $ 100 in taxes and sought a refund in the district court. The government counterclaimed for $ 108,975.98 in unpaid FICA, FUTA, and income taxes, along with penalties and interest.

At trial, GIC's president testified that local miners did not wish to have their taxes withheld. Evidence supported the inference that, because laborers were hired as independent contractors by other small mines in Gila County, the miners would be unwilling to work as regular employees for the Sunflower Mine. The district court concluded that GIC had a reasonable basis for treating its workers as independent contractors within the meaning of the safe haven provisions of § 530, as well as under traditional common law standards. The court therefore entered judgment for GIC and ordered refund of GIC's payments, dismissing the counterclaim. The government appeals.

DISCUSSION

I. SECTION 530 OF THE REVENUE ACT OF 1978; TAX YEARS 1976-78

The IRS contends that the district court committed legal [**4] error in applying § 530's "industry practice" provision. In § 530(a)(1), Congress granted interim relief from withholding and other forms of employer tax liability for certain tax-

3: SECTION 530 OF THE REVENUE ACT OF 1978 (AMENDED)

payers before 1980. 26 U.S.C. § 3401 note. [1] The statute was designed to relieve employers of the burden of surprise or uncertain imposition of retroactive tax liability resulting from an increase in IRS employment-status audits. See, e.g., S. Rep. No. 1263, 95th Cong., 2d Sess. 209-10, reprinted in 1978 U.S. Code Cong. & Admin. News 6761, 6972-73.

1 Section 530(a) provides:

Termination of certain employment tax liability. --

(1) In general. -- If --

(A) for purposes of employment taxes, the taxpayer did not treat an individual as an employee for any period ending before January 1, 1980, and

(B) in the case of periods after December 31, 1978, all Federal tax returns (including information returns) required to be filed by the taxpayer with respect to such individual for such period are filed on a basis consistent with the taxpayer's treatment of such individual as not being an employee, then for purposes of applying such taxes for such period with respect to the taxpayer, the individual shall be deemed not to be an employee unless the taxpayer had no reasonable basis for not treating such individual as an employee.

26 U.S.C. § 3401 note (1979).

[**5] Congress provided that an individual whom the employer did not treat as an employee would be "deemed not to be an employee" for tax purposes "unless the employer had no reasonable basis" for that treatment of the individual. § 530(a)(1)(A) & (B). Section 530(a)(2) provides that an employer's reasonable reliance on any of three supporting elements constitutes a reasonable basis for not treating an individual as an employee. [2] The third provision, [*340] in dispute here, creates a conclusive presumption that an employer had a reasonable basis for not treating an individual as an employee, if the employer did so in reasonable reliance on "long-standing recognized practice of a significant segment of the industry in which such individual was engaged." § 530(a)(2)(C), 26 U.S.C. § 3401 note.

2 Section 530(a)(2) provides:

3: SECTION 530 OF THE REVENUE ACT OF 1978 (AMENDED)

Statutory standards providing one method of satisfying the requirements of paragraph (1). -

For purposes of paragraph (1), a taxpayer shall in any case be treated as having a reasonable basis for not treating an individual as an employee for a period if the taxpayer's treatment of such individual for such period was in reasonable reliance on any of the following:

(A) judicial precedent, published rulings, technical advice with respect to the taxpayer, or a letter ruling to the taxpayer; (B) a past Internal Revenue Service audit of the taxpayer in which there was no assessment attributable to the treatment (for employment tax purposes) of the individuals holding positions substantially similar to the position held by this individual; or

(C) long-standing recognized practice of a significant segment of the industry in which such individual was engaged.

26 U.S.C. § 3401 note.

[**6] The government challenges the district court's application of § 530 on two fronts. First, it contends that the court's definition of the relevant industry was overly narrow; the government argues that the court should have required GIC to have relied on practices of a significant segment of the nationwide industry of mining. Second, the government claims that even if the court was correct to regard small Gila County mining concerns as a discrete industry for purposes of § 530, the court clearly erred by finding that plaintiff met its evidentiary burden.

A. The Scope of the Relevant Industry

To escape tax liability through § 530(a)(2)(C), GIC must show that a "significant segment of the industry" treated miners as independent contractors. The government argues that the industry in which the workers were engaged should be defined to include all mining businesses nationwide. At a minimum, however, the government suggests that the standard should include all small mining concerns in the nation that process and extract ore. We disagree with both of these positions.

Section 530 of the Revenue Act of 1978 does not define "industry." Nor does the Act's extensive legislative history [**7] shed light directly on how Congress

3: SECTION 530 OF THE REVENUE ACT OF 1978 (AMENDED)

intended the term to be construed. Congress' overall purpose in passing the legislation does offer some guidance, however.

Without question, Congress intended to protect employers who exercised good faith in determining whether their workers were employees or independent contractors. Section 530(a)(2)(C) is but one way for an employer to prove it had a "reasonable basis" for not treating its workers as employees for tax purposes. Rev. Proc. 78-35 § 3.01, 1978-2 C.B. 536. The legislative history specifies that "reasonable basis" is to be "construed liberally in favor of taxpayers." H.R. Rep. No. 1748, 95th Cong., 2d Sess. 5, 1978-3 C.B. (Vol. 1) 629, 633; see American Institute of Family Relations, 79-1 U.S. Tax Cas. (CCH) P 9364 (C.D. Cal. 1979). The IRS has embraced Congress' liberal construction directive in its procedural guidelines for § 530. Rev. Proc. 78-35 § 3.01, 1978-2 C.B. 536; see Ridgewell's, Inc. v. United States, 228 Ct. Cl. 393, 655 F.2d 1098, 48 A.F.T.R.2d (P-H) 5673 (Ct. Cl. 1981).

To require the district court to examine nationwide mine employment practices would be cumbersome, and to demand such a showing by a small operator like GIC would thwart congressional intent. [**8] Several dozen small mining concerns with operations similar to the Sunflower Mine exist in Gila County, a geographic area covering 4,400 square miles. The government fails to provide any substantial reason why these small Gila County metallic mineral mines should not be viewed as a discrete industry sufficient to stimulate the kind of reliance protected by § 530. In light of the provision's curative, "remedial character which responded to peculiar circumstances of past deficiencies in the [IRS'] enforcement . . . of the employment tax laws," Donovan v. Tastee Freez (Puerto Rico), Inc., 520 F. Supp. 899, 904 (D. P.R. 1981), we conclude that the district court appropriately interpreted § 530.

B. Evidence of Industry Practice

The government alternatively contends that the district court erred by finding that [*341] the hiring of miners as independent contractors was a recognized practice among a significant segment of the Gila County small mining industry. [3] We review the district court's finding for clear error. E.g. La Duke v. Nelson, 762 F.2d 1318, 1321 (9th Cir. 1985); amended, 796 F.2d 309 (9th Cir. 1986); United States v. McConney, 728 F.2d 1195, 1200 (9th Cir.) [**9] (en banc), cert. denied, 469 U.S. 824, 83 L. Ed. 2d 46, 105 S. Ct. 101 (1984).

3 GIC need not prove the practice was uniformly followed by the industry. Rev. Proc. 78-35 § 3.01(C), 1978-2 C.B. 536.

3: SECTION 530 OF THE REVENUE ACT OF 1978 (AMENDED)

At trial, both Duncan and Thorne, another local mine operator, testified that they always hired laborers as independent contractors. Duncan testified that GIC's practice of contracting for laborers followed the routine practice of the Sunflower Mine's previous owner. Duncan and Thorne also had extensive familiarity with the operations of a number of other small Gila County mines through their roles as officers of a county-wide mining trade association. Their impression, based on meetings with mine owners and numerous visits to other mines, was that all hired laborers on as independent contractors. Duncan also testified that workers who had experience working for other mines were unwilling to work for GIC unless they were treated as contract laborers, because their wages would be lower as employees.

Cross-examination revealed that substantial portions of GIC's evidence were not based on direct personal observation. The government did not move to strike the testimony, however, and that evidence remains part of the [**10] record. [4] The government cannot now complain that such evidence should be excluded from consideration. See United States v. Fernandez, 772 F.2d 495, 499 (9th Cir. 1985) (citing Professional Seminar Consultants, Inc. v. Sino American Technology Exchange Council, Inc., 727 F.2d 1470, 1472 (9th Cir. 1984); United States v. Jamerson, 549 F.2d 1263, 1266-67 (9th Cir. 1977)). Although some of the testimony was hearsay, the district court properly considered it for its probative value. Id.

> [4] The government successfully objected to the introduction of other testimony, which the district court excluded on hearsay grounds.

The government failed to present any evidence of employment practices that cast doubt on GIC's evidence. Moreover, circumstantial nonhearsay evidence supported GIC's assertion that the use of contract laborers was a routine practice among small gold and silver mines in Gila County. The district court did not clearly err in concluding that the treatment of laborers as independent contractors was a long-standing, recognized practice of a significant segment of the industry. Thus, GIC had a reasonable basis for treating its miners as independent contractors [**11] and is relieved of liability for the years 1976-78. § 530(a)(2) (C), 26 U.S.C. § 3401 note.

II. COMMON LAW EMPLOYMENT STANDARDS; TAX YEAR 1979

GIC cannot avail itself of § 530 relief to avoid employment tax liability for 1979. For tax periods after December 31, 1978, relief under § 530 is available only if GIC filed required tax or information returns. § 530(a)(1), 26 U.S.C. § 3401

3: SECTION 530 OF THE REVENUE ACT OF 1978 (AMENDED)

note. [5] GIC conceded that it failed to file information returns for its 1979 workers and is not entitled to § 530 relief for that year.

5 See supra note 1.

Measuring the workers' status by applicable common law standards, see 26 U.S.C. §§ 3121(d)(2) & 3306(i), the district court concluded that GIC also escaped employment tax liability for 1979. The government challenges this conclusion. We review for clear error the court's finding that GIC's laborers were not common law employees. E.g., McGuire v. United States, 349 F.2d 644, 646 (9th Cir. 1965).

Measuring the workers' status by applicable common law standards, see 26 U.S.C. §§ 3121(d)(2) & 3306(i), the district court concluded that GIC also escaped employment tax liability for 1979. The government challenges this conclusion. We review for clear error the court's finding that GIC's laborers were not common law employees. E.g., McGuire v. United States, 349 F.2d 644, 646 (9th Cir. 1965).

Although a variety of factors may be used to analyze employment status for tax purposes, employer control over the manner in which the work is performed, "either actual or the right to it, is the basic test." Air Terminal Cab, Inc. v. United [**12] States, 478 F.2d 575, 579 (8th Cir.), cert. denied, 414 U.S. 909, [*342] 94 S. Ct. 228, 38 L. Ed. 2d 146 (1973); McGuire, 349 F.2d at 646. The Treasury Regulations include the following subsidiary factors to define common law employment status: (1) whether the business has the right to discharge the worker; (2) whether the business furnishes tools to the person rendering the service; (3) whether the business provides the worker with a place to work; and (4) whether the work is performed in the course of the individual's business rather than in some ancillary capacity. See Treasury Regulations on Employment Tax & Collection of Income Tax at Source, 26 C.F.R. §§ 31.3121(d)-1(c)(2), 31.3306(i)-1(b), 31.3401(c)(1)(b) (1987).

Trial testimony established that Duncan, as president of GIC, hired and discharged the workers. There was no indication that the laborers had their own independent businesses, although some also worked for neighboring mines. The jobs did not require sophisticated skills, and GIC provided most of the tools and all heavy equipment. Duncan selected daily crew members, provided safety training, and established strict rules governing conduct in the mining camp. The miners were unable to earn more [**13] than the daily flat-rate wage through their skill, management abilities, or efficiency. See, e.g., Avis Rent A Car System, Inc. v.

3: SECTION 530 OF THE REVENUE ACT OF 1978 (AMENDED)

United States, 503 F.2d 423, 429 (2d Cir. 1974) (cited in Real v. Driscoll Strawberry Associates, Inc., 603 F.2d 748, 754 n.14 (9th Cir. 1979) (listing factors to be considered in determining whether employer-employee relationship exists); Smith v. United States, 75-2 U.S. Tax Cas. (CCH) P 9793, 36 A.F.T.R.2d (P-H) 6174 (N.D. Tex. 1975) (mem.), aff'd per curiam, 568 F.2d 435 (5th Cir. 1978).

GIC did not exercise control over every detail of the work, and GIC contends that payment was on a piecework basis. On the record before us, however, we cannot conclude that Duncan lacked the right to control his laborers. The mere fact that the workers set their own hours and determined when to take breaks did not make them independent contractors. United States v. Silk, 331 U.S. 704, 716-18, 91 L. Ed. 1757, 67 S. Ct. 1463 (1947). The district court clearly erred by finding that GIC demonstrated that its miners were independent contractors. Since common law standards determine the employment status of GIC's workers for 1979, GIC is liable for taxes, penalties, and interest in accordance with the IRS assessment for [**14] that year.

III. LITIGATION COSTS

GIC, as cross-appellant, appeals the district court's denial of litigation costs under 26 U.S.C. § 7430. GIC may only qualify for award of reasonable costs if it was a "prevailing party" within the meaning of § 7430(c)(2)(A). See 26 U.S.C. § 7430(a). A prevailing party must establish that the position of the United States was not substantially justified. Id. § 7430(c)(2)(A)(i). The district court did not abuse its discretion in concluding that GIC failed to make the necessary showing. Cf. Albrecht v. Heckler, 765 F.2d 914, 915 (9th Cir. 1985) (per curiam) (reviewing for abuse of discretion district court's ruling on application for fees under Equal Access to Justice Act, 28 U.S.C. § 2412(d)); Cardwell v. Kurtz, 765 F.2d 776, 781-82 (9th Cir. 1985) (same). We therefore affirm the court's decision to deny GIC's application for litigation costs.

CONCLUSION

On the authority of § 530 of the Revenue Act of 1978, we affirm the district court's dismissal of the government's counterclaim for taxes, penalties, and interest for 1976-78. Because GIC's workers were common law employees, we reverse the district court's decision as to plaintiff's [**15] liability for 1979 and remand for further proceedings consistent with this opinion. Each party will bear its own costs.

AFFIRMED AS TO 1976-78; REVERSED AND REMANDED AS TO 1979.

4: SMOKEY MOUNTAIN SECRETS V U.S.

SMOKY MOUNTAIN SECRETS, INC., Plaintiff v. UNITED STATES OF
AMERICA, Defendant

No. 3:94-cv-121

UNITED STATES DISTRICT COURT FOR THE EASTERN DISTRICT OF
TENNESSEE, KNOXVILLE DIVISION

910 F. Supp. 1316; 1995 U.S. Dist. LEXIS 15271; 95-2 U.S. Tax Cas. (CCH)
P50,573; 76 A.F.T.R.2d (RIA) 6974

September 25, 1995, FILED

COUNSEL: [**1] For SMOKY MOUNTAIN SECRETS, INC., plaintiff: James M
McCarten, Dale C Allen, Woolf, McClane, Bright, Allen & Carpenter, Knoxville,
TN.

For USA, defendant: Michael J Martineau, Trial Attorney, U. S. Department of
Justice, Tax Division, Washington, DC.

For USA, counter-claimant: Michael J Martineau, Trial Attorney, U. S.
Department of Justice, Tax Division, Washington, DC.

For SMOKY MOUNTAIN SECRETS, INC., counter-defendant: James M
McCarten, Dale C Allen, Woolf, McClane, Bright, Allen & Carpenter, Knoxville,
TN.

JUDGES: James H. Jarvis, UNITED STATES DISTRICT JUDGE

OPINION BY: James H. Jarvis

OPINION

[*1317] MEMORANDUM OPINION

This is a tax refund action brought by the plaintiff-taxpayer, Smoky Mountain
Secrets, Inc. (SMS), pursuant to 28 U.S.C. § 1346(a)(1). Plaintiff seeks a refund of
Form 941, Federal Insurance Contribution Act (FICA) taxes and Form 940,
Federal [*1318] Unemployment Tax Act (FUTA) taxes, which plaintiff contends
were assessed erroneously by the United States Department of the Treasury
through the Internal Revenue Service (IRS). The total amount of taxes assessed [1]
is approximately $ 3,888,918. This does not include interest on the assessments.
The jurisdiction of this court is not disputed. This matter was tried before the
undersigned without intervention of a jury on July 20, 1995. The parties were

4: SMOKEY MOUNTAIN SECRETS V U.S.

given additional time within which to file post-trial briefs. After consideration of
the pleadings, the testimony of witnesses, the depositions and exhibits introduced
at trial, the parties' briefs and the applicable law, the court makes the following
findings of fact and conclusions of law. See Rule 52(a), Federal Rules of Civil
Procedure.

> 1 Smoky Mountain Secrets has not actually paid the
> amounts assessed. Rather, it has for each assessment paid an
> amount equal to the employment taxes for one employee
> and immediately sought a refund of that amount. There
> were a total of 10 assessments beginning with the first quar-
> ter of 1989 and ending with the last quarter of 1992. This
> procedure is in full compliance with the IRS' divisible tax
> rule. Each claim for refund has been disallowed by the IRS.
> These and other facts are included in written stipulations
> [Doc. No. 25] filed by the parties.

[**2] Findings of Fact

1. SMS, a Tennessee corporation, markets gourmet foods and condiments, including mustards, salad dressings, jellies and preserves. SMS sells its gourmet foods to
consumers; it does not package and sell its products to other businesses for resale.

2. Sometime during late 1991 or early 1992, defendant, through the IRS, initiated
an audit of SMS which included a review of whether SMS's telemarketers and
delivery persons were properly treated as independent contractors for federal tax
purposes.

3. During the tax years in question, the bulk of SMS's sales orders were solicited
through telephone calls made by plaintiff's telemarketers, although some sales
were made through mail orders received from repeat customers and through on-
the- spot sales by delivery persons. The product orders solicited by the telemarketers were delivered to the customer's home by delivery persons who collected
the amount due.

4. In addition to the telemarketers and delivery persons, all of whom were treated
other than as employees for federal tax purposes during the 1989 and 1990 tax
years, SMS employed workers who were and still are treated as employees for
federal tax purposes. These [**3] employees include home office staff, warehouse
workers, office managers, regional managers, and the officers of the corporation.

5. The telemarketers and delivery persons worked out of sales offices in various

4: SMOKEY MOUNTAIN SECRETS V U.S.

locations in approximately 14 different states during the tax years in question. No walk-in sales were made from these offices. Sales were only made through telephone solicitation and delivery of the package. For each package sold, which SMS defined as requiring actual delivery to and receipt of payment from the customer, the telemarketer received a specific commission, the amount of which depended upon the size of the package sold and the year in which the transaction took place.

6. SMS's delivery persons were an integral part of SMS's sales force; their services did not consist of merely driving to the customer's home and handing over the package. The delivery person had to collect the amount due, which often meant that he or she had to close the sale. Neither the delivery person nor the telemarketer would be paid unless the package was accepted and paid for by the consumer. Thus, the reason SMS's own delivery persons were used instead of common carrier was to obtain the [**4] opportunity to close the sale face-to-face if a delivery was refused. Two of plaintiff's managers, Terry P. Goodall and Barbara Jean Thomas, 2 each of whom had previously worked for SMS as delivery persons, testified that the person delivering the packages was often called upon to close sales, such as when a customer has changed his or her mind, did not know the terms of the sale, or when an unknowledgeable spouse refused to [*1319] accept the package. Mr. Goodall and Ms. Thomas further testified that delivery persons also made sales on a "show-me" basis, in which additional packages are shown and sold to customers and to their neighbors. Consequently, I find that closing the sale was as much an art as was obtaining the order over the telephone in the first place.

> 2 The parties stipulated that the testimony given by Mr. Goodall and Ms. Thomas is consistent with that of all office managers, telemarketers and/or delivery persons working with SMS during the tax years in question, both with regard to SMS's corporate policies and the work of telemarketers and delivery persons.

[**5] 7. Before going to work for SMS, each telemarketer and delivery person was required to sign a written contract. SMS's company president, Charles H. Allen, who along with his wife, Lois Allen, own 100% of the issued and outstanding stock of SMS, testified that it was corporate policy that all salespersons sign a contract before beginning work. The evidence establishes that the contracts clearly set forth that each telemarketer or delivery person would be paid on a commission basis, would not be treated as an employee for federal tax purposes, and that no federal, state or local income or payroll taxes would be withheld. The

4: SMOKEY MOUNTAIN SECRETS V U.S.

earlier forms of the contracts also stated that because the telemarketer or delivery person was not an employee, a Form 1099 would be issued and filed if the individual earned over $ 600 during that year. The parties stipulated that SMS issued a Form 1099, as required by federal tax law, to every telemarketer and delivery person who earned $ 600 or more during the 1989 and 1990 tax years.

8. These written contracts further provided that each telemarketer's or delivery person's remuneration was directly related to the number of sales delivered and for which they [**6] were paid. Each year SMS corporate policy required every telemarketer and delivery person to sign a new contract. It was the responsibility of the manager of each sales office to obtain those documents. And, in fact, the contracts were signed by every telemarketer and delivery person before they started work.

9. Copies of form contracts between SMS and its telemarketers and delivery persons which were used during the years following the 1989 and 1990 tax years were admitted in evidence. As the undisputed testimony confirms, the contracts used in prior years were, in all relevant provisions, substantially the same as those in evidence. The contracts used in the 1989 and 1990 tax years provided that the service provider -- i.e., the telemarketer or delivery person -- would be paid on a per-package-sold basis and that the service provider would not be treated as an employee for federal tax purposes. The parties stipulated, however, that SMS has been unable to produce and does not have in its possession originals or copies of the written contracts for the tax years in question, even though SMS diligently searched for them and even sought to obtain copies or originals from numerous [**7] third parties. The reason SMS was unable to obtain the contracts is that its certified public accountant (CPA), Edgar H. Gee, Jr., advised Mr. Allen, SMS's president, that it would be unnecessary to retain copies after the corporate books had been closed and the required tax returns, including Forms 1099, had been filed for the year. Mr. Gee did not consider it important to keep copies of the contracts between SMS and its sales force because 26 U.S.C. § 3508 does not address retention of contracts in any respect. Nonetheless, because it was SMS's corporate policy that every telemarketer and delivery person sign a new contract each year, and since the undisputed proof at trial indicated that contracts were, in fact, executed by all telemarketers and delivery persons during the tax years at issue, I find that SMS convincingly proved the existence of the contracts and their contents pursuant to Rule 1004(1), Federal Rules of Evidence.

10. Mr. Allen first sought Mr. Gee's advice in 1983, after having read a statement in a business publication which reported the addition of § 3508 to the Internal Revenue Code (the Code). Because he realized that it possibly applied to business-

4: SMOKEY MOUNTAIN SECRETS V U.S.

es such [**8] as his, which utilized the services of "direct sellers" and treated them as independent contractors, Mr. Allen sought the advice of Mr. Gee as to whether the new Code provision would apply to SMS's relationship with its tele-marketers and delivery persons. Mr. Gee is a CPA who has been licensed and in practice for more than 20 years. He received his undergraduate degree in account-ing from Western Kentucky University and a masters in Business Administration from the University of Tennessee at Knoxville. Mr. Gee started his professional career with what was then one of the Big Eight accounting firms. He has had his own practice since 1977. Mr. Gee [*1320] maintains a general accounting prac-tice, concentrating on small businesses, the most significant of which is SMS. He testified at trial that probably one-half of his practice is related to tax accounting and tax advice.

11. Mr. Gee testified that when Mr. Allen first inquired about § 3508 he was ini-tially unfamiliar with the statute's requirements. The reason is that the statute had only recently been enacted. He therefore obtained a copy of the new statute prior to Mr. Allen's initial appointment, found that there were no regulations regarding [**9] § 3508, and analyzed the Code section with Mr. Allen, asking him pertinent questions regarding each of the elements set forth in the statute. Based on the information gleaned from Mr. Allen, Mr. Gee opined that SMS's telemarketers and delivery persons were direct sellers as contemplated by § 3508. Mr. Gee testi-fied that his opinion was based upon Mr. Allen's description of the relevant facts about SMS's business, the manner in which the telemarketers and delivery per-sons would be compensated, and the fact that plaintiff had a written contract with its sales force providing that the telemarketers and delivery persons would not be treated as employees for federal tax purposes. Shortly after his meeting with Mr. Allen, Mr. Gee researched § 3508's legislative history, obtaining copies of the Senate and House committee reports as well as the conference committee report. He gave copies of these reports to Mr. Allen, advising him that he remained of the opinion that SMS's sales force qualified as direct sellers under the statute. Mr. Gee was hired that same year as SMS's CPA with responsibility for closing the books at year-end, preparing financial statements as needed, and filing all [**10] tax returns, including employment tax and information returns.

12. Unknown to Mr. Gee, Mr. Allen also consulted with the CPA who regularly prepared Mr. Allen's personal tax returns, Jerry Lee Sharpe of Middlesboro, Kentucky. Mr. Allen asked Mr. Sharpe the same question regarding the proper tax classification of SMS's telemarketers and delivery persons. Mr. Sharpe, now semi-retired, has been a CPA since 1963. When he began his career, he worked for the IRS as a revenue agent for almost two years. While with the IRS, Mr. Sharpe worked on a number of independent contractor cases. As a CPA in private prac-

4: SMOKEY MOUNTAIN SECRETS V U.S.

tice, the vast majority of his time has been spent on tax-related issues, including some work, primarily related to the coal industry, regarding the issue of independent contractors.

13. Like Mr. Gee, Mr. Sharpe advised Mr. Allen that he believed that SMS's telemarketers and delivery persons were properly classified as independent contractors and not employees. He based this advice, however, upon his prior experience and knowledge of common law factors. Mr. Sharpe was not familiar with and did not discuss with Mr. Allen the application of § 3508. Some years later, Mr. Sharpe called [**11] Mr. Allen regarding this issue after he had attended a three-day continuing professional education course, which was sponsored by the University of Kentucky and taught by IRS instructors. Mr. Sharpe advised Mr. Allen that the course's primary subject involved the IRS's new 20-factor analysis for determining whether workers are employees or independent contractors for federal tax purposes. After again analyzing SMS's sales force in the context of these 20 factors, Mr. Sharpe advised Mr. Allen that the telemarketers and delivery persons were properly characterized as independent contractors.

14. Mr. Gee has continued to perform certain accounting services for SMS since 1983. In addition to the specific advice he gave regarding § 3508, Mr. Gee has represented SMS in state unemployment tax investigations involving the issue of the proper classification of SMS's telemarketers and delivery persons. A number of such investigations took place over the years and, consistent with his initial advice to Mr. Allen, Mr. Gee have taken the position with the states that the telemarketers and delivery persons were statutorily classified as independent contractors. Mr. Gee testified that most, if [**12] not all, of these investigations resulted in findings by the states that SMS's telemarketers and delivery persons were indeed properly treated as independent contractors rather than employees.

15. Based upon the undisputed evidence at trial, I find that SMS has, since its inception, treated all of its telemarketers and delivery [*1321] persons as independent contractors. No telemarketer or delivery person has been treated as an employee for federal tax purposes.

Conclusions of Law

A. Section 3508 -- Statutory Independent Contractors

1. This court has subject matter jurisdiction over this case pursuant to 28 U.S.C. §§ 1340 and 1346(a)(1), and 26 U.S.C. § 7422. Because this is a tax refund suit in which the IRS counterclaims for the unpaid balance of assessments of divisible taxes, the IRS need only show that a timely assessment was made in order to

4: SMOKEY MOUNTAIN SECRETS V U.S.

establish a prima facie case. See Sinder v. United States, 655 F.2d 729, 731 (6th Cir. 1981). Thus, the assessment is initially presumed to be correct, and the taxpayer has the burden of proving that the assessment was wrong. Id. See also United States v. Besase, 623 F.2d 463, 465 (6th Cir.), cert. denied, 449 U.S. 1062, 66 L. Ed. 2d 605, 101 S. Ct. 785 [**13] (1980).

2. Prior to 1982, the question of whether a worker was an independent contractor or an employee for federal tax purposes was a question that was answered almost exclusively under common law. See Cleveland Institute of Electronics, Inc. v. United States, 787 F. Supp. 741 (N.D. Ohio 1992); H.R. Rep. No. 1748, 95th Cong., 2d Sess. 5, 1978-3 C.B. (Vol. 1) 629 (House Report discussing the enactment of the employment tax relief provisions of § 530 of the Revenue Act of 1978). After enacting § 530 of the Revenue Act of 1978 as an interim solution for employment tax controversies, Congress in 1982 made § 530 relief permanent and, to further alleviate the problem for direct sellers and real estate sales persons, enacted 26 U.S.C. § 3508. According to the legislative history, Congress added § 3508 to the Code as a response to the "problems arising from increased employment tax status controversies," and to provide a statutory scheme for assuring the status of certain direct sellers and real estate sales people as independent contractors [for federal tax purposes]." Staff of Joint Comm. on Taxation, 97th Cong., 2d Sess., General Explanation of the Revenue Provisions of [**14] the Tax Equity and Fiscal Responsibility Act of 1982, at 382 (Comm. Print 1982). Importantly, the "statute did not supplant the common law; rather, it merely guaranteed independent contractor status for those taxpayers who met its conditions." Cleveland Institute of Electronics, 787 F. Supp. at 743-44.

3. Section 3508 thus establishes two categories of statutory non- employees: (1) qualified real estate agents and (2) direct sellers. The statute sets forth the general rule that an individual performing services as a "direct seller" shall not be treated as an employee and the person for whom the services are performed shall not be treated as an employer. § 3508(a)(1) and (2).

4. The term "direct seller" is defined in pertinent part in § 3508(b)(2) as any person:

(A) [who]

* * *

        (ii) is engaged in the trade or business of selling (or soliciting the sale of) consumer products in the home or otherwise than in a permanent retail establishment,

4: SMOKEY MOUNTAIN SECRETS V U.S.

(B) substantially all the remuneration (whether or not paid in cash) for the performance of the services described in subparagraph (A) is directly related to sales or other output (including the performance of services) [**15] rather than to the number of hours worked, and

(C) the services performed by the person are performed pursuant to a written contract between such person and the person for whom the services are performed and such contract provides that the person will not be treated as an employee with respect to such services for Federal tax purposes.

The parties have stipulated that SMS's sales (the delivery of its gourmet foods and condiments and receipt of payment) and the solicitation of its sales (by the telemarketers over the telephone) were made either in the home or from other than a "permanent retail establishment" as required by § 3508. The parties further stipulated that SMS's telemarketers were engaged in the business of "soliciting the sale" of plaintiff's product as required by the statute. However, the parties dispute whether or not SMS's delivery [*1322] persons were engaged in the business of soliciting the sale of plaintiff's products. I am of the opinion that they were. In fact, SMS's delivery persons were an indispensable part of selling SMS's products. Delivery persons had to be able to and did "close" sales on a regular basis. Indeed, the extent to which they received remuneration [**16] for their services was very often dependent on their success in closing sales. The telemarketers and delivery persons thus both clearly meet the first prong of the definition of "direct sellers;" they were engaged in the trade or business of selling or soliciting the sale of consumer products in the home or otherwise than in a permanent retail establishment.

5. The next criterion which must be satisfied under § 3508 is that "substantially all the remuneration" paid to the worker be directly related to sales or other output rather than the number of hours worked. SMS compensated its telemarketers and delivery persons on a commission basis -- only if a package was delivered to a customer and the sales price actually collected were the telemarketer and delivery person to be paid. Thus, substantially all of the remuneration of the telemarketers who received a Form 1099 for the 1989 and 1990 tax years was directly related to sales. Similarly, substantially all the remuneration of SMS's delivery persons during the 1989 and 1990 tax years was directly related to sales. SMS has thus met the second prong of § 3508's test.

4: SMOKEY MOUNTAIN SECRETS V U.S.

6. The third requirement of § 3508 is that the services must have [**17] been performed pursuant to a written contract providing that the service provider would not be treated as an employee for federal tax purposes. Although the IRS vigorously contends that SMS has failed to satisfy the written contract requirement of § 3508(b)(2)(C), its argument is unavailing. The IRS would require plaintiff to actually produce the written contracts for the years 1989 and 1990. However, this argument ignores Federal Rule of Evidence 1004(1), which clearly allows other evidence of the contents of an original writing to be introduced assuming all originals have been lost or destroyed. While Congress could have required something more within the terms of § 3508, it did not. The IRS has failed to cite any authority for the proposition that copies of the original contracts must be produced in order for the taxpayer to meet the third prong of § 3508. SMS introduced into evidence copies of form contracts similar in every material respect to those used in the tax years at issue. The contracts specifically provide that SMS's telemarketers and delivery persons will be paid on a commission basis and that the telemarketers and delivery persons would not be treated as employees [**18] for federal tax purposes. SMS required each telemarketer and delivery person to sign these contracts and the evidence clearly reflects that the contracts were, in fact, signed by each telemarketer and delivery person in each of the tax years at issue. Therefore, the third requirement of the statute has been met; the services were performed under a written contract providing that the service provider would not be treated as an employee for federal tax purposes.

7. The IRS also contends that the court may reasonably infer from the existence of written contracts for years subsequent to 1989 and 1990, and the failure of SMS to produce the written contracts for the years at issue, that either no written contracts ever existed for such years or that, if they did exist, the written contracts did not contain the express provisions required by § 3508. Indeed, the IRS goes so far as to argue that the court may properly draw an analogy between the established principle that an adverse inference may be drawn from the failure of a non-hostile witness with direct knowledge of important facts to testify on a party's behalf. While the court could draw such an inference if SMS had adduced no [**19] proof on this issue, that is not the case here. The government itself stipulated that any and all persons whom SMS could call at trial on this issue would testify, as did Mr. Goodall and Ms. Thomas, that each telemarketer and delivery person signed written contracts as a matter of corporate policy. As noted in the leading case of Cleveland Institute of Electronics, Inc., 787 F. Supp. at 749, the legislative purpose underlying enactment of § 3508 was to reduce the number of controversies regarding employment and income tax status of direct sellers and real estate agents. The court therefore must interpret the requirements [*1323] of

4: SMOKEY MOUNTAIN SECRETS V U.S.

§ 3508 in a fashion which will further the statute's purpose. Therefore, because SMS has clearly demonstrated that its telemarketers and delivery persons meet the requirements set forth in § 3508, the court concludes that SMS's sales force were "direct sellers" as that term is used in § 3508 for the tax years 1989 and 1990.

B. Section 530 of the Revenue Act of 1978 -- Professional Advice

8. Section 530 of the Revenue Act of 1978 (the 1978 Act) was enacted by Congress to provide interim relief to certain taxpayers involved in employment tax status [**20] controversies with the IRS. Donovan v. Tastee Freez (Puerto Rico), Inc., 520 F. Supp. 899, 903 (D. P.R. 1981). Section 530 of the 1978 Act is codified as a footnote to 26 U.S.C. § 3401. Congress intended that § 530 would serve as a shelter for taxpayers who had acted in good faith from the potentially harsh retroactive tax liabilities resulting from IRS reclassification of independent contractors as employees. See United States v. MacKenzie, 777 F.2d 811, 815 (2d Cir. 1985), cert. denied, 476 U.S. 1169, 90 L. Ed. 2d 977, 106 S. Ct. 2889 (1986) (citing Ridgewell's Inc. v. United States, 228 Ct. Cl. 393, 655 F.2d 1098, 1101 (1981)). As previously noted, § 530 was later extended indefinitely by the Tax Equity and Fiscal Responsibility Act of 1982.

9. Although the court has previously concluded that the members of SMS's sales staff are properly classified as direct sellers under § 3508, I further conclude that SMS has demonstrated that it is entitled to relief under § 530, even if the telemarketers and delivery persons do not qualify as direct sellers.

10. The government has stipulated and the court finds that SMS has met the first two tests under § 530: that SMS has consistently treated its telemarketers [**21] and delivery persons, as well as all individuals holding similar positions, as independent contractors for federal tax purposes; and that SMS filed all required tax returns, including information returns, in a manner consistent with having treated the telemarketers and delivery persons as independent contractors. Thus, the only remaining question is whether SMS had a reasonable basis for treating its telemarketers and delivery persons as independent contractors. The term "reasonable basis" is to be construed liberally in favor of the taxpayer. See H.R. Rep. No. 1748, 95th Cong., 2d Sess. 5, 1978-3 C.B. (Vol. 1) 629, 633. See also Lambert's Nursery and Landscaping, Inc. v. United States, 894 F.2d 154, 157 (5th Cir. 1990); General Inv. Corp. v. United States, 823 F.2d 337, 340 (9th Cir. 1987).

11. Section 530 provides three non-exclusive methods by which taxpayers can demonstrate a reasonable basis for having treated individuals as independent contractors rather than employees. The first of these statutory safe harbors is reliance

4: SMOKEY MOUNTAIN SECRETS V U.S.

on judicial precedent or published rulings. The second of the statutory safe harbors is reliance on a past IRS audit of the taxpayer in which [**22] there was no assessment attributable to the treatment, for employment tax purposes, of individuals holding positions substantially similar to those held by the workers at issue. The third statutory safe harbor is reliance on the long-standing recognized practice of the worker's industry. See § 530(a)(2). However, the language of § 530(a)(2) refers to the three statutory safe harbors as merely "one method of satisfying the requirements [of the reasonable basis test]." Based upon that language, both the IRS in its procedural guidelines and the courts have held that "[a] taxpayer who fails to meet any of the three [statutory] 'safe havens' may nevertheless be entitled to relief if the taxpayer can demonstrate, in some other manner, a reasonable basis for not treating the individual as an employee."Rev. Proc. 85-18, 1985-1 C.B. 518. See also In re Rasbury, 130 Bankr. 990 (Bankr. N.D. Ala. 1991), aff'd, United States v. Rasbury (In re Rasbury), 141 Bankr. 752 (N.D. Ala. 1992).

12. SMS claims that its reliance on the advice of two professional tax advisors is sufficient to demonstrate a reasonable basis under § 530 for not treating its telemarketers and delivery persons [**23] as employees. I agree. Under the circumstances of this case, reliance upon the professional advice rendered by two CPAs -- Mr. Gee and Mr. Sharpe -- constitutes a reasonable basis for SMS having treated its telemarketers and delivery persons as independent contractors. [*1324] It is undisputed that Mr. Gee explored with SMS's president, Mr. Allen, the facts about SMS's business relevant to the requirements found in § 3508. Mr. Gee testified that he discussed with Mr. Allen that SMS's compensation structure would meet the "substantially all remuneration" requirement, that a written contract was required, and that one existed which met the requirements found in the statute. After determining that the telemarketers and delivery persons would only be compensated on a commission basis and that a written contract meeting the requirements of the statute existed, Mr. Gee advised Mr. Allen that he believed § 3508 applied and that the telemarketers and delivery persons could and should be treated as independent contractors. Thus, not only has Mr. Gee consistently filed all appropriate federal documents related to this status under § 3508, he has also represented SMS in various state unemployment [**24] tax investigations and has consistently taken the successful position with those agencies that the telemarketers and delivery persons qualified as "direct sellers" under § 3508.

13. The IRS attacks SMS's reliance upon Mr. Gee's advice based on the fact that Mr. Gee was unaware of the existence of § 3508 at the time Mr. Allen inquired of him. Because at that time the statute had just been enacted, and based on Mr. Gee's conduct in researching the matter, I am of the opinion that it was reason-

4: SMOKEY MOUNTAIN SECRETS V U.S.

able for Mr. Allen to rely upon the advice of his CPA. Only after he had examined the statute line-by-line in the context of the information provided by Mr. Allen did Mr. Gee opine that SMS had met the essential elements of § 3508.

14. I further conclude that SMS's reliance upon the advice of Mr. Sharpe, who examined the information provided by Mr. Allen in the context of the common law factors governing independent contractor status, was reasonable, thereby further entitling SMS to the protection of § 530. As did Mr. Gee, Mr. Sharpe testified as to his education and experience in similar tax matters and indicated that his advice was based upon the information provided by Mr. Allen. The [**25] IRS's reliance on In re McAtee, 115 Bankr. 180 (N.D. Iowa 1990), is thus misplaced. In that case, the taxpayer's accountant did not testify, nor was his identity disclosed on the record. Moreover, there was no evidence in the record as to exactly what advice the accountant gave the taxpayer or what information the taxpayer gave to the accountant. Id. at 184-85. By contrast, the undisputed testimony in this case indicates that, so far as Mr. Allen knew, Mr. Gee and Mr. Sharpe were fully capable and qualified to render advice on the question asked of them. It is also undisputed that Mr. Allen fully disclosed all pertinent information necessary for his accountants to render that advice.

15. Although the term "reasonable basis" is not defined in the Code or regulations, an analogy may be drawn from those cases interpreting the term "reasonable cause" as it governs the determination of whether income tax penalties should be imposed upon a taxpayer. 3 In determining if reasonable cause exists, the courts and IRS regulations generally look to see whether the taxpayer "exercised ordinary business care or prudence." See, e.g., 26 C.F.R. § 301.6651-1(c)(1). Generally, the courts [**26] have found that reasonable cause exists where the taxpayer relied on the advice of a trusted attorney or accountant. See, e.g., Vorsheck v. Commissioner, 933 F.2d 757 (9th Cir.), cert. denied, 502 U.S. 984, 116 L. Ed. 2d 615, 112 S. Ct. 591 (1991). Indeed, in this regard, the Supreme Court has stated that:

> When an accountant or attorney advises a taxpayer on a matter of tax law, such as whether a liability exists, it is reasonable for the taxpayer to rely on that advice. Most taxpayers are not competent to discern error in the substantive advice of an accountant or attorney. To require the taxpayer to challenge the attorney, to seek a "second opinion," or to try to monitor counsel on the provisions of the Code himself would nullify the very purpose of seeking the advice of a presumed expert in the first place. "Ordinary business

4: SMOKEY MOUNTAIN SECRETS V U.S.

care and prudence" do not demand such actions. 3 Unlike §
530's reasonable basis standard, the reasonable cause test is
not liberally construed in favor of the taxpayer.

[*1325] United States v. [**27] Boyle, 469 U.S. 241, 251, 83 L. Ed. 2d 622, 105
S. Ct. 687 (1985) (emphasis added and citation omitted). Under the circumstances
of this case, then, I conclude that SMS's reliance on the advice of two CPAs is a
reasonable basis for treating its telemarketers and delivery persons as indepen-
dentcontractors, entitling it to the protection of § 530.

C. Section 530 of the Revenue Act of 1978 -- Prior Audit Safe Harbor.

16. The leading case involving the prior audit safe harbor provision under §
530(a)(2)(B) is Lambert's Nursery and Landscaping, Inc. v. United States, 894
F.2d 154 (5th Cir. 1990). The Fifth Circuit set forth the requirements the taxpayer
must satisfy to meet the prior audit safe haven defense. The taxpayer must establish (1) that the IRS conducted a prior audit of the taxpayer for a particular tax
year; (2) that the IRS determined in the prior audit of the taxpayer's workers
were independent contractors; (3) that the workers who were the subject of the
prior audit are "substantially similar" to the workers at issue; and (4) that the
taxpayer treated the two groups of workers in a "substantially similar" fashion.
Unlike the taxpayer in Lambert's Nursery, SMS failed to establish the existence
[**28] of a past IRS audit of SMS. It did establish, however, that Mr. Allen individually, as well as three corporations he owned in the early 1970's, were audited
by the IRS. Mr. Allen nevertheless admitted that he did not know for certain what
year the purported audits took place, or for what tax years the audits were conducted. He also admitted that he has no records reflecting that audits were conducted, or to what tax years the audits pertained. Although he testified generally
that no adverse independent contractor determination was made by the IRS, he
was not able to testify about the precise results of the audits.

17. Accordingly, while there was evidence that Mr. Allen treated SMS's sales force
in the same manner as he had treated his sales force in his prior businesses, the
evidence is insufficient for the court to conclude that SMS was entitled to rely on
the results of the prior audit.

Conclusion

Therefore, because SMS's telemarketers and delivery persons are direct sellers
under 26 U.S.C. § 3508 or, alternatively, because SMS is entitled to the protection
of § 530 on account of its reasonable reliance on professional advice, SMS shall
be awarded judgment in its favor [**29] and against the United States in the

4: SMOKEY MOUNTAIN SECRETS V U.S.

amount of $ 400, which represents the total amount of employment taxes paid for the tax years at issue.

Order accordingly.

James H. Jarvis

UNITED STATES DISTRICT JUDGE

5: QUEENSGATE DENTAL FAMILY PRACTICE V U.S.

QUEENSGATE DENTAL FAMILY PRACTICE, INC., Plaintiff v. UNITED STATES OF AMERICA, Defendant; KEYSTONE HEALTH SERVICES, INC., Plaintiff v. UNITED STATES OF AMERICA, Defendant; COLONIAL FAMILY DENTAL PRACTICE, INC., Plaintiff v. UNITED STATES OF AMERICA, Defendant

Civil Action Nos. 1:CV-90-0918, 1:CV-90-1290, 1:CV-90-1291

UNITED STATES DISTRICT COURT FOR THE MIDDLE DISTRICT OF PENNSYLVANIA

1991 U.S. Dist. LEXIS 13333; 91-2 U.S. Tax Cas. (CCH) P50,536; 68 A.F.T.R.2d (RIA) 5679; Unemployment Ins. Rep. (CCH) P16,279A

September 5, 1991
September 5, 1991, Filed

JUDGES: [*1] William W. Caldwell, United States District Judge.

OPINION BY: CALDWELL

OPINION

MEMORANDUM

Plaintiffs, Queensgate Dental Family Practice, Inc., Keystone Health Services, Inc. (Keystone), and Colonial Family Dental Practice, Inc. (the Corporations), filed a complaint against the United States of America, to recover taxes paid under protest pursuant to the Federal Insurance Contributions Act (FICA) and the withholding provisions of the Federal Unemployment Tax Act (FUTA). Defendant responded with a counterclaim against plaintiffs to enforce judgment and collect the balance of the tax assessments. The parties have cross-moved for summary judgment pursuant to Fed. R. Civ. Pro. 56.

The central issue in this matter is whether dentists who conducted their practices at plaintiffs' facilities may be considered employees or independent contractors for federal employment tax purposes. Defendant contends that the dentists were plaintiffs' employees. To the contrary, plaintiffs argue that the dentists were treated as independent contractors and that plaintiffs reasonably believed that they should be so treated.

Irrespective of whether the dentists were employees or independent contractors, Section 530 of the [*2] Revenue Act of 1978 P.L. 95-600, 92 Stat. 2763; 26

5: QUEENSGATE DENTAL FAMILY PRACTICE V U.S.

U.S.C. § 3401 Note (1979) is "used to protect from civil liability those who reasonably made a determination that a given individual was [or should be treated
as] an independent contractor rather than an employee." United States v.
MacKenzie, 777 F.2d 811, 815 (2d Cir. 1985). Section 530 "is a curative piece of
legislation of a remedial nature based on a standard of good faith reliance intended to provide interim relief for taxpayers involved in employment tax status controversies with the Internal Revenue Service." Donovan v. Tastee Freez (Puerto
Rico), Inc., 520 F. Supp. 899. 903 (D.C. Puerto Rico 1981); H.Rep. No. 95-1748
95th Cong., 2d Sess. 4 (1978); S.Rep. No. 95-1263, 95th Cong., 2d Sess. 209-210
(1978). "Without question, Congress intended to protect employers who exercised good faith in determining whether their workers were employees or independent contractors." General Invest. Corp. v. United States, 823 F.2d 337, 340
(9th Cir. 1987). The Committee Report of the House Ways and Means
Committee, Report No. 95-1748 states as follows:

Generally, the bill grants relief [*3] if a taxpayer had any reasonable basis for
treating workers as other than employees. The committee intends that this reasonable basis requirement be construed liberally in favor of taxpayers. (emphasis
added)

"Congress provided that an individual whom the employer did not treat as an
employee would be 'deemed not to be an employee' for tax purposes 'unless the
employer had no reasonable basis' for that treatment of the individual.'" General
Invest., supra, 823 F.2d at 339.

Pursuant to Section 530, the taxpayer must show: (1) that all federal tax returns
were filed consistent with the taxpayer's treatment of individuals as not being
employees, and (2) that all individuals holding a substantially similar position in
the corporation must not have been treated as employees for tax purposes. Upon
consideration of the record, particularly the stipulated facts, we find that plaintiffs have established a basis for relief under Section 530. The undisputed facts are
as follows. Before Keystone entered into a contract with any dentists (other than
a corporate officer) to perform services at its facilities, the president of Keystone,
Donald R. Paule, telephoned the counsel [*4] of the Pennsylvania Dental Board to
ascertain whether licensed dentists should be treated as employees or independent
contractors by Keystone, which is a non-professional, business corporation.
Although Paule does not recall counsel's name, it is stipulated that John J. Flynn,
then Counsel for the Dental Board, was in all likelihood the person who responded to Paule's inquiries.

Paule was specifically advised by Flynn that: (1) the Dental Board would consider

5: QUEENSGATE DENTAL FAMILY PRACTICE V U.S.

it illegal, under Pennsylvania law, for a nonlicensed business corporation such as Keystone to enter into a relationship or employer/employee with a licensed dentist; and (2) that a practicing dentist must be treated by Keystone as an independent contractor and not as an employee in compliance with the requirements of the Dental Board. See Neill v. Gimbel Brothers, Inc., 330 Pa. 213, 199 A. 178 (1938); Neill v. Bloch, 330 Pa. 222, 199 A. 182 (1938); Neill v. Stern and Company, 330 Pa. 224, 199 A. 182 (1938) (if an unlicensed corporation employs a licensed practitioner, such corporation is guilty of practicing a profession without a [*5] license).

Based upon Paule's good faith inquiry into the manner in which Keystone should treat the dentists, we conclude that plaintiffs had a reasonable basis to believe that the dentists must be treated as independent contractors and not employees, thus satisfying the requirements of Section 530. Defendant contends that relief under Section 530 is inapplicable in this case because Paule cannot show that his reliance upon the word of counsel for the Dental Board was a reasonable basis to avoid paying withholding employment taxes. Specifically, defendant states that "plaintiff's reliance on the alleged advice of counsel for the Board does not rise to a reasonable basis for relief of the tax liabilities under the act." Defendant suggests that the dentist could easily have been treated as employees by simply altering the Corporations from business to professional entities. The Corporations, however, were not deemed professional, because their president, Paule, was not a dentist. For that reason, defendant contends that "as a matter of business convenience, plaintiffs decided not to treat the dentists as employees, even though they had the option of doing so."

We conclude that defendant [*6] has misconstrued Congress' intent in enacting Section 530. Section 530 does not require taxpayers to structure a corporation in a way that would qualify workers as employees. Rather, inquiry is simply whether a taxpayer's beliefs and decisions regarding his treatment of individuals as either employees or independent contractors were reasonable and made in good faith. In the present action, we conclude that plaintiffs have satisfied the reasonable basis test.

Further, the Government contends that this Court first must evaluate whether, in fact, the dentists were employees or independent contractors according to common law, before applying Section 530. We disagree. Section 530 was designed explicitly to eliminate the need for courts to engage in the balancing of complex factual issues in determining whether an individual is an independent contractor or an employee under common law. H.R. Rep. No. 95-1748, 95th Cong., 2d Sess. (1978); Donovan, supra, 520 F. Supp. at 903. Thus, the threshold inquiry is

5: QUEENSGATE DENTAL FAMILY PRACTICE V U.S.

whether under the facts plaintiffs are entitled to claim relief under Section 530. We have concluded they are on that ground alone, summary judgment may be entered in [*7] favor of plaintiffs.

Moreover, the record reveals substantial evidence that plaintiffs intended to and did treat the dentists as independent contractors, both for business and tax purposes. First, the parties have stipulated that all federal tax returns filed by plaintiffs have been consistent with plaintiffs' treatment of the dentists as independent contractors. Second, the dentists have exercised independent control over their practice, fee of corporate direction. Under the common law, an employer-employee relationship is generally found to exist:

when the person for whom the services are performed has the right to control and direct the individual who performs the services, not only as to the result to be accomplished by the work, but also as to the details and means by which the result is accomplished. That is, an employee is subject to the will and control of the employer not only as to what shall be done but how it shall be done.

Section 31.3121(d) -1(c)(2) of the Employment Tax Regulations. Additionally, "if an individual is subject to the control and direction of another merely as to the result to be accomplished by the work and not as to the means and methods for accomplishing [*8] the result, he is an independent contractor." Id. "Individuals such as . . . dentists . . . , engaged in the pursuit of an independent trade, business or profession, in which they offer their services to the public are independent contractors and not employees." Id.

According to the deposition testimony of Dr. Bentivegna, a corporate officer of Keystone:

The doctors practice dentistry according to their own training, background and experience. They develop their own treatment plans. They conduct their own private practice with respect to their patients. They direct staff [dental receptionists] to schedule them appropriately. They direct dental assistants to assist them properly. In that respect they are autonomous.

We [the plaintiff corporations] don't tell them how long they are supposed to schedule, how they can schedule. We don't issue directives. That's not the nature of our relationship.

Moreover, the parties stipulated to the following facts:

Each dentist has discretion to treat and to handle patients as he in his professional

5: QUEENSGATE DENTAL FAMILY PRACTICE V U.S.

experience and opinion deems necessary. The discretion includes (i) scheduling treatments and examinations as needed; (ii) determining [*9] the scope and method of treatment or examination; (iii) determining whether services of a specialist are required; (iv) considering and determining different treatment alternatives; and (v) maintaining the patient's chart for dental services rendered.

The dentist was not required to seek approval from the Corporations for orders of instruments or supplies. The dentist sets his own fee schedule. The Corporations did not set the dentists' fees which theycharged to their patients.

If a dentist desired to refer the patient to another dentist or to seek a consultation with another dentist, he was not required to refer the patient to or to consult with another dentist who conducted his practice at the Corporations.

The Corporations did not provide any dentist with any minimum guaranteed income, any sick leave or any employee benefits. The Corporations did not pay any unemployment compensation tax on the dentists and did not maintain workers' compensation insurance on them. Each dentist retained his own tax advisor or accountant. The Corporations did not provide tax advisors or accountants for the dentists.

These facts (which are only representative of numerous situations which [*10] imply a non-employee relationship in this matter) establish that the dentists planned the treatment of their patients, with no significant right of control by the Corporations. Defendants suggest, as do certain courts, that the "element of control is subject to special considerations if the employment of professional persons is involved." Cody v. Ribicoff, 289 F.2d 394, 398 (8th Cir. 1961). [1] "The method by which physicians work are directed by the standards of their profession and are peculiarly unsuited to direction and close control by an employer." Id. at 393 (citations omitted). Thus, in cases involving professional persons, courts tend to look at factors other than the professional's control over the method of treatment.

> 1 Other courts have continued to utilize the basic "right of control" test, even in cases involving professionals. e.g. McCormack v. Commissioner, 52 T.C.M. 1321, 1326 (1987).

In the present case, it appears that the dentists have demonstrated sufficient [*11] control not simply in dictating the method of treatment, but in ordering supplies, consulting with and referring to other dentists, scheduling fees and hours, offering services to the public, determining how to handle patients who do not pay their fees, maintaining records, paying for entertainment and travel expenses, furnishing their own medical malpractice insurance and training, risking the possibility

5: QUEENSGATE DENTAL FAMILY PRACTICE V U.S.

of lost profits which are based exclusively upon the compensation received from patients, and directing the support staff in light of the individual dentist's needs. We further note that even in those cases in which courts look beyond the right to control the method of treatment, it has been unanimously held that the physicians were independent contractors and not employees. Professional & Executive Leasing, Inc. v. Commissioner, 89 T.C. 225 (1987), aff'd 862 F.2d 751, 753, 754, (9th Cir. 1988); United States v. Azad, 277 F. Supp. 258 (D. Minn. 1966), aff'd, Azad v. United States, 388 F.2d 74, 77-78 (8th Cir. 1968).

We recognize that although the "right of control" test "remains an important index of [*12] the relationship, no single factor is controlling. All of the elements involved in the employment must be balanced in terms of their significance within the entire employment relationship. American Consulting Corporation v. United States, 454 F.2d 473, 477 (3d Cir. 1971). The IRS has endorsed twenty factors which are considered by courts as guidelines in determining whether an employer-employee relationship exists for tax purposes.Revenue Ruling 87-41. 1987- 1 C.B. 296. However, because of the applicability of Section 530, we need not conduct a detailed balancing of these items. We do note, however, that as the guidelines pertain to the facts of this case, although there is some indication of an employer-employee relationship, the great weight of the evidence supports the conclusion that the dentists were independent contractors and not employees of plaintiffs.

For the above reasons, we conclude that the assessments at issue must be stricken and summary judgment will be granted in favor of plaintiffs.

An appropriate order shall issue.

ORDER AND JUDGMENT

AND NOW, this 5th day of September, 1991, upon consideration of the cross-motions [*13] for summary judgment, it is ordered and declared that:

1. Plaintiffs' motion for summary judgment is granted and defendant's motion for summary judgment is denied. Plaintiffs' claims for refunds are granted, with statutory interest thereon, and the assessments in controversy are stricken.

2. Judgment is entered in favor of plaintiffs, Queensgate Dental Family Practice, Inc., Keystone Health Services, Inc., and Colonial Family Dental Practice, Inc., and against defendant, the United States of America.

3. Defendant's counter-claim is denied and dismissed.

4. The Clerk of Court shall close these files.

6: DARRELL HARRIS, INC. V U.S

DARRELL HARRIS, INC., Plaintiff, v. UNITED STATES OF AMERICA, Defendant

No. CIV-90-1282-P

UNITED STATES DISTRICT COURT FOR THE WESTERN DISTRICT OF OKLAHOMA

770 F. Supp. 1492; 1991 U.S. Dist. LEXIS 6820; 91-1 U.S. Tax Cas. (CCH) P50,271; 69 A.F.T.R.2d (RIA) 439; Unemployment Ins. Rep. (CCH) P16,115A

May 7, 1991, Decided
May 7, 1991, Filed

JUDGES: [**1] Layn R. Phillips, United States District Judge.

OPINION BY: PHILLIPS

OPINION

[*1493] ORDER GRANTING DEFENDANT'S MOTION FOR SUMMARY JUDGMENT

LAYN R. PHILLIPS, UNITED STATES DISTRICT JUDGE

I. INTRODUCTION

At issue is defendant United States of America's ("United States") motion for summary judgment filed March 12, 1991. Plaintiff Darrell Harris, Inc. responded on March 26, 1991, to which defendant replied on April 12, 1991. The issues at hand are whether Darrell Harris is an employee of plaintiff Darrell Harris, Inc., and if so whether plaintiff had a reasonable basis to believe Darrell Harris was not an employee so as to avoid a tax penalty for failing to file tax returns and failing to make timely deposits of taxes. The Court rejects plaintiff's contention that defendant's motion was filed out of time. Defendant filed an application to file an outsized brief within the time permitted by the Court's Scheduling Order, and the present motion was reasonably filed after that application was granted by the Court.

II. STANDARD FOR SUMMARY JUDGMENT

The facts presented to the court upon a motion for summary judgment must be construed in a light most favorable to the nonmoving party. Board of Educ. v. Pico, 457 U.S. 853, 864, 73 L. Ed. 2d 435, 102 S. Ct. 2799 (1982); [**2] United

6: DARRELL HARRIS, INC. V U.S

States v. Diebold, Inc., 369 U.S. 654, 8 L. Ed. 2d 176, 82 S. Ct. 993 (1962). If there can be but one reasonable conclusion as to the material facts, summary judgment is appropriate. Only genuine disputes over facts which might affect the outcome of the suit under the governing law will properly preclude the entry of summary judgment. Anderson v. Liberty Lobby, Inc., 477 U.S. 242, 91 L. Ed. 2d 202, 106 S. Ct. 2505 (1986). Finally, the movant must show entitlement to judgment as a matter of law. Ellis v. El Paso Natural Gas Co., 754 F.2d 884, 885 (10th Cir. 1985); Fed. R. Civ. P. 56(c).

Although the Court must view the facts and inferences to be drawn from the record in the light most favorable to the nonmoving party, "even under this standard there are cases where the evidence is so weak that the case does not raise a genuine issue of fact." Burnette v. Dow Chem. Co., 849 F.2d 1269, 1273 (10th Cir. 1988). As stated by the Supreme Court, "summary judgment procedure is properly regarded not as a disfavored procedural shortcut, but rather as an integral part of the Federal Rules as a whole, which are designed 'to secure the just, speedy and inexpensive determination [**3] of every action.'" Celotex Corp. v. Catrett, 477 U.S. 317, 327, 91 L. Ed. 2d 265, 106 S. Ct. 2548 (1986)

(quoting Fed. R. Civ. P. 1).

The Supreme Court articulated the standard to be used in summary judgment cases, emphasizing the "requirement is that there be no genuine issue of material fact." Anderson v. Liberty Lobby, Inc., 477 U.S. 242, 248, 91 L. Ed. 2d 202, 106 S. Ct. 2505 (1986) (emphasis in original). A dispute is "genuine" "if a reasonable jury could return a verdict for the nonmoving party." Anderson, 477 U.S. at 248. The Court stated that the question is "whether the evidence [*1494] presents a sufficient disagreement to require submission to a jury or whether it is so one-sided that one party must prevail as a matter of law." Id. at 251-52. "The mere existence of a scintilla of evidence in support of the [party's] position will be insufficient; there must be evidence on which the jury could reasonably find for the [party]." Id. at 252.

III. UNDISPUTED FACTS

Rule 14(B) of the Western District of Oklahoma provides a framework for determining undisputed facts at the summary judgment stage. The Rule provides:

> The brief in support of a motion [**4] for summary judgment (or partial summary judgment) shall begin with a section that contains a concise statement of material facts as to which movant contends no genuine issue exists. The facts

6: DARRELL HARRIS, INC. V U.S

shall be numbered and shall refer with particularity to those portions of the record upon which movant relies. The brief in opposition to a motion for summary judgment (or partial summary judgment) shall begin with a section which contains a concise statement of material facts as to which the party contends a genuine issue exists. Each fact in dispute shall be numbered, shall refer with particularity to those portions of the record upon which the opposing party relies, and, if applicable, shall state the number of the movant's fact that is disputed. All material facts set forth in the statement of the movant shall be deemed admitted for the purpose of summary judgment unless specifically controverted by the statement of the opposing party.

W.D. Okla. R. 14(B).

A review of United States's brief and Darrell Harris, Inc.'s response reveals the following facts are undisputed within the meaning of Rule 14(B) for the purposes of this motion only:

1. This is a civil action brought by Darrell Harris, [**5] Inc. ("plaintiff") pursuant to title 28, section 1346(a)(1) of the United States Code to recover Internal Revenue taxes and penalties of $ 507.87 and interest of $ 243.25 assessed against and paid by the plaintiff for the taxable quarter ending March 31, 1986.

2. The United States filed a counterclaim against the plaintiff for unpaid federal employment tax assessments, penalties and interest in the amount of $ 4,966.92, plus statutory additions, for the second, third and fourth taxable quarters of 1986 and for all four taxable quarters of 1987.

3. The United States filed a counterclaim against the plaintiff for unpaid FUTA assessments, penalties and interest in the amount of $ 659.54, plus statutory additions, for the tax years ending December 31, 1986, and December 31, 1987.

4. The United States of America is the defendant in this action.

5. The periods in question are all four quarters of both 1986, and 1987.

6. The plaintiff is a professional corporation incorporated under the laws of the State of Oklahoma, and is a "C" corporation for purposes of federal income taxation.

7. The plaintiff was incorporated in order to protect the business assets from

6: DARRELL HARRIS, INC. V U.S

ongoing litigation involving [**6] its only principal, Darrell Harris.

8. The plaintiff began operating in 1982.

9. The plaintiff performed basic accounting services, bookkeeping services, compilations, tax services, including tax planning and tax return preparation.

10. The plaintiff's principal place of business during the period in question, was located at 1732 Northwest 63rd, Oklahoma City, Oklahoma.

11. During the periods in question, Darrell Harris was the sole shareholder, director and president of plaintiff, and resided at 1732 Northwest 63rd, Oklahoma City, Oklahoma.

12. During the periods in question, Darrell Harris performed bookkeeping, accounting work, tax planning, and tax return [*1495] preparation (hereinafter referred to as "accounting services") for the plaintiff.

11. It was also undisputed that the plaintiff claims Darrell Harris' services as president, director and sole shareholder, as well as his accounting services, were provided to the plaintiff in the capacity of an independent contractor; and in the alternative, the plaintiff claims it had a reasonable basis under section 530 of the Revenue Act of 1978 for not treating Darrell Harris as an employee. However, these claims are not facts within the meaning of Rule 14(B).

[**7] 13. In his capacity as president, director and sole shareholder, Darrell Harris presided at the regular meetings of the Board of Directors.

14. In his capacity as president, Darrell Harris made all fundamental decisions of the plaintiff.

15. In his capacity as president, Darrell Harris exercised supervision over the plaintiff's affairs.

16. Darrell Harris was the only individual who supervised, controlled, and directed the business of the plaintiff, including making management decisions.

17. Darrell Harris was the only individual responsible for the affairs of the plaintiff.

18. Darrell Harris was the only individual who performed accounting services for the plaintiff during the periods in question.

19. During the periods in question, Darrell Harris did not perform any account-

6: DARRELL HARRIS, INC. V U.S

ing services for anyone other than the plaintiff.

20. Darrell Harris worked full time for the plaintiff.

21. Darrell Harris had no supervisors.

22. Darrell Harris' services were integral to the operation of the plaintiff.

23. Darrell Harris was entitled to receive compensation not to exceed $ 25,000 for his services as president of the plaintiff for the calendar year 1986.

24. Darrell Harris was entitled to receive [**8] compensation not to exceed $ 50,000 for his services as president of the plaintiff for the calendar year 1987.

25. Darrell Harris had authority to sign corporate checks on behalf of the plaintiff.

26. The only other officer of the plaintiff during the periods in question was Judy Andrewski, an assistant secretary.

27. As assistant secretary, Judy Andrewski also had authority to sign corporate checks on behalf of the plaintiff and also signed the corporate minutes.

28. The only major corporate function performed by Judy Andrewski was signing the corporate minutes.

29. The plaintiff did not rely on a prior audit of its tax return by the Internal Revenue Service ("IRS") in not treating the individual Darrell Harris as an employee.

30. The only judicial precedent, published rulings, or technical advice that the plaintiff relied on in not treating Darrell Harris as an employee wasLetter Ruling 8616002 and Treas. Reg. section 31.3401(c)-1(f).

31.Letter Ruling 8616002 was not issued to the plaintiff by the IRS.

32. In not treating Darrell Harris as an employee, the plaintiff did not rely on a long-standing recognized practice of the accounting and tax industry in which Darrell Harris was [**9] engaged.

33. Plaintiff claims a reasonable basis existed under section 530 of the Revenue Act of 1978 for not treating Darrell Harris as an employee because its cash flow created undue business hardship in paying fixed amounts on a daily basis.

34. The plaintiff and Darrell Harris were located in the same office space during

6: DARRELL HARRIS, INC. V U.S

the periods in issue.

35. The plaintiff's bills for business expenses and Darrell Harris' bills for personal expenses were commingled.

36. The plaintiff paid the entire amount of the commingled bills and treated the portion of the bill allocated to Darrell Harris' personal expenses as an advance to Darrell Harris on the plaintiff's books.

37. The method adopted by the plaintiff in paying expenses would require the plaintiff to allocate substantially more funds to Darrell Harris in order to with-hold money for purposes of federal employment taxes.

[*1496] 38. During the periods in question, the plaintiff did not discuss with any accountant whether or not plaintiff was required to treat Darrell Harris as an employee.

39. During the periods in question, the plaintiff did not discuss whether or not it was required to treat Darrell Harris as an employee with anyone else.

40. [**10] The plaintiff claims it had reasonable cause for failing to file tax returns and for failing to make deposits of taxes pursuant to sections 6651(a) and 6656(a) of the Internal Revenue Code based on a good faith reliance on section 530 of the Revenue Act of 1978.

41. Darrell Harris is a graduate of the University of Oklahoma and a Certified Public Accountant ("CPA"), who has completed between 40-60 hours of account-ing classes in pursuing a Masters of Accountancy degree.

42. Darrell Harris is a former controller of two corporations and a former tax manager in the federal income tax department of Coopers & Lybrand. United States' brief at 4-10 (Mar. 12, 1991); Darrell Harris, Inc.'s response brief at 3 n. 2 (Mar. 26, 1991).

IV. ANALYSIS

A. *Determination of Employee or Independent Contractor Status*

For the reasons set forth below the Court finds Darrell Harris ("Harris") was a statutory, as well as a common law, employee of plaintiff Darrell Harris, Inc., instead of an independent contractor as urged by plaintiff. It is undisputed Harris was the sole shareholder, director, and president of his professional corporation, which was incorporated in 1982 for the purpose of protecting [**11] business

6: DARRELL HARRIS, INC. V U.S

assets from ongoing litigation involving its only principal, Harris. It is also undisputed Harris exclusively performed bookkeeping, accounting work, tax planning, and tax return preparation for plaintiff during the relevant periods of time on a full-time basis and without supervision. In his capacity as president, Harris presided at the regular meetings of the Board of Directors. The only other corporate officer was Harris' wife who served as assistant secretary and had authority to sign corporate checks, but her only corporate function was to sign the annual corporate meeting minutes.

Harris also made all fundamental decisions for plaintiff, exercised exclusive authority over all of plaintiff's affairs, and was the only person who supervised, controlled, and directed the business, including all management decisions. It is further undisputed Harris was entitled to receive $ 25,000 annual salary for his services in 1986, which was doubled to $ 50,000 in 1987. Harris also commingled his personal bills with those of plaintiff, and paid his personal bills as an advance on plaintiff's books.

Plaintiff accrued substantial tax savings by classifying Harris as an independent contractor. [**12] Consequently, plaintiff did not have to pay: (1) Federal Insurance Contributions Act ("FICA") taxes, governed by sections 3101 to 3106 of the Internal Revenue Code, as amended (26 U.S.C.) (the "Code"); (2) Federal Unemployment Tax Act ("FUTA") taxes, governed by sections 3301 to 3311 of the Code; and (3) Income tax withheld at the source ("wage withholding") taxes, governed by sections 3401 to 3406 of the Code. Sections 3121(d) and 3402(a) of the Code provide that the term "employee" includes any officer of the corporation. Section 3306(i) incorporates that definition by reference. An employee is also defined as "any individual who, under the usual common law rules applicable in determining the employer-employee relationship, had the status of an employee." See sections 3121(d)(2), 3306(i) and 3401(c) of the Code. There is no doubt, and no reasonable finder of fact could find otherwise, that under the undisputed facts in this case Darrell Harris was a statutory employee of plaintiff in his role as a corporate officer, and moreover was a common law employee in his role as a provider of services. See Spicer Accounting, Inc. v. United States, 918 F.2d 90, 94, 66 A.F.T.R.2d 5806 (9th Cir. 1990) [**13] (officer who performs substantial services for corporation is an employee and claim of independent contractor was specifically rejected because taxpayer was provided supplies and place to work, work was exclusive, and services [*1497] were integral to corporation); Texas Carbonate v. Phinney, 307 F.2d 289, 291, 293 (5th Cir. 1962) (Taxpayer-officer held to be employee where "he engaged in no business activity for others, and his work for the company was in no sense incidental to a separate or independent business or profession."); accord C.D. Ulrich, Ltd. v. United States, 692

6: DARRELL HARRIS, INC. V U.S

F. Supp. 1053, 1055 (D. Minn. 1988). Only officers who perform no services or perform only minor services and who are not entitled to receive any direct or indirect remuneration are exempted from employee tax status. Treasury Regulations sections 31.3121(d)-1(b)(FICA), 31.3306(i)-1(e)(FUTA) & 31.3401(c)-1(f) (withholding of wages). Darrell Harris fails to qualify for exemption on both prongs of the test.

"Where the record as a whole could not lead a rational trier of fact to find for the non-moving party, there is no 'genuine issue for trial,'" and summary judgment can be granted. [**14] Matsushita Elec. Indus. Co. v. Zenith Radio Corp., 475 U.S. 574, 587, 89 L. Ed. 2d 538, 106 S. Ct. 1348 (1986). Darrell Harris, Inc. has attempted to raise a factual dispute by way of an affidavit regarding the extreme fluctuations of cash flow of the corporation, which prevented establishment of a fixed salary for Darrell Harris. This fact is simply immaterial to the issue of whether Harris was an employee or an independent contractor, and even if it was material, the Court finds the affidavit to be conclusionary and insufficient to defeat summary judgment. Luckett v. Bethlehem Steel Corp., 618 F.2d 1373, 1380 & n. 7 (10th Cir. 1980); Fed. R. Civ. P. 56(e). It does not matter that the determination of whether Darrell Harris was an employee or an independent contractor is a fact question as argued by plaintiff. If there is no genuine dispute as to that fact question, then defendant is entitled to summary judgment as a matter of law on that issue. Anderson v. Liberty Lobby, Inc., 477 U.S. at 251-52; Fed. R. Civ. P. 56(c).

B. Reasonable Basis for Determination of Employee Status and Non-Filing and Non-Payment of Taxes

Next, plaintiff Darrell Harris, [**15] Inc. argues it had a reasonable basis to not treat its only worker as an employee because extreme fluctuations in the corporation's cash flow prevented the establishment of a fixed salary to compensate Harris. However, the United States points out that other than conclusionary allegations, plaintiff has presented no evidence of cash flow problems over the relevant period of time. Without weighing the evidence the Court also notes the incongruence of plaintiff's action of doubling its chief corporate officer's maximum salary from $ 25,000 to $ 50,000 during a time it now asserts it had extreme cash flow problems.

Moreover, instead of paying Harris a fixed salary, plaintiff commingled Darrell Harris' personal bills with its own, and paid the personal bills through salary advances to Harris. As a practical matter Harris was paid the equivalency of a fixed salary, and plaintiff's sleight-of-hand cannot go unnoticed. Also, the United States makes a persuasive argument that the salary advances in effect depleted the

6: DARRELL HARRIS, INC. V U.S

corporate funds and thus prevented direct payment of a fixed salary to Harris. Beyond consideration of Harris' status as a provider of services, plaintiff was required to consider [**16] its corporate officer as a statutory employee for tax purposes, which it did not. This failure alone undercuts plaintiff's good faith argument, which is tenuous at best. Finally, the United States argues the "cash flow problem" defense leads to an absurd result and sets a bad precedent for any other corporation experiencing hard times. The Court agrees that this exception would consume the rule, and should be reserved only for late-payment-of-tax issues where there has been no willful neglect.

Section 530(a)(1) of the Revenue Act of 1978, Pub. L. No. 95-600, 92 Stat. 2763, provides a worker shall not be deemed to be an employee unless the taxpayer had no reasonable basis for not treating the worker as an employee. The statute further provides there are three "safe harbors" that form the basis for an objective reasonable basis standard. These safe harbors are: (1) judicial precedent, published rulings, [*1498] technical advice to the taxpayer or a letter ruling to the taxpayer; (2) a past favorable IRS audit on the same issue; and (3) long-standing, recognized practice of the significant industry in which the individual was engaged.

Plaintiff has argued it relied onLetter Ruling 8616002 (July [**17] 17, 1985). However, this ruling does not qualify as a safe harbor because it was not issued to the taxpayer as required by the Code and is not reasonably relevant to the facts of this case; it therefore provides no reasonable basis for plaintiff's actions. Plaintiff also relies on Treasury Regulation section 31.-3401(c)-1(f), which as previously indicated, excludes from employee status, corporate officers who perform merely minor services for no entitlement of pay. In sharp contrast, Harris provided exclusive, substantial, and integral services for entitlement of substantial pay. It is spurious for a CPA with a Masters Degree in Accountancy with Harris' experience as a former controller of two corporations and a former tax manager in the federal income tax department of a Big Eight accounting firm to claim reliance on this statute. None of the other safe harbors apply to plaintiff as well.

However, a taxpayer may still be entitled to relief under the Act if the taxpayer otherwise had a reasonable basis for treating its worker as an independent contractor.Rev. Proc. 78-35, § 3.01, 1978-2 C.B. 536. This reasonable basis is to be liberally construed in [**18] favor of the taxpayer. General Inv. Corp. v. United States, 823 F.2d 337, 340 (9th Cir. 1987). "Without question, Congress intended to protect employers who exercised good faith in determining whether their workers were employees or independent contractors." Id. But even taking these highly favorable standards into account, the Court believes no reasonable trier of fact could find plaintiff had a reasonable basis to believe Harris was an independent

6: DARRELL HARRIS, INC. V U.S

contractor; to the contrary, plaintiff's belief was wholly unreasonable. The Court rejects plaintiff's "fixed salary" argument as insupportable. As the United States points out, plaintiff's reliance on one court's finding that a taxpayer's financial condition should be considered in determining whether taxes should be timely paid has no applicability to the issue of the proper classification of a worker, which is presented by the instant case. See In re Pool & Varga, Inc., 60 Bankr. 722, 727 (Bankr. E.D. Mich. 1986). Finally, plaintiff argues "thus, Harris, Inc., strenuously asserts it had not only reasonable basis not to treat its workers as employees, but reasonable cause for non-filing and [**19] non-payment of taxes applicable to employees, as well." Plaintiff's brief at 12; see 26 U.S.C. §§ 6651 & 6656. The Court is not certain, but if plaintiff is arguing under the previously cited authority that even if plaintiff is wrong on the employee status issue, which it is, then it should be excused from paying a penalty because it would suffer an undue hardship if it timely paid its taxes, then the Court simply rejects the argument.

First, the theory would not excuse non-filing of taxes, but rather only late payment. In re Pool & Varga, Inc., 60 Bankr. at 727. Here, there was no payment by plaintiff whatsoever regarding the employee status of Harris. Plaintiff's argument, if there is one, is only makeweight in this regard. Second, there is no evidence to support such a hardship argument, except for the conclusionary, self-serving testimony of Harris regarding the "extreme fluctuations in cash flow of Darrell Harris, Inc. . . . ." Plaintiff's brief at app., Affidavit of Darrell R. Harris at 1. Cf. id. at 725-26 (taxpayer had specific evidence showing late payment of taxes, and potential failure of business if taxes were timely paid). Therefore, [**20] the Court finds plaintiff did not "exercise[] ordinary business care and prudence and was nevertheless unable to file the return within the prescribed time," and therefore the delay is not due to reasonable cause. Treasury Regulations section 301.6651-1(c)(1). Finally, plaintiff cannot prove its failure to pay taxes was not due to "willful neglect", and the failure was "due to reasonable cause." Section 6651(a)(1); section 6656(a).

[*1499] V. CONCLUSION

Accordingly, the Court finds summary judgment is GRANTED to defendant United States. Plaintiff's complaint is therefore dismissed with prejudice, and judgment is granted to the United States on its counterclaim as it requested. Defendant United States is hereby ORDERED to file a final entry of judgment consistent with this Order and the local rules. W.D. Okla. R. 23(A). The case is hereby STRICKEN from the Court's May 1991, trial docket.

IT IS SO ORDERED THIS 7TH DAY OF MAY 1991.

7: CRITICAL CARE REGISTERED NURSING INC. V U.S.

CRITICAL CARE REGISTER NURSING, INC., Plaintiff, v. UNITED STATES OF AMERICA, et al, Defendants

Civil Action No. 89-7640

UNITED STATES DISTRICT COURT FOR THE EASTERN DISTRICT OF PENNSYLVANIA

776 F. Supp. 1025; 1991 U.S. Dist. LEXIS 13310; 91-2 U.S. Tax Cas. (CCH) P50,481; 68 A.F.T.R.2d (RIA) 5716

September 19, 1991, Decide
September 23, 1991, Filed

COUNSEL: [**1] JEFFREY COOPER, ESQ., BARRY H. FRANK, ESQ., MESIROV, GELMAN, JAFFE, CRAMER & JAMIESON, Philadelphia, Pennsylvania.

UNITED STATES OF AMERICA, ET AL by: Joseph F. Minni, Esq., Trial Attorneys, Washington, D.C., Michael J. Salem.

JUDGES: Raymond J. Broderick, United States District Judge.

OPINION BY: BRODERICK

OPINION

[*1026] MEMORANDUM

Plaintiff Critical Care Registered Nursing, Inc. ("Critical Care") commenced this action against defendants United States of America; Fred Goldberg, Commissioner of the Internal Revenue Service; and J. Robert Starkey, Regional Commissioner of the Internal Revenue Service (referred to hereinafter as "United States") to recover federal employment taxes assessed by the Internal Revenue Service ("IRS") and paid by Critical Care for the taxable years 1982 and 1983. The United States filed a counterclaim for additional taxes it claimed were owed by Critical Care. The case was tried to a jury which, after a four day trial, found for Critical Care. Judgment was entered for Critical Care in the amount of $ 5,188.00, pursuant to stipulation by the parties. Judgment was also entered against the United States on its counterclaim.

The United States has now filed a motion for judgment notwithstanding [**2] the verdict or, in the alternative, a new trial. For the reasons stated below, this Court

7: CRITICAL CARE REGISTERED NURSING INC. V U.S.

will deny both motions of defendant United States.

Plaintiff Critical Care is a business which provides specialized registered nurses to hospitals in need of temporary additional staffing for emergency rooms and intensive care units. Critical Care contracts with hospitals to supply nurses according the hospitals' requests for particular shifts, and contracts with nurses to work those shifts. Evidence at trial established that Critical Care does not prescribe for the nurses the work they are to perform at the hospitals, nor does it furnish uniforms, transportation, journals, sick pay, vacation pay, pensions, bonuses, insurance or licenses to its nurses. In addition to being registered with Critical Care, the nurses are permitted to be also employed directly by hospitals and/or be registered with other similar nursing agencies or registries. Further, the nurses may choose when, where and how often they work. Critical Care contends, and the jury found at trial, that it properly treated its nurses as independent contractors, and therefore was not liable for the employment taxes it had paid to the [**3] government but was, instead, entitled to a refund.

The United States now asserts in its motion for judgment notwithstanding the verdict or, in the alternative a new trial, that Critical Care is liable as a matter of law for the federal employment taxes assessed by the IRS. Asserting a presumed validity of the IRS assessments, the United States claims that Critical Care failed to produce evidence sufficient to overcome this presumed validity and thus, contrary to the jury findings at trial, failed to meet its burden of proof.

This case is governed by Section 530 of the Revenue Act of 1978, Pub.L. 95-600, 92 Stat. 2763, 2885-86 [*1027] (November 6, 1978) (codified at 26 U.S.C. § 3401 note (1982) (as amended). Section 530 (a) (1) provides:

Controversies Involving Whether Individuals are Employees for Purposes of Employment Taxes

(a) Termination of certain employment tax liability.--

(1) In general. --If--

(A) for purposes of employment taxes, the taxpayer did not treat an individual as an employee for any period, and

(B) in the case of periods after December 31, 1978, all Federal tax returns (including information returns) required to be filed by the taxpayer with respect to such individual [**4] for such period are filed on a basis consistent with the taxpayer's treatment of such individual as not being an employee, then for purposes of

7: CRITICAL CARE REGISTERED NURSING INC. V U.S.

applying such taxes for such period with respect to the taxpayer, the individual shall be deemed not to be an employee unless the taxpayer had no reasonable basis for not treating such individual as an employee.

Section 530 (a) (1) (emphasis added).

In addition, Section 530 (a) (2) provides three statutory 'safe havens' for the taxpayer. Pertinent to the present case, it states in part:

(2) * * * a taxpayer shall in any case be treated as having a reasonable basis for not treating an individual as an employee * * * if the taxpayer's treatment of such individual for such period was in reasonable reliance on any of the following:

* * *

(C) long-standing recognized practice of a significant segment of the industry in which such individual was engaged.

Section 530 (a) (2).

Even the "safe havens" of Section 530 (a) (2), however, are not the exclusive ways of meeting the reasonable basis requirement: "A taxpayer who can demonstrate a reasonable basis for the treatment of an individual in some other manner also is entitled to termination [**5] of employment tax liabilities." H.R.Rep.No. 95-1748, 95th Cong., 2d Sess. 3-4 (1978) (referred to hereinafter as "House Report"). As also stated inRev. Proc. 85-18, 1 C.B. 518, Sec. 3.01 (C) (1985) (referred to hereinafter as "Rev. Proc. 85-18"), "A taxpayer who fails to meet any of the three 'safe havens' may nevertheless be entitled to relief if the taxpayer can demonstrate, in some other manner, a reasonable basis for not treating the individual as an employee."

Thus, the Congressional mandate is clear that there are several avenues by which a taxpayer may prove, under Section 530, that it had a reasonable basis for not treating a worker as an employee.

Further, according to the House Report, Section 530 was intended "generally, [to] grant[] relief if a taxpayer had any reasonable basis for treating its workers as other than employees. The committee intends that this reasonable basis requirement be construed liberally in favor of the taxpayers." House Report at 631-32. As also stated inRev. Proc. 85- 18 Sec. 3.01 (c), "[The House Report] indicated that 'reasonable basis' should be construed liberally in favor [**6] of the taxpayer." Liberal construction in favor of the taxpayer was deemed necessary to pro-

7: CRITICAL CARE REGISTERED NURSING INC. V U.S.

vide interim relief to taxpayers involved in employment tax status controversies, many of which found retroactive tax liability through the reclassification of workers as employees who had previously been classified as independent contractors. Until Congress could develop a comprehensive, permanent solution to the many complex issues involved, the House Report stated, the reasonable basis requirement under Section 530 was to be construed "liberally" and was to be granted "if a taxpayer had any reasonable basis for treating its workers as other than employees." House Report at 631-32.

Congress has not, to date, passed a comprehensive Act to supersede Section 530. Congress has, instead, extended the provisions of Section 530 indefinitely, through the provisions of the Tax Equity and Fiscal Responsibility Act of 1982, 1982-2 C.B. 462, 536. Under this Act, according to Revenue Procedures issued by the IRS, Section 530 as amended continues to provide that "if, for purposes of the employment taxes [*1028] * * * , a taxpayer did not treat an individual as an employee for any period, then the [**7] individual will be deemed not to be an employee for that period, unless the taxpayer had no reasonable basis for not treating the individual as an employee."Rev. Proc. 85-18, Sec. 2.01.

The United States, in its motion for judgment notwithstanding the verdict or, in the alternative a new trial, contends that Critical Care failed to produce evidence at trial sufficient to overcome a presumed validity of the IRS assessments, and therefore failed to meet its burden of proof. This Court has considered this statement as an assertion by the United States that, contrary to the jury's finding, Critical Care did not carry its burden of establishing by a preponderance of the evidence that it had a reasonable basis, pursuant to Section 530, for not treating [*1029] its nurses as employees.

Congress has not defined "reasonable basis" for the purposes of Section 530 (a) (1), which is the section of general applicability. See Section 530 (a) (1), supra. After analyzing the statute and legislative history, however, this Court has concluded that, for purposes of Section 530 (a) (1), a taxpayer may establish that it had a reasonable basis for not treating its workers as [**8] employees by utilizing the traditional common law rules for determining whether workers are employees or independent contractors. However, under the Congressional mandate of Section 530, the taxpayer need only show that, under the common law rules, its treatment of its workers was reasonable. That is, under Section 530, the taxpayer's burden has been lessened and the taxpayer need only show a reasonable basis for not treating its workers as employees under the traditional common law rules.

This conclusion is based on the fact that relief under Section 530, according to

7: CRITICAL CARE REGISTERED NURSING INC. V U.S.

the House Report, was deemed necessary when strict enforcement of the common law rules resulted in the reclassifications of workers and the liability of taxpayers for employment taxes that had not been previously withheld and paid to the Treasury. Before this time, audits had been superficial or sporadic, and had only occasionally entailed examination of employment status issues; most taxpayers had relied on "their own judgment, industry practice, or, in a few industries, published Revenue Rulings." House Report at 632. Liability, many taxpayers insisted, was due to a change in position by the IRS through the strict [**9] application of the traditional common law factors. Id. Section 530, thus, was intended to be an interim solution for controversies between the Internal Revenue Service and taxpayers involving whether certain individuals are employees under interpretations of the common law by * * * (2) allowing taxpayers who had a reasonable basis for not treating workers as employees in the past, to continue such treatment without incurring employment tax liabilities * * * while the committee works on a comprehensive solution, * * *

House Report at 632 (emphasis added). Relief under Section 530, then, was intended to allow taxpayers who had had a reasonable basis "in the past," that is, under the traditional common law rules as existed before the increased enforcement by IRS, for the tax treatment of their workers to continue such treatment until Congress had resolved the many issues involved. See House Report at 631, and House Report at 632, quoted supra. Relief, further, was to be granted if a taxpayer had "any reasonable basis for treating workers as other than employees," id. at 633, and this reasonable basis requirement was to be "construed liberally in favor of the [**10] taxpayers." Id. This Court therefore concludes that "reasonable basis" for the purposes of Section 530 (a) (1) may be established by a showing by the taxpayer that, under the traditional common law rules, it had a reasonable basis for not treating its workers as employees.

In determining whether plaintiff Critical Care had a reasonable basis for not treating its nurses as employees, this Court instructed the jury that it was to consider two issues. The first was whether Critical Care had a reasonable basis for not treating its nurses as employees under the applicable traditional common law factors for determining whether a worker is an employee or independent contractor, of which the most important is the right to control, though no one factor is controlling. American Consulting Corp. v. United States, 454 F.2d 473, 477 (3d Cir. 1971). See also Treasury Regulation $ 31.3121(d)-1(c) (26 C.F.R. § 31.3121(d)-1(c) (generally, employer/employee relationship exists when person for whom services are performed has right to control and direct not only result but also details and means by which result is to be accomplished; on the other hand, generally, employer/independent [**11] contractor relationship exists when work-

7: CRITICAL CARE REGISTERED NURSING INC. V U.S.

er is subject to control merely as to result and not means and methods for accomplishing result). The second was whether Critical Care, in not treating its nurses as employees, had reasonably relied on a long-standing recognized practice of a significant segment of the industry in which the nurses were engaged. The first issue, of course, is based on Section 530 (a) (1), see supra, and the second is based on the third of the three "safe havens" of Section 530 (a) (2), see supra.

The jury was instructed that if it found that Critical Care had a reasonable basis for not treating the nurses a employees during 1982 and 1983 under the traditional common law factors, then the jury was to answer yes to question number one of the interrogatory, which was:

Has the plaintiff, Critical Care, proved by a preponderance of the evidence that in 1982 and 1983 it had a reasonable basis for not treating the nurses in question as employees under the traditional factors discussed in the Court's charge?

Interrogatories to the Jury, question number one.

The jury was instructed that if it answered question number one in the affirmative, then it was not [**12] to proceed to question number two. The jury answered question number one in the affirmative.

This Court, in examining the record, finds that there is ample evidence on which the jury could reasonably have found by a preponderance of the evidence that Critical Care had a reasonable basis under Section 530 (a) (1) for not treating its nurses as employees for the taxable years 1982 and 1983. Evidence was presented from which the jury could conclude that Critical Care neither directed and controlled, nor had the right to direct and control, the nurses in the performance of their duties at the hospitals. That is, Critical Care did not prescribe, nor did it have the right to prescribe the nurses' duties or the methods and means by which the nurses were to perform those duties at the hospitals. Critical Care gave no instructions to the nurses as to how the nurses were to perform their duties, and provided no training except for a brief orientation that was designed by a particular hospital and given only when a nurse had not previously worked at that hospital. Further, evidence was presented that the nurses performed no services for Critical Care on Critical Care's premises, and that the [**13] nurses were free to choose when and from whom they would accept work, and were permitted to be registered with Critical Care in addition to their regular jobs with hospitals or their registration with other agencies. From these and other factors ample in the record, this Court holds that there was more than sufficient evidence presented at trial from which the jury could conclude that Critical Care satisfied, by a prepon-

7: CRITICAL CARE REGISTERED NURSING INC. V U.S.

derance of the evidence, the dictates of Section 530 (a) (1) as to a reasonable basis for not treating its nurses as employees. Accordingly, the defendant United States' motion for judgment notwithstanding the verdict will be denied.

Since there was no miscarriage of justice in this case, defendant United States' motion for a new trial will also be denied.

ORDER

AND NOW, this 19th day of September, 1991, the Defendant, United States of America, et al., having filed a Motion for Judgment Notwithstanding the Verdict or, in the alternative, for a New Trial; for the reasons set forth in this Court's Memorandum of September 19th, 1991;

IT IS ORDERED: Defendant United States of America's Motion for Judgment Notwithstanding the Verdict or, in the alternative, for a New [**14] Trial, is DENIED.

8: REAG, INC. V U.S.

REAG, INC., Plaintiff and Counterclaim Defendant, v. UNITED STATES OF AMERICA, Defendant and Counterclaim Plaintiff.

No. CIV-91-1267-C

UNITED STATES DISTRICT COURT FOR THE WESTERN DISTRICT OF OKLAHOMA

801 F. Supp. 494; 1992 U.S. Dist. LEXIS 16351; 92-2 U.S. Tax Cas. (CCH) P50,475; 71 A.F.T.R.2d (RIA) 1524

August 28, 1992, Decided
August 28, 1992, Filed and Entered

JUDGES: [**1] CAUTHRON

OPINION BY: ROBIN J. CAUTHRON

OPINION

[*495] MEMORANDUM OPINION

I. INTRODUCTION

This case was tried to the Court on August 10-11, 1992. Plaintiff appeared through counsel, James H. Rice of Midwest City, Oklahoma. Defendant appeared through counsel Dennis M. Duffy and Jay P. Golder both with the Department of Justice in Washington, D.C. Having heard testimony of witnesses and considered all properly admitted exhibits, the Court enters the following opinion which shall constitute its findings of fact and conclusions of law.

This case involved a failure to withhold federal social security and unemployment taxes for real estate appraisers. The government claimed that the taxes were supposed to be paid because the workers were employees of plaintiff. REAG claimed that no taxes were due and owing because the workers were independent contractors.

II. LEGAL ISSUES

1. Whether on the facts presented, the appraisers were employers or independent contractors.

2. Whether on the facts presented, REAG reasonably relied on a long-standing recognized practice of a significant segment of the appraisal industry.

8: REAG, INC. V U.S.

3. Whether on the facts presented, REAG treated any person holding a [**2] position substantially similar to the appraisers as an employee.

4. Whether on the facts presented, REAG had a reasonable basis for treating the appraisers as independent contractors.

5. What is a significant segment of the appraisal industry for purposes of the "safe harbor" under Section 530 of the Revenue Act of 1978? See 26 U.S.C. ("I.R.C.") § 3401 note.

6. If REAG qualifies for the safe harbor, need REAG only show that it had a reasonable basis for not treating the appraisers as employees under the common law rules applicable in determining the employer-employee relationship rather than bearing the burden of proof by a preponderance of the evidence on this issue?

III. STIPULATIONS

On September 3, 1990, a delegate of the Secretary of the Treasury made assessments in the total amount of $ 47,686.26 against REAG, Inc. REAG paid $ 150 and timely filed an administrative claim for a refund, which was denied by the IRS. REAG brought this suit against the United States seeking a refund of its $ 150 payment.

The United States properly filed a counterclaim against REAG for the unpaid portion of the assessments in the total amount of $ 47,536.26, [**3] plus statutory interest and additions accruing after the dates of the assessments.

REAG is in the business of conducting real estate appraisals. During the years in question, approximately 70 to 80 percent of REAG's appraisal work related to residential property, with the remainder relating to commercial property.

[*496] REAG was incorporated in 1981 and was owned during the period in question by John W. (Bill) Strong, Robert Borders and Kenneth Stepp. Strong has held a professional appraiser designation from the Society of Real Estate Appraisers since the incorporation of REAG.

During the years 1986 and 1987, substantially all of REAG's appraisal work that was performed by persons REAG alleges to have been independent contractors was performed by Jack Carson, Richard C. (Chris) Borders, Ernest Helaire and Steve Ranney (collectively "Workers").

According to REAG's records, REAG paid the Workers the following amounts in 1986 and 1987:

8: REAG, INC. V U.S.

Worker	1986	1987
Jack Carson	$ 60,932.00	$ 57,605.25
Chris Borders	$ 23,847.75	$ 39,922.50
Ernest Helaire	$ 42,409.00	$ 43,807.44
Steve Ranney	$ 16,837.50	$ 25,832.50

REAG was responsible for all of the negotiations with potential clients, [**4] including discussions involving fee quotes, work time frame and the specific assignment of jabs to the Workers. The work files relating to the appraisals were the property of REAG.

The Workers could utilize the resources of REAG in preparing appraisals for REAG. In addition to having access to REAG's offices and secretarial staff, the Workers had access to REAG's cost databases. The billing invoices for residential appraisals were sent to clients on REAG's letterhead and required payments to be made directly to REAG. The Workers were paid for their appraisal work regardless of whether REAG was paid by its client. REAG withheld a portion of Ranney's paycheck and held it in trust for Ranney as a savings plan.

REAG did not rely on a prior tax audit for its treatment of the Workers as independent contractors. REAG did not rely upon judicial precedent, published rulings, respective technical advice, or a letter ruling to REAG in connection with its decision not to treat its appraisers as employees.

In the event that the appraisers are found to be employees rather than independent contractors and REAG is found not to qualify for the safe harbor under Section 530 of the Revenue Act [**5] of 1978 for the years at issue, REAG owes the United States the following amounts, as of September 3, 1990, less its payment of $ 150, any amount attributable to inclusion in their calculation of payments to Jack Carson in excess of the FICA limit of $ 43,800 in 1987, and any amount collected by the IRS and applied to the liabilities at issue, adjusted to date for interest:

8: REAG, INC. V U.S.

3 *FICA and Withholding Taxes*

QUARTER	TAX	INTEREST
1st, 1986	2,265.48	1,282.86
2nd, 1986	6,121.79	3,235.84
3rd, 1986	2,546.02	1,258.48
4th, 1986	1,778.76	819.61
1st, 1987	3,449.38	1,480.05
2nd, 1987	5,188.36	2,059.91
3rd, 1987	3,620.06	1,319.65
4th, 1987	4,656.96	1,534.39
TOTALS	$ 29,626.81	$ 12,990.79

3 *Federal Unemployment Taxes*

QUARTER	TAX	INTEREST
12-31-86	1,824.44	840.66
12-31-87	1,807.89	595.67
TOTAL	$ 3,632.33	$ 1,436.33

[*497] In the event REAG prevails, the United States owes it the amount of its $ 150 payment, plus any additional amounts paid or collected and applied to the liability at issue, and interest on these amounts, subject to the provisions of I.R.S. § 6402.

IV. FINDINGS OF FACT

The Court hereby incorporates all of the above stipulations as [**6] findings of fact.

REAG is a real estate appraisal firm. It solicits and receives orders for appraisals from property owners, lenders, and others and engages other appraisers to perform some of the appraisals. The appraisers inspect the property; consult various records of sales and values of comparable properties; analyze income and expense data on income-producing property; and prepare a report determining an appraised value for such property.

REAG accrued substantial tax savings by classifying its non-owner appraisers as independent contractors for tax purposes during the years at issue, 1986-1987.

8: REAG, INC. V U.S.

Consequently, REAG did not have to pay: (1) Federal Insurance Contributions Act ("FICA") taxes, governed by sections 3101 to 3106 of the Internal Revenue Code, as amended (the "Code"); and (2) Federal Unemployment Tax Act ("FUTA") taxes, governed by sections 3301 to 3311 of the Code.

However, REAG did treat its owner-officers, who also conducted appraisals, as employees. The IRS audite REAG, determined that the full-time, non-owner appraisers should have properly been treated as employees subject to withholding and employment taxes, and asserted deficiencies.

All federal tax [**7] returns, including, in particular, Forms 1099, required to be filed by REAG with respect to each of its non-owner appraisers were filed on a basis consistent with REAG's treatment of each such appraiser as not being an employee from the inception of REAG's business through 1987.

John W. Strong, Robert E. Borders, and Kenneth A. Stepp (the "Owners") are the founders, only stockholders, officers, and managers of REAG. Each has been consistently treated by REAG as an employee from its inception. All other persons performing appraisal services for REAG have been consistently treated by REAG as independent contractors.

Each of the non-owner appraisers was not an employee of REAG, as that term is used in Sections 3121(d)(2), 3306(i) and 3401(c) of the Internal Revenue Code, under the common law rules applicable in determining the employer-employee relationship, both generally and, specifically, pursuant to application of the twenty common law factors set forth inRev. Rul. 87-41, 1987-1 C.B. 296, in 1986 and 1987. See In re Rasbury, No. CV-91-H-2445-W, 92-1 USTC (CCH) P 50,195, at 83,775 n.14, 1992 U.S. Dist. LEXIS 3836, [**8] at *22 n.14 (N.D. Ala. 1992). This finding is reinforced by the results of REAG's survey. This finding provides an independent ground for REAG to prevail in this action.

[*498] The non-owner appraisers were skilled professionals who carried out their appraisal assignments independently, worked when and where they chose with no set hours, and were compensated solely on a fee-spli basis. These Workers received no inservice training from REAG and had to pay for their own continuing professional education. The Workers received no fringe benefits, except that they were permitted, at their own request and expense, to participate in REAG's health insurance program.

The non-owner appraisers determined the manner in which they carried out the appraisals that they performed. They also determined the bottom line figure as to the appraised value of the subject property, which was submitted to the client.

8: REAG, INC. V U.S.

Robert Borders is a partner of REAG and was a credible witness. He testified that appraisals were reviewed on a very limited basis, but if errors were found, then the appraiser was instructed to correct the inaccuracy. REAG was very concerned with its reputation and strived to not let appraisals [**9] that were deemed to be unethical, unprofessional, or inaccurate be sent to clients. Although REAG retained the right to accept, reject, or modify an appraisal, if the individual appraiser was adamant, then REAG would be stuck with the appraisal, but the individual appraiser might not be used anymore. Of approximately 10,000 to 12,000 appraisals, substantially less than one percent (1%) had to be modified. Some larger clients required the appraisal to be reviewed.

The Workers were provided work space at REAG and were not assigned specific offices, but each generally used the same offices on a consistent basis. These offices might also be shared on a limited basis by the part-time independent contractors. At one point the Workers were asked to remove their personal effects from the offices so that they would not appear to be employees. The Workers could work at home if they chose. The Workers had keys to the building. During the pertinent time in question, the

Workers were employed almost exclusively by REAG and generally worked over forty (40) hours weekly. The Workers were provided business cards from REAG, but other part-time workers were not. The IRS has not challenged [**10] the independent contractor status of the part-time appraisers. Some of these appraisers did not use the tools provided by REAG, but were paid the same way as the Workers on a fee-split basis.

The appraisers did not solicit their own clients. If an appraiser was terminated then REAG would get another appraiser to finish the job. REAG Workers were asked not to solicit REAG clients if the Workers left REAG. The Workers could hire their own assistants.

The most important aspect of the Workers' tasks was the appraisal. An important tool was the computer database subscriptions, which were provided by REAG as were plat maps of Oklahoma City. However, it was possible, although impractical, to make appraisals from court records as was done prior to the widespread use of computers in the industry. The Workers were trained and experienced professionals, and the most important tool of their trade was inside each appraiser's head. See In re Rasbury, 92-1 USTC (CCH) P 50,195, at 83,776 n.22, 1992 U.S. Dist. LEXIS at *23 n.22. The Workers provided their own cameras, measuring tape, and automobiles, but were paid a higher fee-split percentage [**11] for having to travel out of the market to conduct an appraisal and for expenses such as

8: REAG, INC. V U.S.

plat maps for out-of-market areas. In contrast, in at least one other firm, employees, as opposed to independent contractors, were permitted to use company vehicles to perform appraisals. REAG provided film and paid for developing. REAG provided telephones, and paid rent on the building. The Workers received business and personal phone messages at the REAG office, and received mail there as well. The completed appraisal forms were the property of REAG.

The Workers had signed contracts with REAG that evidence that they intended to be treated as independent contractors. The Workers were provided absolutely no paid fringe benefits like life insurance or sick or vacation leave. REAG paid the Workers semi-monthly based on a percentage of the fee charged to clients, and prior to the clients paying their bills. REAG had an errors and omissions policy that covered the Workers.

Steve Ranney testified that at the time he was hired he was told that he could not work for anyone else and believed that he would be fired if he did so. Nevertheless, Ranney testified that he did engage in outside employment [**12] during the time he worked for

REAG. Ranney was provided a computer cost database service at his [*499] other job although he was considered to be an independent contractor at that job. The Court did not find Ranney to be a completely credible witness. His answers lacked spontaneity. Ranney also owes the IRS money for delinquent taxes. REAG treated the appraisers as independent contractors in reasonable reliance on a long-standing recognized practice of a significant segment of the appraisal industry. This finding provides a second independent ground for REAG to prevail on its claim. The survey conducted by Market Analysis Group establishes that a significant segment of the independent fee appraisal firms in the relevant geographic area treated their non-owner appraisers as independent contractors during the relevant period.

The relevant market is the non-owner appraisers who either work exclusively or almost exclusively for real estate appraisal firms in the Oklahoma City metropolitan area. The practices during 1981 to 1987 represent long-standing practices in the relevant industry. Fifteen out of twenty, or 75%, of the survey respondents treated non-owner appraisers as independent [**13] contractors who either work exclusively or almost exclusively for real estate appraisal firms in the Oklahoma City metropolitan area. The percentage was slightly less if the employees were part-time--thirty out of forty-two, respondents or 71%. In the years 1981-82 the figures regarding independent contractors were higher: thirteen out of fifteen respondents or 87%.

8: REAG, INC. V U.S.

The survey lacked responses from 64 firms:

37 firms were in business in 1981-82, but were not in the 1990-91 phone book .
  utilized for the survey

7 firms gave no response

13 firms were unable to be contacted

7 firms are no longer in business and were not surveyed

64 total firms were not included in the survey results.

The Court finds that even if these 64 firms all treated their similarly situated workers as employees and not independent contractors, then plaintiff's statistics regarding independent contractors would still represent a significant portion of the relevant industry. However, it is more likely, and therefore the Court so finds, that the firms who did not participate in the survey treated their workers as independent contractors in the same proportion as those firms who responded to the [**14] survey.

The testimony of each of the Owners and witnesses, with the exception of Charles L. Monnot III of Market Analysis Group who did not testify on the subject, bolsters the finding that a significant segment of the independent fee appraisal firms in the relevant geographic area treated their non-owner appraisers as independent contractors during the relevant period. See General Inv. Corp. v. United States, 823 F.2d at 341. While a finding that the Workers were independent contractors under the common law factors is not dependent on the survey results, those results further reinforce the finding that the Workers were indeed independent contractors.

The personal observations of REAG's owners in conjunction with the application of the common law factors, as well as the survey results amply provide a reasonable basis for REAG treating the non-owner appraisers as independent contractors. This finding provides a third and separate basis for REAG to prevail in this action.

VI. CONCLUSIONS OF LAW

Jurisdiction of this Court is proper pursuant to 28 U.S.C § 1346(a)(1), venue is proper, and the Court has jurisdiction [**15] of the parties and subject matter. As

8: REAG, INC. V U.S.

pleaded in its complaint and in the final pretrial order, plaintiff's sole claim is for a refund of federal taxes. [*500] The determination of the tax by the Commissioner is prima facie correct unless overcome by a sufficient quantum of evidence. Welch v. Commissioner, 290 U.S. 111, 115, 78 L.Ed. 212, 54 S.Ct. 8 (1933). The taxpayer has carried its burden of proof with respect to the issues before the Court on three separate grounds: 1) the Workers were common law independent contractors; 2) REAG reasonably relied on a long-standing recognized practice of a significant segment of the industry in which such individual was engaged; and 3) REAG otherwise had a reasonable basis for not treating the Workers as employees. See generally, Marvel v. United States, 719 F.2d 1507, 1516 (10th Cir. 1983); Beatty v. Halpin, 267 F.2d 561, 564 (8th Cir. 1959); Chase Mfg., Inc. v. United States, 446 F. Supp. 698, 701 (E.D. Mo. 1978); In re McAtee, 115 Bankr. 180, 184 (N.D. Iowa 1990); In re Pearson, 86 Bankr. 179, 180 (Bankr. E.D. Mo. 1988). [**16]

REAG has carried its burden of proof by a preponderance of the evidence on each of the three independent grounds for demonstrating a reasonable basis for its treatment of the Workers as independent contractors. However, REAG is only required to carry its burden of proof by a lesser standard. See Critical Care Registered Nursing, Inc. v. United States, 776 F. Supp. 1025, 1028, 91-2 USTC P 50,481, at 89,830-31 (E.D. Pa. 1991) (rejecting IRS's argument that a preponderance of the evidence standard is necessary for the taxpayer to prove a reasonable basis and finding that the appropriate standard was lessened in conformity with Congress's intent of liberal construction for the taxpayer of the pertinent provision of the Tax Code); see also General Inv. Corp. v. United States, 823 F.2d 337, 340 (9th Cir. 1987) ("The IRS has embraced Congress' liberal construction directive in its procedural guidelines for § 530."); Ridgewell's Inc. v. United States, 228 Ct. Cl. 393, 655 F.2d 1098, 1105 (Ct. Cl. 1981) ("The 'reasonable basis' test is to be construed liberally in favor of the taxpayer.") (citations [**17] omitted); Darrell Harris, Inc. v. United States, 770 F. Supp. 1492, 1498 (W.D. Okla. 1991) (granting summary judgment to the IRS despite the "highly favorable standards" that Congress intended for the taxpayer); In re McAtee, 115 Bankr. at 184 (employers exercising good faith were without question intended by Congress to be protected from adverse tax consequences). There is no practical objective method to carry out Congress's directive of liberally construing the applicable tax provision other than lowering the hurdle of the taxpayer's burden of proof. The Court therefore holds that a taxpayer need only show a substantial rational basis for its decision to treat the Workers as independent contractors in order to prevail. *

* The Court is aware of the seemingly amorphous nature of a

8: REAG, INC. V U.S.

standard of review that is quantitatively less than a preponderance of the evidence. However, logically, the burden on the taxpayer must be some quantum more than the IRS' prima facie showing of correctness, but less than a preponderance. Certainly if the evidence weighed out evenly, then under such a standard the taxpayer would still prevail.

While a change of the burden of proof standard to some measure less than a preponderance gives this Court apprehension of the unfamiliar, it is not inconsistent with reviews of agency decisions that are familiar. See, e.g., United States v. Custodian of Records, S.W. Fertility Ctr., 743 F. Supp. 783, 787 (W.D. Okla. 1990) (the Court's role in reviewing the enforcement of an administrative subpoena by the government is strictly limited to a determination of whether the Court's process would be abused). The only difference in this case is that the advantageous deference usually accorded only to the government agency is instead given to the taxpayer as is expressly directed by Congress under this circumstance. Cf., e.g., FDIC v. Butler, No. CIV-87-2553-P, 1988 U.S. Dist. LEXIS 18103, at *5 (W.D. Okla. Nov. 4, 1988) (holding that FDIC Receiver was entitled to the nearly impenetrable defenses of FDIC corporate).

The Court's conclusion is also congruent with established precedent in the lop-sided playing field of the tax laws where it is usually the IRS that is given more than an equal share of litigation advantages, such as trial and appellate counsel, as well as costs, paid at taxpayers' expense, starting with a prima facie showing of tax assessment correctness, the placement of the burden of proof on the taxpayer, and the limitation of judicial decisions as precedent over other taxpayers. E.g., Welch v. Commissioner, 290 U.S. at 115; Beatty v. Halpin, 267 F.2d at 564; Stern & Co. v. State Loan & Fin. Corp., 205 F. Supp. 702, 706 (D. Del. 1962).

[**18] An employee is defined as "any individual who, under the usual Common law rules [*501] applicable in determining the employer-employee relationship, had the status of an employee." See I.R.C. §§ 3121(d)(2), 3306(i) & 3401(c).

The IRS has compiled a non-exclusive list of twenty factors that are used in the analysis of the status of workers: 1) instructions from the supervisor; 2) training;

8: REAG, INC. V U.S.

3) integration; 4) services personally rendered; 5) hiring, supervision and paying assistants; 6) continuing relationship; 7) set hours of work; 8) mandatory full time employment; 9) working on employer's premises; 10) set order of tasks to be performed; 11) oral or written reports; 12) payment by the hour, week, or month; 13) payment of business and/or travel expenses; 14) furnishing of tools and materials; 15) significant investment; 16) realization of profit or loss; 17) working for more than one firm at a time; 18) making service available to general public; 19) right to discharge; and 20) right to terminate.Rev. Rul. 87-41, 1987-1 C.B. 296 (1986 & 1987).

Other factors might include industry practice or custom, the intent of the parties and how they [**19] viewed the relationship, the existence of written and signed independent contractor forms, and whether employee-type benefits were provided. In re Rasbury, 92-1 USTC (CCH) P 50,195, at 83,775 n.14, 1992 U.S. Dist. LEXIS at *22 n.14.

No one factor is controlling, nor is the list complete, and the degree of importance of each factor depends on the occupation and the factual context in which services are rendered. United States v. Silk, 331 U.S. 704, 716, 91 L. Ed. 1757, 67 S. Ct. 1463 (1947), superseded by statute on other grounds as stated in Illinois Tri-Seal Prods., Inc. v. United States, 173 Ct. Cl. 499, 353 F.2d 216, 224-28 (Ct. Cl. 1965) (per curiam); E & W Auto, Inc. v. United States, No. 72- C-584, 75-1 USTC (CCH) P 9295, at 86,639 (E.D. Wis. Jan. 22, 1975); see alsoPriv. Ltr. Rul. 9001033 (Oct. 10, 1989) (persuasive, but non-precedential). Although no one factor is controlling, employer control over the manner in which the work is performed is the fundamental test. General Inv. Corp. v. United States, 823 F.2d at 341; American Consulting Corp. v. United States, 454 F.2d 473, 477 & n.12 (3d Cir. 1971); [**20] In re Imholte, 118 Bankr. 103, 107 (Bankr. D. Alaska 1990).

The mere existence of the right to control and direct the specific manner in which an individual works towards the desired end product is the relevant factor for inquiry. Moreover, it is the ultimate right to control the details and not the actual exercise of such supervision that is determinative. E.g., McGuire v. United States, 349 F.2d 644, 646 (9th Cir. 1965); accord Service Trucking Co. v. United States, 347 F.2d 671, 672 (4th Cir. 1965).

REAG did not have the right to control and direct the Workers as to the result to be accomplished or as to the details, manner, and means by which that result was accomplished. See In re Hamlin, Nos. 23473-B-2 to 23475- B-2, 74-2 USTC (CCH) P 9578, at 84,823 (D. Kan. July 11, 1974); E & W Auto, Inc. v United States, 75-1 USTC (CCH) P 9295, at 86,638-39. Even if REAG did have the right

8: REAG, INC. V U.S.

to control the result to be accomplished by the appraisers, then REAG did not have the right to control the means and methods used by the [**21] Workers in determining the appraisal, which is vital to a determination of independent contractor status under all of the circumstances of this case. See Illinois Tri-Seal Prods., Inc. v. United States, 353 F.2d at 228 & n.20; Critical Care Registered Nursing, Inc. v. United States, 776 F. Supp. at 1025 at 1029, 91-2 USTC P 50,481, at 89,831 (citing Treas. Reg. § 31.3121(d)-1(c) (26 C.F.R. § 31.3121(d)-1(c))); American Institute of Family Relations v. United States, No. CV 72-1402-WMB, 79-1 USTC (CCH) P 9364, at 86,878 (C.D. Cal. Feb. 22, 1979); Standard Life & Accident Ins. Co. v. United States, No. CIV-74-150C, 75-1 USTC (CCH) P 9352, at 86,841 (W.D. Okla. Feb. 27, 1975) (Chandler, J.).

Section 530(a)(1) of the Revenue Act of 1978, Pub. L. No. 95-600, 92 Stat. 2763, provides that an "individual shall be deemed not to be an employee unless the taxpayer had no reasonable basis for treating such individual as an employee." Section 530(a)(2) further provides:

[*502] For purposes of paragraph (1), a taxpayer shall in any case be treated as having a reasonable [**22] basis for not treating an individual as an employee for a period if the taxpayer's treatment of such individual for such period was in reasonable reliance on any of the following:

(A) Judicial precedent, published rulings, technical advice with respect to the taxpayer, or a letter ruling to the taxpayers;

(B) A past Internal Revenue Service audit of the taxpayer in which there was no assessment attributable to the treatment (for employment tax purposes) of the individuals holding positions substantially similar to the position held by this individual; or

(C) Long-standing recognized practice of a significant segment of the industry in which such individual was engaged.

I.R.C. § 3401 note. Of the three expressed safe harbors, REAG has relied only on the long-standing recognized practice of a significant segment of the relevant industry in subpart C.

In order for the safe harbor to apply, the following conditions must be satisfied: (a) at all times since January 1, 1978 through 1987, REAG must not have treated any worker holding a position substantially similar to the position of the Workers at issue as an employee; (b) REAG must not have treated any of the Workers at issue [**23] as an employee at any time; (c) all federal tax returns, including

8: REAG, INC. V U.S.

information returns, required to be filed by the taxpayer with respect to such Workers for such period have been filed on a basis consistent with REAG's treatment of such Workers as not being employees; and (d) REAG had a reasonable basis for not treating the Workers at issue as employees. Id. REAG has met each of these conditions.

The survey admitted into evidence was trustworthy and was properly conducted according to generally accepted survey principles. The survey demonstrates that a significant segment of the industry has had a long-standing recognized practice of treating non-owner appraisers as independent contractors. See generally, United States v. Generes, 405 U.S. 93, 105-06, 31 L. Ed. 2d 62, 92 S. Ct. 827 (1972) (noting that "significant" is distinctly less than "dominant"). The survey is the only practical manner for REAG to meet its proof on this issue and is admitted over the United States' hearsay objection. See Brunswick Corp. v. Spinit Reel Co., 832 F.2d 513, 522-23 & nn.5-6 (10th Cir. 1987); Randy's Studebaker Sales, Inc. v. Nissan Motor Corp., 533 F.2d 510, 520 & n.16 (10th Cir. 1976); [**24] Standard Oil Co. v. Standard Oil Co., 252 F.2d 65, 75 (10th Cir. 1958); Fed. R. Evid. 803(24). The survey results were bolstered by the testimony of the appraiser witnesses. The United States called no expert witness to challenge the survey. The United States neither conducted its own survey, nor presented persuasive evidence of employment practices that cast a shadow of a doubt on REAG's evidence. See General Inv. Corp. v. United States, 823 F.2d at 341. While there is no burden on the United States to come forward with any evidence to the contrary, such a failure to do so only substantiates the taxpayer's position that its actions were indeed reasonable. And, a taxpayer who fails to meet any of the above-mentioned three "safe havens may nevertheless demonstrate, in some other manner, a reasonable basis for not treating the individual as an employee."Rev. Rul. 83-152 (citing H.R. Rep. No. 95-1748, 95th Cong., 2nd Sess. 5 (1978), 1978-3 C.B. (Vol. 1) 629, 633);Rev. Proc. 78-35, § 3.01, 1978-2 C.B. 536. This reasonable [**25] basis is to be liberally construed in favor of the taxpayer. General Inv. Corp. v United States, 823 F.2d at 340. "Without question, Congress intended to protect employers who exercised good faith in determining whether their workers were employees or independent contractors." Id. REAG has demonstrated a reasonable basis for not treating the appraisers as employees under the common law rules applicable to determining the employer-employee relationship, as well as the other circumstances of this case. See Illinois Tri-Seal Prods., Inc. v United States, 353 F.2d at 218 (in close cases the view of the workers as to their own status is very significant).

[*503] Finally, the Court rejects the United States' argument that REAG is precluded from treating the non-owner appraisers as independent contractors

8: REAG, INC. V U.S.

because the corporation treated the owner-officer appraisers as employees. The owners have managerial control and ownership of the corporation and perform substantial duties and therefore are substantially distinct from the non-owner appraisers who are merely workers for the corporation. The Court concludes that these two [**26] groups of workers are therefore not similarly situated. See Spicer Accounting, Inc. v. United States, 918 F.2d 90, 94 (9th Cir. 1990) (officer who performs substantial services for corporation is an employee and claim of independent contractor was specifically rejected because taxpayer was provided supplies and place to work, work was exclusive, and services were integral to corporation); Texas Carbonate Co. v. Phinney, 307 F.2d 289, 293 (5th Cir.) (Taxpayer-officer held to be employee where "he engaged in no business activity for others, and his work for the company was in no sense incidental to a separate or independent business or profession."), cert. denied, 371 U.S. 940, 9 L. Ed. 2d 275, 83 S. Ct. 318 (1962); Darrell Harris, Inc. v. United States, 770 F. Supp. at 1496-97 (holding that a sole shareholder, director, and president of an accounting corporation was considered an employee instead of an independent contractor for federal employment tax law purposes because he performed substantial services for the corporation); C.D. Ulrich, Ltd. v. United States, 692 F. Supp. 1053, 1055 (D. Minn. 1988) [**27] (a corporate officer is to be treated as an employee if more than-minor services are rendered).

V. CONCLUSION

For the reasons discussed herein, the Court finds, and holds in favor of plaintiff REAG, Inc. on both plaintiff's claim against the United States of America, and on defendant's counter-claim. A judgment shall enter.

IT IS SO ORDERED THIS 28 DAY OF AUGUST 1992.

ROBIN J. CAUTHRON

UNITED STATES DISTRICT JUDGE

ENTERED IN JUDGEMENT DOCKET ON 8/28/92

9: J AND J CAB SERVICE V U.S.

J&J CAB SERVICE, INC., Plaintiff, v. UNITED STATES OF AMERICA, Defendant.

CIVIL ACTION NO. 1:93CV234-V

UNITED STATES DISTRICT COURT FOR THE WESTERN DISTRICT OF NORTH CAROLINA, ASHEVILLE DIVISION

1998 U.S. Dist. LEXIS 5630; 98-1 U.S. Tax Cas. (CCH) P50,360; 81 A.F.T.R.2d (RIA) 1656

March 29, 1998, Decided
March 30, 1998, Filed

DISPOSITION: [*1] Plaintiff's request for reasonable litigation costs under 26 U.S.C. § 7430 GRANTED. Judgment entered in favor of Plaintiff and case dismissed.

COUNSEL: For J & J CAB SERVICE, INC., plaintiff: T. Scott Tufts, Brian F.D. Lavelle, Roy W. Davis, Jr., Van Winkle, Buck, Wall, Starnes & Davis, P. A., Asheville, NC USA.

For USA, defendant: Thomas Holderness, Michael J. Martineau, U.S. Department of Justice, Washington, DC USA.

For USA, counter-claimant: Thomas Holderness, U. S. Dept. of Justice, Washington, DC USA.

For J & J CAB SERVICE, INC., counter-defendant: T. Scott Tufts, Brian F.D. Lavelle, Roy W. Davis, Jr., Van Winkle, Buck, Wall, Starnes & Davis, P. A., Asheville, NC USA.

JUDGES: RICHARD L. VOORHEES, UNITED STATES DISTRICT COURT JUDGE.

OPINION BY: RICHARD L. VOORHEES

OPINION

MEMORANDUM OPINION AND ORDER

THIS MATTER is before the Court for ruling upon proposed findings of fact and recommendations for disposition of Plaintiff's request for an award of

9: J AND J CAB SERVICE V U.S.

reasonable litigation costs as submitted by Chief Magistrate Judge Carl Horn. Pursuant to 28 U.S.C. § 636 and the standing order of designation, this Court had referred Plaintiff's request for fees and costs to Chief Magistrate Judge Horn for recommended disposition (doc. 44). In accordance with the briefing schedule established by the magistrate judge, the parties have fully briefed the issues (docs. 45, 46, 47, 48, 49). On September 8, 1997, Chief Magistrate Judge Horn recommended that the Court grant Plaintiff's fee request in its entirety, that is, in the amount of $ 68,967.75, and further recommended that the award be increased to include any reasonable costs and fees incurred by Plaintiff as a result of further briefing in response to objections raised by [*2] Defendant to the recommended award (doc. 50). By supplemental Memorandum and Recommendation, the magistrate judge corrected the requested amount to $ 106,710.00 (docs. 51, 52, 54). Defendant filed objections to the recommendation and Plaintiff responded in opposition (docs. 53, 55, respectively). Plaintiff incurred additional costs in reviewing and replying to Defendant's opposition to Plaintiff's fee request, and has requested additional fees of $ 2,234.50 and expenses of $ 768.00 (doc. 55, Supplemental Affidavit, Exhs. I-2 and J-2). Plaintiff's total attorneys' fee and expenses request under Section 7430 now totals $ 109,712.50. After consideration of the record, briefs of the parties, and relevant case authority, and for the reasons stated below, the Court affirms the recommendation of the magistrate judge.

STANDARD OF REVIEW

The Federal Magistrates Act provides that a district court shall make a de novo determination of those portions of the report or specific proposed findings or recommendations to which objection is made. 28 U.S.C. § 636. The parties were notified that the failure to file objections to the magistrate judge's Memorandum and Recommendation with the [*3] district court would constitute a waiver of the right to de novo review by the district court, Nettles v. Wainwright, 677 F.2d 404, 410 (5th Cir. 1982), and would preclude the parties from raising such objections on appeal. Thomas v. Arn, 474 U.S. 140 at 149, 106 S. Ct. 466 at 472, 88 L. Ed. 2d 435; United States v. Schronce, 727 F.2d 91 (4th Cir.), cert. denied, 467 U.S. 1208, 81 L. Ed. 2d 352, 104 S. Ct. 2395 (1984). "The statute [28 U.S.C. § 636(b)(1)(C)] does not on its face require any review at all, by either the district court or the court of appeals, of any issue that is not the subject of an objection." Thomas v. Arn, 474 U.S. 140, 149, 106 S. Ct. 466, 472, 88 L. Ed. 2d 435 (1985); Camby v. Davis, 718 F.2d 198, 200 (4th Cir. 1983); Keeler v. Pea, 782 F. Supp. 42, 43 (D.S.C. 1992). De novo review is not required or necessary when a party makes general or conclusory objections that do not direct the court to a specific error in the magistrate judge's proposed findings and recommendations. Orpiano

9: J AND J CAB SERVICE V U.S.

v. Johnson, 687 F.2d 44, 47 (4th Cir. 1982). In any event, the district judge retains responsibility for the final determination and outcome of the case. Wallace [*4] v. Housing Authority of the City of Columbia, 791 F. Supp. 137, 138 (D.S.C. 1992). Accordingly, the undersigned will conduct a careful review of the entirety of the magistrate judge's recommendation, and a de novo review of the portions of the recommendation to which specific objections have been filed.

OBJECTIONS BY DEFENDANT

Defendant raised the following specific objections to the magistrate judge's recommendation: 1) that the Magistrate Judge's determination that the government's position was not substantially justified is erroneous; 2) that the Magistrate Judge erroneously concluded that Plaintiff was entitled to actual attorneys' fees; and 3) that the Magistrate Judge erroneously concluded that Plaintiff was entitled to recover all costs (doc. 53). The Court will conduct a de novo review of these objections.

DISCUSSION

Administrative costs and litigation costs are available to a prevailing plaintiff in an administrative or court proceeding brought against the United States in connection with the determination, collection or refund of any tax, interest, or penalty under Title 26, subject to certain limitations and findings. 26 U.S.C. § 7430, et seq. [*5] Plaintiff has the burden of demonstrating, among other things, that it was the prevailing party, that Defendant's position was not substantially justified, and that the requested sum is reasonable and adequately supported with appropriate documentation. Id. Plaintiff must satisfy its burden in this regard, and Defendant must be given an opportunity to rebut same. See Bowles v. U.S., 947 F.2d 91 (4th Cir. 1991); In re Rasbury, 24 F.3d 159 (11th Cir. 1994).

When deciding a request for reasonable litigation costs under Section 7430, the district court has considerable discretion in determining whether the government's position was substantially justified and in determining the amount of the award. In re Rasbury, 24 F.3d at 166-67; Bowles v. United States, 947 F.2d at 94. The Supreme Court has stated that a request for attorneys' fees should not result in a second major litigation. Pierce v. Underwood, 487 U.S. 552, 108 S. Ct. 2541, 2549, 101 L. Ed. 2d 490 (1988).

The government does not dispute that Plaintiff was the prevailing party in this action, therefore, the issues to be determined are whether the government's position was substantially justified, and whether [*6] the requested attorneys' fees and litigation costs are reasonable, consistent with cases interpreting Section 7430,

9: J AND J CAB SERVICE V U.S.

and adequately supported by documentation. Courts look to cases interpreting fee awards under the EAJA for guidance in interpreting Section 7430. Pierce v. Underwood, 487 U.S. 552, 565, 108 S. Ct. 2541, 2549, 101 L. Ed. 2d 490 (1988)(EAJA "substantially justified" standard means reasonable basis in law and fact).

Additionally, the legislative history of Section 7430 sets forth some factors a court may consider in determining whether the position of the government was unreasonable: (1) whether the government used the costs and expenses of litigation against its position to extract concessions from the taxpayer that were not justified under the circumstances of the case, (2) whether the government pursued the litigation against the taxpayer for purposes of harassment or embarrassment, or out of political motivation, and (3) such other factors as the court finds relevant. Bowles v. United States, 947 F.2d at 94, quoting In re Testimony of Arthur Andersen & Co., 832 F.2d 1057, 1060 (8th Cir. 1987). These factors, with "all the facts and circumstances surrounding [*7] the proceeding," provide guidance to the court. In re Arthur Andersen, 832 F.2d at 1060. It is clear that the Court is permitted to step back and take an overall view of the government's conduct in deciding an award under Section 7430.

Substantial Justification

The Supreme Court has held that the term "substantially justified" means "justified in substance or in the main," that is, justified to a degree that could satisfy a reasonable person. This standard is consistent with a "reasonable basis both in law and fact." Commissioner, INS v. Jean, 496 U.S. 154 at 158, 110 L. Ed. 2d 134, 110 S. Ct. 2316, quoting Pierce v. Underwood, 487 U.S. 552, 565-566, 101 L. Ed. 2d 490, 108 S. Ct. 2541 (1988). The reasonableness of the government's position is based upon the record as developed in the underlying civil action prior to final adjudication, and no further discovery of the government's position is necessary. Commissioner, INS v. Jean, 496 U.S. at 160 n.8.

In granting Plaintiff's motion for summary judgment, the Court found that Defendant did not prevail on a single issue or argument which it put before the court. Although a loss in itself does not subject the United States to a fee award, a total loss [*8] at the summary judgment stage does reveal something regarding the merits of the government's position.

Regarding the contested issue of whether Plaintiff had made "payments" to its drivers, which would have triggered the requirement for Plaintiff to have filed informational returns on its drivers as a prerequisite to Section 530 relief,

9: J AND J CAB SERVICE V U.S.

Defendant argued that "With respect to the payment of fares, plaintiff and the drivers were in a principal/agent relationship. Defendant rationalized that "Since title to all funds vested in Plaintiff originally, the driver's share ultimately came from plaintiff." Ultimately, Defendant concluded that, "Thus, as the drivers' principal, plaintiff made payments to its drivers." (doc. 33, pgs. 4-5).

Regarding the "assumed agency" theory advanced by the government, this Court found:

> Defendant has stated a legal conclusion as if it were an established fact. [footnote omitted] As noted by the Court in its recent Howard's Yellow Cabs ruling, Defendant has presented no material facts, case law, or legislative history of § 530 in support of its assertion that the drivers were acting as Plaintiff's agents when they collected fares from the public. [*9] This objection is without merit.

(Doc. 44, pg. 17).

In addressing Defendant's objection to the definition of payment utilized by the magistrate judge, this Court stated:

> Defendant argues that the magistrate judge erred by relying upon the definition of payment as set forth in Manchester Music. In Manchester Music, the court was called upon to determine whether the IRS's decision to assess penalties against the plaintiff for failing to file informational returns (Form 1099) and for intentional disregard of information return filing requirements was correct. As in the instant case, the determinative issue was whether Manchester Music, in dividing the revenues from the machines with the proprietors of establishments where Manchester Music had placed coin operated video games, pinball machines, and juke boxes, made "payments" to the proprietors which triggered the 1099 filing requirement. The plaintiff and the proprietors had contractually agreed to divide equally the revenues (profits and losses) from the machines, and any expenses were allocated evenly between the parties. Plaintiff provided the machines in exchange for the proprietors' agreement to use exclusively [*10] plaintiff's machines.
>
> The court reasoned that the issue could be decided by either focusing on the legal definition of "payment," or by determining

9: J AND J CAB SERVICE V U.S.

whether the proceeds originally belonged to plaintiff in their entirety, such that the proceeds constituted income to the plaintiff. The court found that only the half of the proceeds to which the plaintiff had a right could be considered income to it, and, therefore, the transfer of the other half to the proprietors cannot constitute a "payment" to the proprietors. Discussing the legal definition of "payment" under Internal Revenue Code Regulation 1.6041(f), the court determined that a "payment" is not considered to have been made unless and until the moneys are first "reduced to the taxpayer's possession." That is, "a payment occurs with the transfer of possession, dominion, or control over money or its equivalent from a person who up to that point had been exercising such prerogatives over the same to another who is due the funds." The Manchester Music court found that, based upon the contractual agreement between plaintiff and the proprietors, as well as the actual method of division of the proceeds, neither party exercised dominion [*11] and control over the proceeds until the moneys were divided, such that no "payment" occurred.

Defendant disagrees with the Manchester Music court's analysis of Internal Revenue Code Regulation 1.6041(f), contending that the definition of payment utilized by the court, and relied upon by Chief Magistrate Judge Davis, is flawed with inconsistent reasoning. Defendant does not support its position with case authority. Further, Defendant's analysis is based upon its presumption that the drivers were acting as agents of Plaintiff when they collected fares, leading to the conclusion that Plaintiff had legal possession of all fares at all times. This position has been discussed and rejected earlier in this opinion.

Like the Manchester Music court, this Court finds that Plaintiff did not exercise control over all the proceeds such that the proceeds could be considered income to Plaintiff, or that the division of proceeds between Plaintiff and its drivers constituted a "payment" under the legal definition thereof. Manchester Music is valid authority and its facts are closely analogous to those of the instant case. This reasoning is also consistent with the Fourth Circuit's determination [*12] in Magruder v. Yellow Cab Co., 141 F.2d 324 (4th Cir. 1944)(money received by drivers from fare-paying public does not constitute "wages" paid by Yellow

9: J AND J CAB SERVICE V U.S.

Cab). Accordingly, the magistrate judge's reliance on Manchester
Music was proper, and Defendant's objections are overruled.

(Doc. 44, pgs. 18-20).

Defendant contended that the Magistrate Judge erroneously found that there was
no question of material fact concerning Plaintiff's basis for not treating its drivers
as employees. After reviewing the recommendation of the magistrate judge, this
Court overruled Defendant's objection.

Under Section 530(a)(2)(C), Plaintiff will be presumed to have acted with a reasonable basis if Plaintiff reasonably relied upon a long-standing recognized practice of a significant segment of the taxicab industry in treating the drivers as not
being employees. General Investment Corp. v. United States, 823 F.2d 337 (9th
Cir. 1987). This provision is to be construed liberally in favor of the taxpayer. Id.
Section 530 requires the "taxpayer to come forward with an explanation and
enough evidence to establish prima facie grounds for a finding of reasonableness
... this threshold burden [*13] is relatively low, and can be met with any reasonable showing. Once the taxpayer has made this prima facie showing, the burden
then shifts to the IRS to verify or refute the taxpayer's explanation." McClellan v.
United States, 900 F. Supp. 101 (E.D.Mich. 1995)(underlining added).

Without citation to case authority, Defendant contends that Plaintiff's survey and
other evidence is meaningless to establish reasonable reliance by Plaintiff. Case
authority cited by Plaintiff is clearly contrary to Defendant's position. In REAG,
Inc. v. United States, 801 F. Supp. 494, 92-2 U.S. Tax Cas. (CCH) 50,475 (W.D.
Okla. 1992), Plaintiff relied upon the results of a 1991 survey to establish that a
significant segment of the appraisal industry in the Oklahoma City area treated
their non-owner appraisers as independent contractors during the relevant period,
1981 to 1987. In General Investment Corp. v. United States, 823 F.2d 337 (9th
Cir. 1987), the Court found that trial testimony by GIC's president and one additional mine owner 1) that they "always hired" laborers as independent contractors, 2) that it was the routine practice of the previous owners to hire laborers as
independent contractors, [*14] and 3) that their impressions, based upon meetings with other mine owners, was that all hired the laborers as independent contractors, was sufficient to establish that the treatment of laborers as independent
contractors was a long-standing recognized practice of a significant segment of
the industry. The court did not find that Section 530 required that plaintiff's evidence be gathered, analyzed, or discussed in 1973, when GIC made the decision
to treat the laborers as independent contractors. See also, REAG, Inc. V. United
States, 801 F. Supp. 494, 1992-2 U.S. Tax Cas. (CCH) P50,475 (W.D. Okla.

9: J AND J CAB SERVICE V U.S.

1992); In re Rasbury, 130 B.R. 990, 1003 (Bankr. N.D. Ala. 1991), aff'd, 141 B.R. 752 (N.D. Ala. 1992).

Defendant's position is contrary to the liberal construction Congress intended in interpreting § 530, and contrary to established case authority, as cited by Plaintiff in its original brief and supplemental brief in support of summary judgment. The undersigned agrees with Chief Magistrate Judge Davis that Plaintiff has presented overwhelming evidence of a reasonable basis for its treatment of its drivers as non-employees. The Court finds that Defendant's objection is without merit.

[*15] (Doc. 44, pgs. 21-23).

After rejecting each of Defendant's arguments, this Court concluded as follows:

In sum, the Court finds that Plaintiff has established that it has met all of the requirements to be entitled to § 530 relief from liability for past employment taxes.

Plaintiff did not treat any of its drivers as an employee for any time during the relevant period; Plaintiff filed all required tax returns consistently with its treatment of its drivers as non-employees (Plaintiff was not required to file Forms 1099 because Plaintiff did not make "payment" to its drivers); and Plaintiff had a reasonable basis for not treating its drivers as employees, relying upon industry practice, advice from its accountants, and determinations by the Sheriff and Magistrate (see doc. 24, Ex. 3, Bosworth Survey, responses by 24 cab companies; Ex. 2, Queen Affidavit; Ex. 24, Queen deposition testimony; Ex. 8, Defendant's Responses to Plaintiff's Request for Admissions; Ex. 17, Howard Survey; Ex. 29, Preacher deposition testimony).

(Doc. 44, pg. 23).

As evidenced by the language used in this Court's opinion, it was clear to this Court, based upon uncontested facts and the applicable [*16] law, that Plaintiff was at all times entitled to the safe harbor provisions of Section 530, which was specifically enacted as a remedial statute to protect taxpayers from arbitrary action of the IRS which had been evidenced in the past. Instead of analyzing and applying Section 530 in a manner consistent with its purpose and case authority, the government bombarded the Plaintiff, and then this Court, with strained, unsupported arguments, and ignored the relevant case authority repeatedly cited by Plaintiff. This Court has no hesitation in finding that the government's position, during both the administrative proceedings and in this litigation, was not justified to a degree that could satisfy a reasonable person, and, therefore, such

9: J AND J CAB SERVICE V U.S.

position did not demonstrate a reasonable basis in law and fact. Commissioner, INS v. Jean, 496 U.S. 154 at 158, 110 L. Ed. 2d 134, 110 S. Ct. 2316. Accordingly, the Court finds that Plaintiff has met its burden of demonstrating that the government's position in this case was not substantially justified, and that it is, therefore, entitled to an award of its reasonable litigation costs. 26 U.S.C. § 7430, et seq.

Attorneys' Fees and Litigation Costs

Defendant objects that the [*17] magistrate judge erroneously determined that Plaintiff was entitled to recover all requested attorneys' fees and litigation costs. The magistrate judge found that the following factors were present in the instant case which justified an award in excess of the statutory rate: the cost of living has increased in Western North Carolina; the issues persistently raised by the IRS, without substantial justification, required and resulted in retention of counsel with advanced degrees and training in tax litigation; that there is a limited avail-ability of such counsel in the Lenoir, North Carolina area, and, accordingly, it is necessary to pay local counsel a higher hourly rate; and, that no lesser award of fees and costs would further the clear federal policies protecting citizens from unreasonable expenses proximately caused by unjustified government conduct (doc. 50, pgs. 5-6).

Defendant filed the following objections to the above recommendation: 1) the court is limited by the statutory cap of $ 75.00 per hour as the attorneys' hourly rate; 2) the costs for non-attorney personnel and other costs, such as copying, postage, and telephone, are not recoverable; 3) the magistrate judge's reference [*18] to "furthering federal policies" as a factor in his fee determination was improper because the court is limited to the remedy ($ 75.00 per hour) specified by Congress; and, 4) with respect to Plaintiff's accountant charges, only the $ 1947.66 for preparation of the survey is compensable (doc. 53, pgs. 7-14).

The Court has reviewed the documentation submitted by Plaintiff in support of its reasonable litigation costs. Plaintiff submitted a 24 page brief and hundreds of pages of exhibits and appendices in support of its request (docs. 46, 47, 55). The affidavits are detailed as to time, date, nature of work performed, hourly rate, and costs incurred. In fact, the government does not contend that Plaintiff's attor-neys' fees or the hours expended are unreasonable for the type of work performed or the results obtained.

It is clear that the Court has discretionary authority under Section 7430 to award an attorneys' fee in excess of $ 75.00 per hour. Bode v. United States, 919 F.2d

9: J AND J CAB SERVICE V U.S.

1044 (5th Cir. 1990)($ 150 per hour); Smoky Mountain Secrets, Inc. v. United States, 1996 U.S. Dist. LEXIS 18408, 78 A.F.T.R.2d (RIA) 7603 (E.D.TN 1996)($ 150.00 per hour); McConaughy v. United States, 833 F. Supp. 534 (D. MD. [*19] 1993)($ 150 per hour); Reag, Inc. V. United States, 1993 U.S. Dist. LEXIS 3656, 93-1 U.S. Tax Cas. (CCH) P50,199 (W.D.OK 1993)($ 100.00 per hour). The magistrate judge recommended an award to Plaintiff of its requested attorneys' fees for the following individuals at the following rates: 1 T. Scott Tufts ($ 100.00 to $ 160.00 per hour); Brian F.D. Lavelle ($ 150.00 to $ 185.00 per hour); Roy W. Davis, Jr. ($ 160.00 to $ 185.00 per hour); Albert Sneed ($ 170.00 to $ 185.00). Plaintiff's attorneys submitted affidavits of other attorneys in the Asheville, North Carolina area which attest to the reasonableness of these rates for attorneys of similar qualifications, experience, and ability. Defendant does not attempt to rebut the affidavits submitted by Plaintiff which indicate that Plaintiff could not have obtained the necessary legal expertise to successfully litigate this action in the Asheville, North Carolina area, for less than the hourly rates charged by its attorneys (doc. 47, Appendix D).

1 Plaintiff's attorneys' hourly rates increased over the period of representation in this case, October 1993 to the present.

[*20] In support of a limitation of Plaintiff's award to the $ 75.00 cap, Defendant argues that "Obviously a specialty in tax and litigation cannot be a special factor for cases governed by Section 7430 or else the exception would swallow the rule." (Doc. 54, pg. 10). However, cases cited by Defendant do recognize that a specialty in tax law can qualify as a special factor, and that the determination is made on a case by case basis, at the discretion of the district judge. In Bode, the Fifth Circuit explained as follows:

... The district court in this case, however, could have found that a special skill and expertise in tax were, under Pierce, "needful for the litigation in question." Pierce, 487 U.S. at 572, 108 S. Ct. at 2554.

Our decision today is distinguishable from Mattingly [Mattingly v. United States, 711 F. Supp. 1535, 1542 (D.Nev. 1989)] and Kim [Kim v. United States, 709 F. Supp. 932, 933 (N.D.Cal. 1989)] because we are not holding that a specialty in tax law, whether or not the underlying merits of the tax case actually require a tax specialist, automatically constitutes a special factor under section 7430. We do find, however, that the uncontroverted [*21] evidence is sufficient to establish that the Taxpayers could not have obtained qualified attorneys who could handle the complex nature of the underlying merits in this case--attorneys with a special expertise in tax law--for substantially less than the hourly rate of $ 150 awarded

9: J AND J CAB SERVICE V U.S.

by the district court, and certainly not for $ 75 per hour. We do not find that the district court erred in departing from the statutory cap of $ 75 per hour for Mr. Urquardt's time.

Bode v. United States, 919 F.2d at 1050-1051. The Court agrees with the magistrate judge that Plaintiff has submitted sufficient evidence to support a departure from the statutory cap of $ 75 for its attorneys. The Court will award attorneys' fees at the hourly rate submitted by Plaintiff's attorneys.

Defendant asserts that Plaintiff is not entitled to recover for cost of work performed by paralegals. Paralegal costs are recoverable under Section 7430. Miller v. Alamo, 983 F.2d 856, 862 (8th Cir. 1993)(If such hours were not compensable, then attorneys may be compelled to perform the work done by paralegals, thereby increasing the cost of the litigation); Worthington v. United States, 882 F. Supp. 509, 511 [*22] (E.D.N.C. 1994). Although Defendant does cite to cases wherein paralegal fees were not recovered, this determination is a matter committed to the discretion of the district judge who conducted the litigation. Plaintiff's paralegal costs will be allowed.

Defendant contends that with respect to expenses claimed for Plaintiff's accountant, only the costs of preparation of the survey ($ 1947.66) are recoverable. Section 7430(c)(1) specifies three types of expenses that are recoverable. The statute provides for recovery of "reasonable court costs," reasonable expenses of expert witnesses," and "reasonable cost of any study, analysis, engineering report, test, or project ... found by the court to be necessary, ..." 26 U.S.C. § 7430 (c)(1)(A) and (B). These costs are included within the broader category of "reasonable litigation costs", and the type of expenses listed in the statute are not intended to be an exhaustive list of recoverable expenses. Miller v. Alamo, 983 F.2d at 862 n.4.

While Defendant apparently concedes that the cost of preparation of the survey of cab companies is compensable under the statute, it offers no argument or explanation in support of its position that [*23] the other accountant expenses, including research and conferences with Plaintiff's attorneys, totaling $ 850.00, are not also compensable as a study, analysis, or project necessary to preparation of the case.

Defendant relies upon Worthington v. United States, 882 F. Supp. 509, 511 (E.D.N.C. 1994) in support of its position. However, recovery of the accountant's fee was denied in Worthington because the plaintiffs had failed to offer any explanation or argument in support of their request. Defendant's reliance on this case

9: J AND J CAB SERVICE V U.S.

is not persuasive under the facts of the instant case. Defendant's objection is without merit, and the Court will, in its discretion, award to Plaintiff the accountant expenses incurred in litigating this action.

Defendant objects to the magistrate judge's finding "that no lesser award of fees and costs would further the clear federal policies protecting citizens from unreasonable expenses proximately caused by unjustified government conduct." It is clear that Congress vested the Court with substantial discretion in determining a proper fee award under Section 7430, and that a reviewing court considers the propriety of the award under an abuse of discretion [*24] standard. The purpose of statutes such as EAJA and Section 7430, which direct a court to award fees and other expenses of litigation to a private party who prevail in litigation against the United States, was addressed by the Supreme Court in Commissioner, INS v. Jean, 496 U.S. 154, 110 L. Ed. 2d 134, 110 S. Ct. 2316 (1990) The purpose is to eliminate for the average person the financial disincentive to challenge unjustified governmental actions. "The Government's general interest in protecting the federal fisc [footnote omitted] is subordinate to the specific statutory goals of encouraging private parties to vindicate their rights and 'curbing excessive regulation and the unreasonable exercise of governmental authority.'" Commissioner, INS v. Jean, 496 U.S. at 164-165.

Section 530, the statute which Defendant failed properly to apply in the instant case, is a remedial statute which is to be construed in favor of the taxpayer. What should have been a "safe-haven" for Plaintiff became a five-year court battle during which Plaintiff expended over $ 100,00.00. The Court is certainly allowed to consider the purposes for which statutes were enacted and to apply the statutes in [*25] a manner which furthers those purposes. Contrary to Defendant's objection, the Court is not simply substituting its judgment for that of Congress by awarding a party who prevails against the government all of its requested litigation costs without warrant of the circumstances of the case. Defendant's objection is without merit.

In addition to the fact that Plaintiff prevailed on all of its claims, there are certain additional factors in this case which the Court considers relevant to its determination that the government's position was not substantially justified and that Plaintiff is entitled to recover the total amount of its litigation costs. Plaintiff is a small business located in Asheville, North Carolina. The catastrophic retroactive tax assessments by the IRS certainly had the potential for destroying Plaintiff's business, a potential which was certainly known to Defendant during the administrative proceedings and throughout this litigation. To this potential calamity, Defendant now seeks to add for Plaintiff the burden of a sizeable residue of

9: J AND J CAB SERVICE V U.S.

unpaid litigation costs. Defendant's position in this case and the resulting five years of litigation lends credence to Plaintiff's [*26] allegation that the IRS targeted it, as a small business, to use as a "guinea pig" to further its own agenda, in spite of the enactment of Section 530 as a bulwark against such action.

By Notice dated November 17, 1997, the Memphis Service Center of the IRS sent a "Reminder of Overdue Tax" to Plaintiff for all tax quarters and years currently before this Court (except for 9/30/89). The Notice demanded that Plaintiff pay a total of $ 367,314.17 in tax, penalty and interest by November 27, 1997 (doc. 56). Defendant's claims for these amounts was rendered unenforceable by this Court in its Memorandum Opinion and Order filed June 9, 1997. Despite Plaintiff's success in this litigation, Defendant persists in hounding Plaintiff for payment of taxes which were improperly assessed, in apparent disregard or ignorance of this Court's Order. Defendant's conduct is not well-regarded by the Court.

Although the Court is not identifying the above circumstances as "special factors" per se, these are circumstances of the litigation which the Court finds relevant to its fee award determination. See Bowles v. U.S., 947 F.2d 91 (4th Cir. 1991).

Under the authority of Hensley v. Eckerhart, 461 [*27] U.S. 424, 437, 76 L. Ed. 2d 40, 103 S. Ct. 1933 (1983), the district court is required to consider the relationship between the amount of the fee awarded and the results obtained, in order to recognize and discount fee requests which are exorbitant or unfounded. In the instant case, Plaintiff prevailed on all claims and succeeded in setting aside retroactive tax assessments, penalties and interest totaling $ 274,483.44, plus obtaining a refund of the $ 11,937.89 in taxes and penalties which it had paid under protest. Plaintiff's total litigation costs request of $ 109,712.50 is plainly not excessive relative to the $ 286,421.33 liability which Plaintiff faced. Accordingly, the Court finds that the fee awarded is reasonable and consistent with the results obtained.

ORDER

Based upon the foregoing, the Court adopts in their entirety the recommendations of the magistrate judge. Plaintiff's request for reasonable litigation costs under 26 U.S.C. § 7430 is **GRANTED**. Accordingly, **IT IS ORDERED** that Plaintiff is awarded fees and litigation expenses in the amount of $ 109,712.50, in addition to the relief provided in this Court's Memorandum and Order filed previously (doc. [*28] 44). Judgment for Plaintiff will follow.

IT IS SO ORDERED THIS the 29th day of March, 1998.

9: J AND J CAB SERVICE V U.S.

RICHARD L. VOORHEES

UNITED STATES DISTRICT COURT JUDGE

JUDGMENT

By Memorandum and Order filed June 12, 1997 (doc. 44), this Court GRANTED Plaintiff's Motion For Summary Judgment and ordered that the $ 11,937.89 in assessments which Plaintiff paid to the IRS under protest be refunded, together with interest as provided by law, and that Defendant be enjoined from enforcing collection of the amounts it assessed as stated in its "Notice[s] Of Intent To Levy . . . ." dated September 24, 1993. By Memorandum and Order filed simultaneously herewith, this Court GRANTED Plaintiff's request for reasonable litigation costs under 26 U.S.C. § 7430.

Accordingly, it is hereby ORDERED, ADJUDGED, and DECREED that Judgment be entered in favor of Plaintiff and that this case be dismissed on the merits; Defendant is to refund to Plaintiff $ 11,937.89 in taxes and penalties previously paid by Plaintiff, with interest thereon as provided by law, 28 U.S.C. § 2411; and Defendant is further ordered to pay to Plaintiff the sum of $ 109,712.50 in litigation costs.

[*29] **IT IS SO ORDERED THIS** the 29th day of March, 1998.

RICHARD L. VOORHEES

UNITED STATES DISTRICT COURT JUDGE

10: BOLES TRUCKING, INC., V U.S.

BOLES TRUCKING, INC., Appellee/Cross-Appellant, v. UNITED STATES OF AMERICA, Appellant/Cross-Appellee

No. 95-1826, No. 95-2088

UNITED STATES COURT OF APPEALS FOR THE EIGHTH CIRCUIT

77 F.3d 236; 1996 U.S. App. LEXIS 2626; 96-1 U.S. Tax Cas. (CCH) P50,112; 77 A.F.T.R.2d (RIA) 909

January 11, 1996, Submitted
February 22, 1996, Filed

PRIOR HISTORY: [**1] Appeal from the United States District Court for the District of Nebraska. 8:CV92-00120, 8:CV92-120. Honorable Lyle E. Strom, District Judge.

COUNSEL: Counsel who presented argument on behalf of the appellant was Tamara L. Schottenstein, Washington, D.C.. Additional attorneys appearing on the brief were Gary R. Allen and William S. Estabrook.

Counsel who presented argument on behalf of the appellee was Howard N. Kaplan, Omaha, NE. Additional attorney appearing on the brief was Michael S. Mostek.

JUDGES: Before BEAM and MORRIS SHEPPARD ARNOLD, Circuit Judges, and JONES, * Senior District Judge.

> * The HONORABLE JOHN B. JONES, Senior District Judge, United States District Court for the District of South Dakota, sitting by designation.

OPINION BY: JONES

OPINION

[*237] JONES, Senior District Judge

This appeal involves the attempt by the United States to collect employment taxes from plaintiff Boles Trucking, Inc.

10: BOLES TRUCKING, INC., V U.S.

The appeal by the United States presents two issues: first, what is the taxpayer's burden of proof when it asserts it had a "reasonable basis" for improperly classifying employees as independent contractors under Section 530 of the Revenue Act of 1978, 26 U.S.C. § 3401 note (Section 530) and secondly, whether the evidence was sufficient to support the jury's finding of a "reasonable basis". We find that the district court improperly instructed the jury on taxpayer's burden of proof, and reverse and remand on the appeal by the United States. In doing so, we do not reach the sufficiency of the evidence claim made by the United States.

Taxpayer's cross-appeal presents the issue of whether the district court [**2] properly assessed penalties against it because of its failure to pay employment taxes on behalf of David B. Boles (Boles), taxpayer's owner and [*238] president. We affirm on the issue raised in the cross-appeal.

I.

Taxpayer is a Nebraska corporation engaged in the business of leasing truck tractors, or "power units," to interstate trucking carriers. At all times relevant to this case, Boles was the sole stockholder, director, and president of taxpayer. In the relevant period from January 1984 through December 1987, taxpayer leased its tractors to Bee Line Motor Express, Inc. or to its successor, Cornhusker Motor Lines, Inc. Under the terms of the lease agreements taxpayer was to supply drivers with each leased tractor.

Although the lease agreements provided that the drivers were to be "employees" of taxpayer, during the years in question taxpayer treated its drivers as independent contractors. For tax purposes this means the taxpayer did not withhold any federal income (withholding tax or "WT") or Federal Insurance Contributions Act (FICA) taxes from the amount it paid to its drivers, nor did it make any payments of Federal Unemployment Tax Act (FUTA) taxes to the Internal Revenue [**3] Service. Rather than W-2's, taxpayer issued Forms 1099 to its drivers each year.

Boles was compensated by way of interest-free "loans against future profits" instead being paid a salary or wages. Under this arrangement the taxpayer was not withholding income taxes or FICA or FUTA taxes relative to Boles. There was also evidence that taxpayer paid many of Boles' personal living expenses and purchased a Lincoln Continental automobile for Boles' exclusive use.

Taxpayer underwent an employment tax examination in 1987 which resulted in the Commissioner of the I.R.S. reclassifying the truck drivers who worked for taxpayer as employees rather than independent contractors. The I.R.S. subse-

10: BOLES TRUCKING, INC., V U.S.

quently made assessments against the taxpayer for unpaid WT, FICA, and FUTA taxes, along with interest and penalties for years 1984 through 1987. The assessments also reflected the I.R.S.'s determination that Boles himself was an employee of taxpayer and that loans and other payments he received were actually wages.

In October 1991, taxpayer paid a small portion of the taxes, interest and penalties allegedly owed and thereafter filed administrative claims for a refund of the same. After the administrative [**4] claims were denied, taxpayer filed the present action against the United States seeking a refund of the taxes, interest, and penalties paid, along with a determination that it was not liable for the remaining taxes, interest, and penalties assessed against it. The United States filed a counterclaim for the outstanding balance of the unpaid taxes, interest, and penalties. The issues tried to the jury were: (1) whether taxpayer's drivers were employees or independent contractors; and (2) if taxpayer's treatment of its drivers as independent contractors was erroneous, whether it had a reasonable basis for such treatment pursuant to Section 530. 2

> 2 The parties agreed prior to trial that the district court would make the determination of whether the loans and other benefits received by David Boles from taxpayer were, in fact, taxable income. The parties further agreed that once the jury made its determinations regarding the classification and section 530 issues, the district court would determine the amount of money, if any, owed by the respective parties.

[**5] The jury found that taxpayer's drivers were employees. The jury went on to find that taxpayer had a reasonable basis for not treating the drivers as employees. When asked to state the basis for its finding on the latter issue, the jury made check marks by two of the four options; the long-standing practice of a significant segment of the industry and the advice of a CPA or tax return preparer.

II.

Under the Internal Revenue Code, an employer is required to pay one-half of the total FICA taxes assessed against its employees, and withhold from paychecks those FICA taxes owed by the employees themselves. 26 U.S.C. §§ 3101, 3102(a), 3402(a). Also, the employer is obligated to pay FUTA taxes for its employees. 26 U.S.C. § 3101. However, [*239] these obligations are incumbent upon an employer only if its workers are determined to be "employees" under the Tax Code.

Section 530 was created by Congress in 1978 to alleviate what was perceived as overly zealous pursuit and assessment of taxes and penalties against employers

10: BOLES TRUCKING, INC., V U.S.

who had, in good faith, misclassified their employees as independent contractors. In Re Rasbury, 130 Bankr. 990 (Bankr. N.D. Ala. 1991). The statute is a relief provision [**6] and provides an alternative method by which to avoid employment tax liability where a taxpayer cannot establish his workers are or were independent contractors. Section 530(a)(1) provides in pertinent part that although a taxpayer mistakenly classified its workers as other than employees, "the individual [worker] shall be deemed not to be an employee unless the taxpayer had no reasonable basis for not treating such individual as an employee."

The statute goes on to explain methods by which a taxpayer may show it had a "reasonable basis" for the improper classification of its workers. Section 530(a)(2) provides that reasonable reliance on any of three "safe harbors" or "safe havens" shall be treated as a reasonable basis for not treating an individual as an employee. The provision states:

For the purposes of paragraph (1), a taxpayer shall in any case be treated as having a reasonable basis for not treating an individual as an employee for a period if the taxpayer's treatment of such individual for such period was in reasonable reliance on any of the following:

(A) judicial precedent, published rulings, technical advice with respect to the taxpayer, or a letter ruling [**7] to the taxpayer;

(B) a past Internal Revenue Service audit of the taxpayer in which there was no assessment attributable to the treatment (for employment tax purposes) of the individuals holding positions substantially similar to the position held by this individual; or

(C) long standing recognized practice of a significant segment of the industry in which such individual was engaged.

In addition to the three specific safe haven rules, a taxpayer may take advantage of Section 530 by demonstrating that it had some other reasonable basis for treating its workers as independent contractors. H.R. Rep. Not. 95-1748, 95th Cong., 2d Sess. 5 (1978), reprinted in 1978-3 C.B. (vol. 1) 629, 633 (hereinafter House Report). As stated in Rev.Proc. 85-18, 1 C.C. 518, Sec. 3.01(c), "A taxpayer who fails to meet any of the three 'safe havens' may nevertheless be entitled to relief if the taxpayer can demonstrate, in some other manner, a reasonable basis for not treating the individual as an employee."

III.

10: BOLES TRUCKING, INC., V U.S.

Despite the relative breadth and complexity of the employment tax statutes discussed above, we are faced in the government's appeal with the narrow question
of [**8] what is the taxpayer's burden in proving it had a reasonable basis for
not treating its workers as employees under Section 530.

The district court instructed the jury that should it reach the reasonable basis
issue, the taxpayer was not required to prove this issue by a preponderance of the
evidence. The instruction concluded, " To prove reasonable basis, [taxpayer] need
only show that the existence of a reasonable basis is just as likely true than not
true. In other words, even if the evidence weighs out evenly, you must find that
[taxpayer] had a reasonable basis for not treating the drivers as its employees."

The government contends these instructions erroneously shifted the burden of
proof on the issue to the government. While we are not convinced the court's
instruction actually shifted the burden to the government, we nevertheless conclude the instruction erroneously stated the taxpayer's burden.

We start with the well-established principle that the Commissioner's determination of tax liability is entitled to a presumption of correctness and that the burden
is on the taxpayer to prove that the determination is erroneous. Helvering v.
Taylor, 293 U.S. 507, 55 S. Ct. 287, [**9] 79 L. Ed. 623 (1935); Day v.
Commissioner, 975 F.2d 534, 537 (8th Cir. 1992). It is further well established
that the quantum of proof required is that of a preponderance of the evidence.
Mattingly v. [*240] U.S., 924 F.2d 785, 787 (8th Cir. 1991). These general principles apply as well to the Commissioner's classification of a taxpayer's workers as
employees, i.e., once such a determination is made, it is the taxpayer's burden to
prove, by a preponderance of the evidence, that its workers are or were independent contractors. Beatty v. Halpin, 267 F.2d 561, 563 (8th Cir. 1959); Kiesel v.
U.S., 545 F.2d 1144, 1146 (8th Cir. 1976). The district court's instructions in this
regard were correct and the jury found the taxpayer had not satisfied its burden.

The taxpayer sought relief via Section 530 urging that when Section 530 is
involved, a lesser standard of proof is permitted for the taxpayer to prevail. It
should first be noted that nothing in the text of Section 530 itself suggests that
the taxpayer's traditional burden is to be altered when applying this statute. As
previously indicted, Section 530 permits a taxpayer/employer who had wrongly
failed to treat its [**10] workers as employees for tax purposes to avoid employment tax liability. This is done by the taxpayer showing it had a "reasonable
basis" for doing so. Under the clear text of the statute, "reasonable basis" is what
must be proved by the taxpayer - it is not an expression regarding the level of
proof or quantum of evidence. Congress's silence as to an altered burden must be

10: BOLES TRUCKING, INC., V U.S.

taken as meaning the traditional burdens apply, i.e., a taxpayer's reasonable basis must be proved by a preponderance of evidence. See, Grogan v. Garner, 498 U.S. 279, 286, 111 S. Ct. 654, 659, 112 L. Ed. 2d 755, (1991) (interpreting section 523 of the Bankruptcy Code to require a defrauded creditor to prove his claim by a preponderance of the evidence based on lack of Congressional directives to the contrary).

Nor does the legislative history of Section 530 lend support to the notion that the traditional burden of proof is to be altered. There can be no doubt that Section 530 is provision favorable to taxpayers and may serve to relive significant tax burdens. Section 530 was intended "generally, [to] grant[] relief if a taxpayer had any reasonable basis for treating its workers as other than employees. The committee [**11] intends that this reasonable basis requirement be construed liberally in favor of the taxpayers." House Report at 631-32. Taxpayer argues that the statutory language and legislative history "demonstrates that Congress fully intended that section 530 be interpreted and enforced quite differently than the norm in other tax cases where the Government is presumptively correct." We do not agree.

Liberal construction of Section 530 is not inconsistent with maintaining the taxpayer's traditional burden. Liberal construction may be effected in a variety of ways that have nothing to do with the taxpayer's burden of proof, including: 1) consideration of a wide range of conduct serving to establish reasonable basis; 2) broadly interpreting the scope of the safe havens specifically enumerated in the statute; and 3) leniently construing the term "reasonable."

The taxpayer relies in part on Critical Care Register Nursing, Inc. v. U.S., 776 F. Supp. 1025 (E.D.Pa. 1991). In Critical Care, the United States moved for judgment notwithstanding the verdict after a jury found that the taxpayer in that case had a reasonable basis for treating its workers as independent contractors instead of [**12] employees. Id. at 1028. While the court engaged in an extended discussion of the statute and its relatively taxpayer-friendly legislative history, there is no indication the court interpreted Section 530 to alter the burden of proof or shift the burden to the government. To the contrary, it is apparent the evidence was analyzed with the traditional preponderance standard being placed on the taxpayer. For example, the court submitted the issue to the jury via a special interrogatory which stated, "Has the plaintiff, Critical Care, proved by a preponderance of the evidence that in 1982 and 1983 it had a reasonable basis for not treating the nurses in question as employees...?" Critical Care, 776 F. Supp. at 1029 (emphasis added). Further, the court's holding based on the record was that "there was more than sufficient evidence presented at trial from which the jury

10: BOLES TRUCKING, INC., V U.S.

could conclude that Critical Care satisfied, by a preponderance of the evidence, the dictates of Section 530(a)(1) as to a reasonable basis for not treating its nurses as employees." Id. (emphasis added). The district court's opinion [*241] in Critical Care does not support the jury instruction given in the [**13] present case.

REAG, Inc. v. U.S., 801 F. Supp. 494 (W.D. Okl. 1992), is also cited by taxpayer as supporting its argument on this issue. In that case the court noted that "REAG has carried its burden of proof by a preponderance of the evidence on each of the three independent grounds for demonstrating a reasonable basis for its treatment of the Workers as independent contractors. However, REAG is only required to carry its burden of proof by a lesser standard." Id. at 500 (citing Critical Care, supra). By the REAG court's reading, Section 530 and its legislative history required the court to "... lower[] the hurdle of the taxpayer's burden of proof." Id. The court articulated this "lesser standard" by stating that "a taxpayer need only show a substantial rational basis for its decision to treat the Workers as independent contractors in order to prevail." Id. Language in the currently-challenged instruction was likely derived from commentary found in a footnote of the REAG case, which states in part:

> The Court is aware of the seemingly amorphous nature of a standard of review that is quantitatively less that a preponderance of the evidence. However, [**14] logically, the burden on the taxpayer must be some quantum more than the IRS' prima facie showing of correctness, but less than a preponderance. Certainly if the evidence weighted out evenly, then under such a standard the taxpayer would still prevail.

REAG, 801 F. Supp. at 500 note.

We believe the REAG court misinterpreted Section 530 and its legislative history and decided this issue wrongly. As previously indicated, there is nothing in the statute or its legislative history which supports the idea that the burden of proof under Section 530 is different than other tax cases. "Rational basis" for not treating workers as employees is what must be shown by the taxpayer; "[Substantial] rational basis" is not the level of proof required. Under the present facts it was taxpayer's burden to prove that its workers were properly classified as independent contractors by a preponderance of the evidence. Failing that, it became the taxpayer's burden to prove by a preponderance of the evidence that it had a rational basis for improperly classifying the workers. The district court's burden of proof instruction was reversible error.

10: BOLES TRUCKING, INC., V U.S.

This court has stated that "It has long [**15] been generally recognized that it is reversible error to place the burden of proof on the wrong party or to place an unwarranted burden of proof on one party. Voigt v. Chicago & Northwestern Railroad Co., 380 F.2d 1000, 1004 (8th Cir. 1967).

IV.

The taxpayer's cross-appeal alleges the district court committed reversible error by imposing penalties on the taxpayer for its failure to file tax returns attributable to "loans" or other fringe benefits recharacterized as salary to David Boles. The district court determined that David Boles was an employee of the taxpayer and should have been treated as such for employment tax purposes. Taxpayer does not challenge this determination. The district court went on to impose additions to the taxes due for taxpayer's failure to file returns or pay the taxes at the time they were due. Taxpayer contends the imposition of penalties in addition to the taxes was in error. We disagree.

Where an employer fails to file timely employment or unemployment tax returns or fails to make deposits of taxes, the Code provides for additions to the tax in the way of penalties. 26 U.S.C. § 6651(a)(1), 26 U.S.C. § 6656(a). The addition to taxes under [**16] § 6651 has been described as mandatory unless it is shown that the taxpayer's actions were due to reasonable cause and not due to willful neglect. Id.; Rubber Research, Inc. v. Commissioner, 422 F.2d 1402, 1407 (8th Cir. 1970). To escape the penalties, "the taxpayer bears the heavy burden of proving both (1) that the failure did not result from 'willful neglect,' and (2) that the failure was 'due to reasonable cause.'" U.S. v. Boyle, 469 U.S. 241, 245, 105 S. Ct. 687, 689-90, 83 [*242] L. Ed. 2d 622 (1985); Rubber Research, 433 F.2d 1403 at 1407. 3

> 3 Regarding our standard of review on this issue, the Supreme Court has stated that "Whether the elements that constitute 'reasonable cause' are present in a given situation is a question of fact, but what elements must be present to constitute 'reasonable cause' is a question of law." U.S. v. Boyle, 469 U.S. 241, 249, 105 S. Ct. 687, 692 n.8, 83 L. Ed. 2d 622 (1985) (emphasis in the original). We construe the district court's decision as analyzing whether the taxpayer presented evidence to establish the presence of reasonable cause, and thus review the decision under the clearly erroneous standard. It should be noted however that our conclusion on this issue would be the same even if we reviewed the issue de novo.

10: BOLES TRUCKING, INC., V U.S.

[**17] In this case the evidence showed that Boles was the sole owner of the taxpayer, as well as serving as its president, secretary and treasurer. In short, the evidence presented indicated that Boles alone ran taxpayer in all respects, both day to day and long term. During the time in question Boles did not draw a salary, but instead caused taxpayer to make him interest-free loans by writing checks payable to himself or to "cash" on taxpayer's checking account. Taxpayer also paid some of Boles' personal living expenses and paid for an automobile for Boles' exclusive use. Boles had no other employment other than with taxpayer, and his sole source of income was the money he received from taxpayer. Given its treatment of its drivers as independent contractors, the taxpayer was operating as a corporation without any employees for tax purposes.

In an effort to establish reasonable cause and the lack of willful neglect, the taxpayer argued below that he relied on the advice of his tax preparers in not paying taxes attributable to Boles' wages. The district court heard all of the evidence and rejected this contention.

Reasonable cause requires the taxpayer to demonstrate that he exercised [**18] "ordinary business care and prudence" but nevertheless was "unable to file the return within the prescribed time." 26 C.F.R. § 301.-6651(c)(1) (1984); U.S. v. Boyle, 105 S. Ct. at 690. Additionally it was the taxpayer's burden to show that its actions were not due to willful neglect, which has been interpreted as meaning a "conscious, intentional failure or reckless indifference." U.S. v. Boyle, 105 S. Ct. at 690. While a taxpayer may establish reasonable cause (and/or lack of willful neglect) by showing that it reasonably relied on the advice of an accountant or tax preparer, Chared Corp. v. U.S., 69-2 U.S. Tax Cas. (CCH) P9535 (N.D. Tex., 1969), aff'd. 446 F.2d 745 (5th Cir. 1971), ordinary business care and prudence on the part of the taxpayer are still required. Obviously, reliance on the advice of others must be reasonable to make out a showing of reasonable cause. Boles received no income other than that received from the taxpayer. For the years in question, Boles was running a corporation with no employees for federal tax purposes. Under the facts of this case, we agree with the district court that taxpayer failed to meet its burden of showing reasonable cause. The district court's [**19] determination is affirmed on this issue.

V.

In conclusion, we affirm the judgment of the trial court assessing penalties on taxpayer's failure to pay employment taxes on the money and fringe benefits given to David Boles. We reverse the judgment entered on the jury's verdict finding that taxpayer had a reasonable basis for treating its drivers as independent contractors, and we remand for a new trial on this issue.

11: APOLLO DRYWALL, INC. V U.S.

APOLLO DRYWALL, INC., Plaintiff, v. UNITED STATES OF AMERICA,
Defendant.

Case No. 5:91cv 16

UNITED STATES DISTRICT COURT FOR THE WESTERN DISTRICT OF
MICHIGAN, SOUTHERN DIVISION

1993 U.S. Dist. LEXIS 5611; 96-1 U.S. Tax Cas. (CCH) P50,196; 71 A.F.T.R.2d
(RIA) 1689

April 6, 1993, Decided
April 6, 1993, Filed

SUBSEQUENT HISTORY: [*1] Adopting Order of

June 3, 1993, Reported at: 1993 U.S. Dist. LEXIS 12106.

JUDGES: Scoville

OPINION BY: JOSEPH G. SCOVILLE

OPINION

*REPORT AND RECOMMENDATION ON APPLICATION FOR FEES AND
EXPENSES*

This was a civil action brought by a taxpayer against the United States for recovery of payroll taxes paid under protest. The central issue in the case was whether drywallers working for the plaintiff corporation were properly classified as independent contractors or employees. The case was resolved shortly before trial by stipulated judgment, in which the United States abandoned its position and agreed to the complete refund of the disputed taxes, plus penalties and interest. Within thirty days of the entry of the judgment, plaintiff filed an application for fees and expenses. The United States opposes the motion. The matter has been referred to me. As magistrate judges apparently do not have the authority to make dispositive rulings on post-trial motions for the assessment of fees in the Sixth Circuit, I am proceeding by report and recommendation. See Perez v. Secretary of Health and Human Services, 881 F.2d 330, 336 n.1 (6th Cir. 1989).

Plaintiff's motion for the assessment of attorney's fees and expenses is brought pursuant to 26 U.S.C. § 7430. [*2] That statute applies to court proceedings brought by or against the United States in connection with the determination, col-

11: APOLLO DRYWALL, INC. V U.S.

lection, or refund of taxes. It empowers the court to award a prevailing party reasonable administrative and litigation costs, including attorney's fees, if that party
can establish that the position of the United States in the proceeding was not "substantially justified." In order to be entitled to an award under this statute, the
moving party must show: (1) that all administrative remedies available within the
Internal Revenue Service have been exhausted; (2) that he or she is a "prevailing
party" as defined in 26 U.S.C. § 7430(c); (3) that the position of the United States
in the proceeding was not "substantially justified"; and (4) that the claimed litigation costs were reasonable. See Kenagy v. United States, 942 F.2d 459, 463 (8th
Cir. 1991). The burden of showing that each factor has been met rests upon the
moving party. Id. In its response to the motion, the United States concedes that
plaintiff properly exhausted administrative remedies and that the plaintiff was the
prevailing party [*3] in this litigation. The United States does contend, however,
that its position was substantially justified and that plaintiff's claimed expenses are
unreasonable. For the reasons set forth below, I find that plaintiff has sustained its
burden to show entitlement to fees and expenses, and recommend an award,
reduced in conformity with the limitations set forth in the statute.

Factual Background

Plaintiff, Apollo Drywall, Inc., is a small drywall company, completely owned by
Barbara Rutledge. Plaintiff is classified as a "women's business enterprise" (WBE)
by the State of Michigan. Mrs. Rutledge's husband owns and operates a separate
business, Spartan Drywall.

In early 1988, the Internal Revenue Service began an investigation of plaintiff's
compliance with federal tax laws requiring employers to make income tax withholding and pay social security (FICA) and federal unemployment (FUTA) taxes
on the wages of their employees. The investigation was conducted by Barbara
Rinehart, a Revenue Officer of the IRS. Ms. Rinehart determined that in 1986,
plaintiff had eight employees and used fourteen persons treated as independent
contractors. In 1987, the company had seven employees [*4] and twenty-three
independent contractors. Her investigation focused on plaintiff's decision to treat
some of its drywallers as subcontractors. In conducting her investigation, Ms.
Rinehart spoke to Barbara Rutledge, reviewed documents and took statements
from a number of the alleged independent contractors.

When interviewed, Ms. Rutledge explained that the unsteady nature of her business precluded her from maintaining a large staff of employed drywallers. Instead,
she kept a small staff of employed drywallers that she could count on to be at the
job site when needed. These persons were treated as employees for tax purposes

11: APOLLO DRYWALL, INC. V U.S.

and had the right to receive unemployment compensation when they were not working. The rest of the drywalling was done by independent contractors, who typically worked for a number of drywall companies.

The information gleaned by Ms. Rutledge pointed very strongly to independent contractor status. Each drywaller filed income tax returns indicating self-employment, usually on Schedule C. Plaintiff did not provide them training or supervision. Of course, plaintiff was required to direct the workers to the job site and to explain the result desired for each job. [*5] Past that, it appeared that plaintiff provided no supervision, did not keep track of hours worked, and allowed each worker to follow his own methods. Some contractors had drywalling businesses and employees of their own, and all did work for other drywall companies.

As with any inquiry as complex as this, there were some contrary indications. The interview of Pete Hughes (Rinehart Dep. Ex. 11) indicated that Mr. Hughes wanted to be an employee but the company refused him that status. He stated that there was no difference between him and the employed drywallers. Nevertheless, other factors on his interview sheet tended to prove independent contractor status. Likewise, the statement of Virgil Romig contained some answers tending to show employee status. For example, in question 16, he indicated that he would be bound to tell the company if the customer wanted additional work from him. In addition, in question 31, he indicated that the company could not sue him. Yet, numerous other answers indicated independent contractor status, including lack of supervision, ownership of own tools, and the ability to hire and fire his own workers.

Ultimately, Ms. Rinehart concluded that all plaintiff's [*6] workers were employees and not independent contractors. The principal reason underlying her decision appears to be that the independent contractors were performing the same basic job as plaintiff's employees and therefore should be considered employees. (See Supporting Statement, Rinehart Dep. Ex. 3 at p. 3). Consequently, Ms. Rinehart determined that the independent contractors should have been treated as employees, and she made an assessment of back taxes against plaintiff in the amount of $ 25,754.00, including interest and penalty, for the years 1986 and 1987.

Plaintiff paid this amount under protest in July of 1990. Plaintiff pursued its administrative remedies by requesting a refund and seeking an appellate conference. Plaintiff was represented by counsel in this endeavor. On September 12, 1990, plaintiff's counsel submitted a 25-page brief analyzing the facts and the law relevant to the independent contractor question. Plaintiff's request for refund was rejected at the appellate level. However, the IRS offered to settle by conceding the 1986 taxes in exchange for a concession by plaintiff on the 1987 taxes. This offer, which represent-

11: APOLLO DRYWALL, INC. V U.S.

ed roughly a 50-50 compromise, was apparently [*7] not based on any difference between the years 1986 and 1987. Rather, it seems to have represented a compromise based on the perceived merits of the case. Plaintiff rejected the offer.

On April 1, 1991, plaintiff filed its complaint in the present action. The parties proceeded with discovery, which was accomplished with the court's intervention being required on only two occasions. In February of 1992, the parties arbitrated their dispute pursuant to W.D. Mich. L.R. 43. The arbitrator, after reviewing the evidence, found in favor of plaintiff and awarded plaintiff a refund of all taxes and interest. The award also included some amount for attorney's fees, apparently reduced to provide the United States with an incentive to settle. The United States rejected the award and demanded a trial de novo.

In May of 1992, the United States moved for summary judgment on two issues. First, the United States sought a declaration that the "safe harbor" provisions of section 530(a) of the Revenue Act of 1978 were not available to plaintiff. Second, the United States argued that plaintiff was not entitled to receive a credit for taxes that were actually paid by the independent contractors if [*8] they were to be reclassified as employees. Judge David W. McKeague conducted a hearing on the motion on June 26, 1992. The judge denied the motion with regard to plaintiff's ability to rely on the safe harbor defense, but granted the motion as to the unavailability of a credit for taxes paid. [1]

> 1 Because the government did not prevail, the question of a cred-
> it to plaintiff was mooted.

The matter was scheduled for jury trial in July of 1992. Shortly before the trial, the parties informed the court that the matter would be resolved by consent judgment. A judgment was entered on July 21, 1992, in favor of plaintiff awarding a refund of $ 17,502.00 in taxes, $ 1,557.00 in penalties, and $ 7,053.00 in interest.

Substantial Justification For Government's Position

The first contested issue in this case is whether plaintiff has proved that the government's position was not "substantially justified" within the meaning of 26 U.S.C. § 7430(c)(4). This standard was copied by Congress [*9] from the Equal Access to Justice Act (EAJA). See Kenagy v. United States, 942 F.2d 459, 464 (8th Cir. 1991). In construing both EAJA and section 7430, the courts have adopted a standard of objective reasonableness. See Pierce v. Underwood, 487 U.S. 552, 565 (1988) (Under EAJA, substantially justified means "justified in substance or in the main -- that is, justified to a degree that could satisfy a reasonable person."); Beaty v. United States, 937 F.2d 288, 292 (6th Cir. 1991) (under section 7430,

11: APOLLO DRYWALL, INC. V U.S.

position of United States is substantially justified if objectively reasonable). The government's position is substantially justified "if a reasonable person could think it correct, that is, if it has a reasonable basis in law and fact." United States v. Real Property Located at 2323 Charms Rd., 946 F.2d 437, 441 (6th Cir. 1991) (quoting Pierce, 487 U.S. at 566 n.2). The Supreme Court has indicated that objective indicia, such as the terms of settlement and the stage at which the merits were decided are relevant in determining reasonableness. Pierce, 487 U.S. at 568. [*10] Ultimately, however, an examination of actual merits of the government's litigating position is usually required. Id. at 568-570. [2]

> 2 Relying on legislative history, the government argues that the court should consider as a factor whether the government used the costs and expenses of litigation to extract unjustified concessions from the taxpayer and whether the government pursued litigation for purposes of harassment or out of political motivation. (See Brief in Opposition, docket # 53, at 4). These factors do not appear in the statute or in any controlling case authority. Consequently, although such egregious behavior would certainly be relevant to a finding of unreasonableness, it is not necessary that these factors be present as a prerequisite for an award under section 7430.

The question, therefore, is whether the United States was reasonable in asserting that the drywallers in question were employees of plaintiff. Under the Internal Revenue Code, a person is an employee for FICA [*11] and FUTA purposes if the individual has the status of an employee under common law rules. 26 U.S.C. § 3121(d), 3402. Under case law and regulations, the relationship of employer and employee exists when the person for whom services are performed has the right to control and direct the individual who performs the services, not only as to the result to be accomplished by the work but also as to the details and means by which that result is accomplished. 26 C.F.R. § 31.3401(c)-1(b); see Lanigan Storage & Van Co. v. United States, 389 F.2d 337, 338 (6th Cir. 1968). The Supreme Court established in United States v. Silk, 331 U.S. 704 (1947), that numerous factual inquiries may be relevant to the central question of right to control. Following Silk and other cases, the Internal Revenue Service has synthesized twenty common law factors to be analyzed as elements showing the existence of control. See, e.g., Rev. Rul. 87-41, 1987-1 Cum. Bull. 296, 298-99. These factors include the length of employment, opportunity for profit or loss, right [*12] to discharge workers, substantial investment by the worker, skill or training required, right to employee assistance, integration of the worker's business into the employer's, and method of payment. See, generally, Annot., What Constitutes

11: APOLLO DRYWALL, INC. V U.S.

Employer-Employee Relationship For Purposes of Federal Income Tax Withholding, 51 A.L.R. Fed. 59 (1978). No single factor is controlling. See Bartels v. Birmingham, 332 U.S. 126 (1947).

Applying these factors to the facts now of record, I conclude that the United States was unreasonable in asserting that the drywallers in question were employees of plaintiff. The administrative record compiled by Revenue Officer Rinehart pointed unequivocally towards independent contractor status. The income tax returns of the workers showed that they considered themselves to be independent contractors, used federal identification numbers rather than their social security numbers, and paid taxes accordingly. Plaintiff made Form 1099 filings for each independent contractor. Ms. Rinehart's factual investigation supported independent contractor treatment, as virtually all relevant common-law factors [*13] indicated the lack of the requisite control by plaintiff over these workers. Significantly, most of the contractors indicated on their questionnaires (Rinehart Dep. Ex. 11) that they had the right to hire someone if they thought it was necessary to get the job done, and that plaintiff would not have the right to hire or fire assistants for them (question no. 17). Plaintiff did not provide training or close supervision, except for dictating the desired end results. Although no case in such a fact-specific area is free from all doubt, the record before the IRS provided no reasonable support for a finding of employee status. See Lanigan Storage & Van Co. v. United States, 389 F.2d 337 (6th Cir. 1968); Kurio v. United States, 281 F. Supp. 252 (S.D. Tex. 1968) (drywall construction workers held not employees of contractor). 3

> 3 The strongest evidence in support of the government's position appears in the interviews of Hughes, Sich, and Romig. Viewing all relevant factors, it appears clear that even these workers were independent contractors, although their situations could be argued as being ambiguous. Nevertheless, the ambiguities in their situations did not justify the action of the IRS in reclassifying all plaintiff's workers to employee status. If the IRS had merely reclassified these workers, it could tenably argue that its position was reasonable, although probably incorrect. In the present circumstances, in which the IRS relied on ambiguity in the situations of three workers to reclassify all of them, the position of the IRS appears patently unreasonable.

[*14] The administrative position of the IRS, as formulated by Ms. Rinehart, was contrary to the manifest weight of the common-law factors relevant to independent contractor status. The position appears to have been based upon a complete misreading (and perhaps even perversion) of the "safe harbor" provisions of sec-

11: APOLLO DRYWALL, INC. V U.S.

tion 530(a) of the Revenue Act of 1978. (Section 530 is found in the legislative notes following 26 U.S.C. § 3401). Section 530(a) of the Revenue Act of 1978 was enacted by Congress in reaction to the perceived inconsistent and arbitrary action of the Internal Revenue Service in reclassifying independent contractors as employees. Congress intended the section to serve as a safe haven sheltering employers who had acted in good faith in treating workers as independent contractors. Section 530(a) provides, in general, that if an employer did not treat an individual as an employee for employment tax purposes, the employer's treatment of that person would not be upset "unless the taxpayer had no reasonable basis for not treating such individual as an employee." Section 530(a)(2) goes on to list three specific statutory "safe harbors" by which [*15] the employer could prove that it acted with a reasonable basis. If the employer falls within the safe harbor, application of the common law test is unnecessary and the employer is automatically spared a reclassification of the workers. If the company cannot claim protection under one of the safe harbors, then the twenty common law factors must be used to determine employee status. See In re Rasbury, 130 Bankr. 990, 1010-11 (Bankr. N.D. Ala. 1991).

Section 530(a) precludes an employer's reliance upon the safe harbor provision if the employer has treated an individual holding a substantially similar position as an employee. § 530(a)(3). Apparently relying on this provision, Revenue Officer Rinehart of the IRS determined that plaintiff was not eligible for safe harbor treatment, as plaintiff had drywallers on its payroll performing substantially the same job as those workers claiming to be independent contractors. This was a reasonable interpretation of section 530(a). However, rather than rejecting the safe harbor defense and proceeding to a common-law analysis of employee status, Ms. Rinehart appeared to conclude that the similarity in functions between [*16] plaintiff's employees and independent contractors required, as a matter of law, that all independent contractors be reclassified to employee status. (See Rinehart Dep. Ex. 3, at 3: "The examining agent's position appears to be that since some workers were considered employees, and all workers were doing the same job (hanging drywall), they should all be considered employees.").

This is an illogical construction of section 530(a), and it turns the statutory provision on its head. Disqualification from the safe harbor protections of the act does not, by any stretch of the imagination, automatically direct a finding of employee status; it just means that the workers are not automatically independent contractors. Hence, an analysis of the common-law factors is necessary. "If a company cannot claim protection under one of the safe harbor provisions, then IRS is free to scrutinize the employer's classification against 20 'common law' factors." H.R. Rep. No. 979, 101st Cong., 2d sess. (1990) (quoted in In re Rasbury, 130 Bankr.

11: APOLLO DRYWALL, INC. V U.S.

at 1010). Instead of viewing plaintiff's disqualification from the safe harbor provision as requiring a common-law analysis, the [*17] IRS apparently took the unwarranted position that disqualification from the safe harbor protection automatically justified the reclassification to employee status. As Judge McKeague found at the summary judgment hearing, the position of the IRS defies all logic. The mere fact that a defense is not available does not mean that a claimant wins automatically. It just means that claimant must prove its case.

In arguing that its litigation position was substantially justified, the United States raises several untenable arguments. First, it points out that plaintiff bore the burden of proof to show independent contractor status. This observation is correct, but unavailing. If the implication of defendant's position were followed, the IRS could take virtually any position it wished at the administrative level, assess taxes, and require taxpayers to bring suit, in which the taxpayers would have the burden of proof. The mere fact that the taxpayer has the burden of proof does not justify the taking of an unreasonable litigation position.

In a related vein, the United States points out that both parties pursued discovery until late in the case. Again, this observation is correct but unavailing. [*18] The United States has pointed to no new information uncovered during discovery that caused an eleventh hour change in the government's position. As far as I can tell, the government had virtually the same information at the administrative stage as it did by the end of the litigation. Likewise, the government does not help its position by pointing to two "facts" that were confirmed late in the litigation (Brief, p. 9). The United States argues that it was not until January of 1992 that plaintiff ultimately confirmed that its employed drywallers were properly treated as employees, and it argues that only at the deposition of plaintiff's president was it confirmed that employed and independent contractor drywallers all did the same jobs. Neither of these facts were ever an issue. There was no likelihood that plaintiff would suddenly recant and confess that its employed drywallers were actually independent contractors. Likewise, it was patent from the outset that all drywallers did basically the same job. This so-called "ammunition" was available to the government when the first shots were fired in this skirmish, as early as 1988.

In summary, I find that any reasonably objective person [*19] viewing the facts known to the United States throughout this litigation would conclude that the drywallers were independent contractors and not employees. The mere fact that the safe harbor provision was not available to plaintiff is immaterial, as the common-law factors pointed clearly to this conclusion. The effort expended by plaintiff from the time of the administrative appeal was made necessary only because of the unreasonable insistence by the IRS on an untenable position.

11: APOLLO DRYWALL, INC. V U.S.

Reasonableness of Claimed Fees

The second disputed issue is the reasonableness of the fees claimed by plaintiff. Plaintiff claims $ 22,930.50, consisting of $ 3,687.00 for fees and costs incurred at the administrative level; $ 9,928.50 incurred for litigation through arbitration; $ 7,095.00 incurred from arbitration through the entry of judgment; and $ 2,220.00 for post-judgment fees and expenses, including preparation of the application for fees. Attorney time was billed at the rate of $ 110 an hour for time expended in 1989 and $ 120 per hour thereafter.

I find that plaintiff's application for fees is inconsistent with section 7430 in two major respects. Each is discussed below.

1.

First, the [*20] statute provides that attorney's fees "shall not be in excess of $ 75 per hour unless the court determines that an increase in the cost of living or a special factor, such as the limited availability of qualified attorneys for such proceeding, justifies a higher rate." 26 U.S.C. § 7430(c)(1)(B)(iii). The affidavit of plaintiff's counsel and attachments establish that the claimed rate of $ 120 per hour is "reasonable" as that term is usually defined in attorney's fee proceedings. That is, the rate is within the range generally charged by attorneys of like experience on similar matters. This, however, is not the statutory test. This statute, like the EAJA, establishes a $ 75 per hour limit. As the Sixth Circuit has remarked in the EAJA context, "the $ 75 statutory rate is a ceiling and not a floor." Chipman v. Secretary of Health and Human Services, 781 F.2d 545, 547 (6th Cir. 1986). The statute provides only two exceptions to this ceiling -- increases in the cost of living and special factors. Plaintiff has not proved the existence of either exception.

The main thrust of plaintiff's presentation is that the claimed [*21] $ 120 per hour rate is fair and reasonable in light of prevailing market conditions. The Supreme Court has squarely held that this fact does not constitute a "special factor." In Pierce v. Underwood, 487 U.S. 552 (1988), the Court construed the identical provision of the EAJA. The Court found that Congress thought $ 75 an hour was generally "quite enough public reimbursement for lawyer's fees, whatever the local or national market might be." 487 U.S. at 572. Consequently, it is not sufficient to merely prove that the claimed fee in excess of the statutory maximum is reasonable. The moving party must show the existence of some special circumstance, and that showing has not been made here. [4]

4 Relying on Powell v. Commissioner, 891 F.2d 1167 (5th Cir. 1990), plaintiff argues that the rate must merely be reasonable.

11: APOLLO DRYWALL, INC. V U.S.

> Powell was decided under a former version of the statute, which
> did not contain the $ 75 cap. 891 F.2d at 1168 n.1. The cap was
> added by Pub. L. 99-514 in 1986.

[*22] Likewise, plaintiff has not shown entitlement to relief under the cost-of-living provision of section 7430. The Sixth Circuit has held, in the EAJA context, that the district court must first determine whether the claimed fee is justified by the prevailing market rate for attorney services of the kind and quality rendered in the case and next should consider whether cost-of-living increases justify an award in excess of $ 75 per hour. See Begley v. Secretary of Health and Human Services, 966 F.2d 196, 199-200 (6th Cir. 1992). In the present case, plaintiff has shown that the claimed fees fall within the fair range of prevailing market rates for like services. Plaintiff has not, however, made a factual showing concerning any change in the cost-of-living after 1986, the date of the enactment of the relevant amendment to 26 U.S.C. § 7430. Although there obviously has been an increase in the cost of living since that time, the court is left to speculate on the present record concerning the exact increase. As this is a matter of proof, not speculation or guesswork, I conclude that plaintiff has failed to prove entitlement [*23] to a cost-of-living increase.

2.

Section 7430 denies a prevailing party recovery of litigation costs "with respect to any portion of the administrative or court proceeding during which the prevailing party has unreasonably protracted such proceedings." 26 U.S.C. § 7430(b)(4). Applying this statutory provision, I find that the award of fees to plaintiff should be reduced to account for two instances in which plaintiff contributed to the unnecessary expense and delay of this lawsuit.

First, plaintiff filed a motion to compel the production of documents on October 28, 1991, without certifying in the motion that a personal conference had been held with opposing counsel in a good-faith effort to resolve the discovery dispute, as required by Local Rule 27(d). This required the court to enter an order (docket # 11) holding the motion in abeyance, directing the parties to confer by telephone to resolve the dispute, and requiring the filing of a statement setting forth the results of the discovery conference. The order cancelled a hearing previously scheduled for resolution of the motion. The time records submitted by plaintiff disclose that 2 1/2 [*24] hours was spent in conference and preparation of the discovery statement (Billing of 1/16/92, entry of 12/3/91). Plaintiff should not be allowed to recover for this time.

11: APOLLO DRYWALL, INC. V U.S.

Second, the government should not be forced to reimburse plaintiff for opposing the government's motion for summary judgment concerning the availability of a credit for payments made by the independent contractors under section 3402(d). Plaintiff's billings dated June 1 and July 1, 1992, indicate that sixteen hours was spent in researching and briefing plaintiff's response to the government's motion. Without any further detail, I can only assume that one-half the time was spent on the tax credit issue and the other on the safe harbor issue. In his oral ruling, Judge McKeague found that plaintiff's position on the tax credit issue was completely unsupported by the Internal Revenue Code. Eight hours of attorney time expended in June and July of 1992 should therefore be disallowed.

Conclusion

I find that plaintiff has borne its burden of showing entitlement to fees and expenses under section 7430 for proceedings before the IRS and this court. The hourly rate for attorney's fees, however, should be reduced [*25] to $ 75, as plaintiff has not demonstrated the existence of either of the statutory exceptions to that ceiling rate. In addition, the award should be reduced by 10 1/2 hours to account for plaintiff's own conduct in increasing expense and delay.

Although plaintiff has provided copies of attorney time billings, plaintiff has not provided a summary totalling the hours expended or the out-of-pocket costs claimed, nor has plaintiff shown fees separately from expenses in a summary. Plaintiff should file a summary showing total hours expended, minus the 10 1/2 hours disallowed, multiplied by the $ 75 statutory rate. The summary should also separately itemize expenses. I recommend that plaintiff be awarded fees and expenses in accordance with that summary.

Dated: April 6, 1993

Joseph G. Scoville

U.S. Magistrate Judge

NOTICE TO PARTIES

Any objections to this Report and Recommendation must be filed and served within ten days of service of this notice on you. 28 U.S.C. § 636(b)(1)(C); Fed. R. Civ. P. 72(b). All objections and responses to objections are governed by W.D. Mich. L.R. 13(b). Failure to file timely objections may constitute a waiver [*26] of any further right of appeal. United States v. Walters, 638 F.2d 947 (6th Cir. 1981); see Thomas v. Arn, 474 U.S. 140 (1985).

12: REVENUE RULING

Revenue Ruling 77-279

Rev. Rul. 77-279; 1977-2 C.B. 12; 1977 IRB LEXIS 80

July 1977

[*1]

SUBJECT MATTER: Section 61.-Gross Income Defined

APPLICABLE SECTIONS:

26 CFR 1.61-1: Gross income. (Also Sections 62, 162, 170, 1401, 3121, 3306, 3401; 1.62-1, 1.162-1, 1.170-2, 1.1401-1, 31.3121 (d)-1, 31.3306 (i)-1, 31.3401 (c)-1.)

TEXT:

Child care services in own home. Factual situations illustrate the tax treatment of amounts received and amounts expended for child care provided by individuals in their own homes; Rev. Rul. 56-70, 1956-1 C.B. 460 superseded.

Advice has been requested as to the Federal income tax consequences and the Federal employment or self-employment tax consequences in connection with day care services performed by taxpayers under the circumstances described below.

Situation 1. Under the auspices of a charitable organization formed to provide day care for needy children, an individual takes care of such children in the individual's home during the working hours of the children's parents. The individual has complied with the state's licensing requirements for day care services. The charitable organization rather than the individual designates the children assigned to the individual. The individual furnishes a hot lunch and morning and afternoon snacks daily for the children and provides suitable furniture, toys, and activities [*2] for them. The individual receives no payment of any kind from the parents, but the organization gives the individual $13 per week per child to repay the estimated amount of out-of-pocket expenses in connection with the day care services rendered. These payments do not exceed actual expenses. The organization makes periodic inspections to insure that the children assigned to the individual are receiving proper care. The organization has the authority to remove the children from the care of the individual if proper care is not provided.

The parents of children enrolled in the program have no voice in the selection of the individual who cares for the children. They pay the organization, according to

12: REVENUE RULING

their ability, for the cost of administering and providing the day care services, such payments ranging from $2 to $21 per week per child. The organization is recognized by the Internal Revenue Service as one that is exempt from Federal income tax under section 501 (c) (3) of the Internal Revenue Code of 1954 and one to which contributions are deductible under section 170 (c).

Situation 2. An individual takes care of a child whose parents work during the day, as discussed in Rev. Rul. 56-70, 1956-1 C.B. 460. [*3] The parents leave the child at the individual's home in the morning before going to work and call for the child in the evening upon returning from work. The parents rely upon the individual's judgment in caring for the child and issue no instructions other than relative to diet, health and rest, and occasionally relative to special foods, medicines, etc., that the child may require from time to time. The individual is told whom to contact in case of emergency. The individual personally determines the amount of attention the child requires, the types of meals to be served, and the manner in which to cope with any situation likely to arise in rendering child care services. The individual is free to perform household chores at any time during which the child does not require personal attention, such as, while the child is taking an afternoon nap. The individual receives a fixed weekly fee from the parents for these services. However, the individual is not held out to the public as engaging in day care work, and is not required to obtain a license for such work under state law.

Section 61 (a) of the Code and the Income Tax Regulations thereunder provide that, except as otherwise provided [*4] by law, gross income means all income from whatever source derived.

Section 162 (a) of the Code provides that there shall be allowed as a deduction all the ordinary and necessary expenses paid or incurred during the taxable year in carrying on a trade or business. Under this provision an employee or a self-employed individual may deduct the ordinary and necessary expenses of carrying on a trade or business. If the trade or business does not consist of the performance of services by the taxpayer as an employee, such deduction is an allowable deduction from gross income in computing adjusted gross income under section 62 (1). However, if the trade or business consists of the performance of services by the taxpayer as an employee, the deduction is allowable only if the taxpayer itemizes deductions or if the expenses fall into one of the categories set forth in section 62 (2).

Section 170 of the Code provides that subject to certain limitations a deduction shall be allowed for any charitable contribution (as defined in section 170 (c))

12: REVENUE RULING

payment of which is made within the taxable year. Section 1.170A-1 (g) of the Income Tax Regulations provides, in part, that unreimbursed out-of-pocket expenditures [*5] made incident to the rendition of services to a charitable organization may constitute a deductible contribution.

The Federal employment taxes of the Federal Insurance Contributions Act, the Federal Unemployment Tax Act, and the Collection of Income Tax at Source on Wages (Chapters 21, 23, and 24, respectively, subtitle C of the Code) are imposed on the wages paid to an employee by an employer. An individual is an employee for Federal employment tax purposes if the individual has the status of employee under the usual common law rules applicable in determining whether an employer-employee relationship exists. Guides for determining whether an employer-employee relationship exists are found in three substantially similar sections of the employment tax regulations, namely sections 31.3121 (d)-1 (c), 31.3306 (i)-1, and 31.3401 (c)-1.. These sections state that generally, the relationship of employer and employee exists when the person for whom the services are performed has the right to control and direct the individual who performs the services, not only as to the result to be accomplished by the work but also as to the details and means by which that result is accomplished. That is, an [*6] employee is subject to the will and control of the employer not only as to what shall be done but how it shall be done. In this connection, it is not necessary that the employer actually direct or control the manner in which the services are performed; it is sufficient if the employer has the right to do so.

Section 1401 of the Code imposes taxes on the self-employment income of an individual derived from any trade or business carried on by such individual.

The individual rendering child care services in Situation 1 does not have a profit motive and is not, in fact, making a profit. The charitable organization rather than the individual designates the children assigned to the individual. The organization has a purpose of providing day care services for needy children and of locating individuals to provide such day care services. The organization has a continuing responsibility to supervise the care provided by an individual after the assignment of children to the individual's home and the organization does, in fact, supervise the care provided by the individual. Also, the organization has the authority to remove children from the care of an individual who does not provide proper care. [*7] Therefore, the individual in Situation 1 is rendering gratuitous services to the charitable organization in providing day care services for needy children.

Consequently, the expenses incurred by the individual in Situation 1 in providing

12: REVENUE RULING

day care services are directly connected with and solely attributable to the rendition of gratuitous services to the charitable organization. These expenses are incurred on behalf of and for the use of the charitable organization. Thus, the payments from the charitable organization represent reimbursements or advances for such expenses incurred on behalf of the organization by the individual. In addition, there is no employment relationship between the organization and the individual, and the individual is not engaged in an independent trade or business.

Accordingly, in Situation 1:

(a) The payments received from the charitable organization are not includible in the gross income of the individual as long as the payments do not exceed the expenses incurred by the individual in caring for the children.

(b) The individual's expenditures in providing day care services are not deductible business expenses under section 162 of the Code.

(c) The individual is entitled [*8] to a charitable contribution deduction within the limitations of section 170 for any unreimbursed out-of-pocket expenses incurred in providing day care.

(d) The payments received from the charitable organization are not subject to employment taxes or self-employment taxes.

See Rev. Rul. 77-280, 1977-2 C.B. 14, page 14, this Bulletin, Situations 1 and 2, for a discussion of similar payments to foster parents.

The individual rendering child care services in Situation 2 does have a profit motive. The individual receives a weekly fee for services from the parents of the child. Thus, the individual is engaged in a trade or business. Under the facts of this case, however, there does not exist a sufficient right of control on the part of the parents to establish, for employment tax purposes, the relationship of employer and employee between the parents and the individual who cares for the child. Thus, the individual is not engaged to perform services as an employee, but is engaged in an independent trade or business.

The individual receives a fixed weekly fee for services rendered. There is no agreement between the individual and the parents of the child that a portion of each payment is intended as a reimbursement [*9] of expenses incurred in caring for the child.

Accordingly, in Situation 2:

12: REVENUE RULING

(a) The entire amount of each payment received by the individual from the parents of the child is includible in the individual's gross income.

(b) The ordinary and necessary expenses incurred by the individual in carrying on this trade or business are deductible business expenses under section 162 of the Code, subject to the limitations of section 280A. Further, such expenses may be deducted from gross income to arrive at adjusted gross income under section 62 (1).

(c) The payments received by the individual are gross income derived from a trade or business for purposes of the self-employment tax imposed by section 1401.

Rev. Rul. 56-70, 1956-1 C.B. 460 is superseded since its contents are amplified and included in this ruling.

13: WESTERN NEURO V U.S.

WESTERN NEURO RESIDENTIAL CENTERS, INC., Plaintiff vs. UNITED STATES OF AMERICA, Defendant

CIVIL ACTION NO. SA-CV-01-645-AHS(ANx)

UNITED STATES DISTRICT COURT FOR THE CENTRAL DISTRICT OF CALIFORNIA, SOUTHERN DIVISION

2002 U.S. Dist. LEXIS 9608; 2002-1 U.S. Tax Cas. (CCH) P50,368; Unemployment Ins. Rep. (CCH) P16,713B

February 26, 2002, Decided
February 28, 2002, Filed, Entered

DISPOSITION: [*1] Motion of Plaintiff for Summary Judgment, GRANTED. Judgment, together with interest and attorneys' fees as awarded after subsequent Motion, entered in favor of plaintiff and against defendant.

COUNSEL: For WESTERN NEURO RESIDENTIAL CENTERS INC, plaintiff: Jeffrey Cooper, Alexander S. Helderman, Schnader Harrison Segal & Lewis, Jeffrey Cooper, Alexander S. Helderman, SCHNADER HARRISON SEGAL & LEWIS LLP, Philadelphia, Pennsylvania.

For WESTERN NEURO RESIDENTIAL CENTERS INC, plaintiff: Stephen H Dye, Schnader Harrison Segal & Lewis, San Francisco, CA.

For WESTERN NEURO RESIDENTIAL CENTERS INC, plaintiff: Carter H Dukes, Huckaby Scott & Dukes, Birmingham, AL.

For UNITED STATES OF AMERICA, defendant: Assistant US Attorney, AUSA, Office of US Attorney, Santa Ana, CA.

For UNITED STATES OF AMERICA, defendant: Edward M Robbins, Jr, Michael N Wilcove, AUSA, Office of US Attorney, Los Angeles, CA.

For UNITED STATES OF AMERICA, defendant: Herbert H Henry, III, G Douglas Jones, Sharon [*2] D Simmons, AUSA - Office of US Attorney, Birmingham, AL.

For UNITED STATES OF AMERICA, defendant: Marc J Korab, US Department of Justice, Washington, DC.

For UNITED STATES OF AMERICA, counter-claimant: Assistant US Attorney, AUSA, Office of US Attorney, Santa Ana, CA.

13: WESTERN NEURO V U.S.

For UNITED STATES OF AMERICA, counter-claimant: Edward M Robbins, Jr, Michael N Wilcove, AUSA, Office of US Attorney, Los Angeles, CA.

For UNITED STATES OF AMERICA, counter-claimant: Herbert H Henry, III, G Douglas Jones, Sharon D Simmons, AUSA - Office of US Attorney, Birmingham, AL.

For UNITED STATES OF AMERICA, counter-claimant: Marc J Korab, US Department of Justice, Washington, DC.

For WESTERN NEURO RESIDENTIAL CENTERS INC, counter-defendant: Jeffrey Cooper, Schnader Harrison Segal & Lewis, Philadelphia, PA.

For WESTERN NEURO RESIDENTIAL CENTERS INC, counter-defendant: Stephen H Dye, Schnader Harrison Segal & Lewis, San Francisco, CA.

For WESTERN NEURO RESIDENTIAL CENTERS INC, counter-defendant: Carter H Dukes, Huckaby Scott & Dukes, Birmingham, AL.

Michael Wilcove, Esquire, Trial Attorney, U.S. DEPARTMENT OF JUSTICE, Washington, DC.

JUDGES: Alicemarie H. Stotler, U.S. DISTRICT [*3] COURT JUDGE.

OPINION BY: Alicemarie H. Stotler

OPINION

PLAINTIFF WESTERN NEURO RESIDENTIAL CENTER, INC.'s STATE-MENT OF UNCONTROVERTED FACTS AND CONCLUSIONS OF LAW

UNCONTROVERTED FACTS

1. Western Neuro Residential Centers, Inc. ("Western Neuro") is a business corporation organized and existing pursuant to the laws of the State of Delaware. (Compl. P1, Ex. 1 to Pl's Points & Auth.).

2. Western Neuro's Employer Identification Number is 33-0287913. (Compl. P3, Ex. 1; Amend Ans. and Counterclaim P3, Ex. 2 to Pl's Points & Auth.).

3. During the audit years in question, 1991 through 1995, Western Neuro was a corporate subsidiary of Continental Medical Systems, Inc. ("CMS") and was one of many similar subsidiary corporations throughout the United States which operated freestanding for-profit rehabilitation hospitals. (Misitano Dep. at 3:14-21,

13: WESTERN NEURO V U.S.

21:23-24:24, 104:1-13, Ex. 3 to Pl's Points & Auth.). [1]

> 1 By agreement of counsel, the depositions of Anthony Misitano, Deborah Myers Welsh, Robert Ortenzio, Patricia Rice and Scott Romberger, taken in other similar actions may be used as if taken in this action.

[*4] 4. In order to provide rehabilitation hospital services to assist people with injuries or disabilities to reach their maximum level of independence and to assist patients and family members in developing a knowledge of the patient's needs, Western Neuro contracted with the physicians to serve as Medical Directors. (Compl. P7, Ex. 1; Misitano Dep. at 21:10-19, Ex. 3; Welsh Dep. at 11:28-12:6, Ex. 4 to Pl's Points & Auth.; Def.'s Resp. to Pl.'s Req. for Admis. P1-5, Ex. 5 to Pl's Points & Auth.).

5. Western Neuro was subjected to an employment tax audit by the IRS for the tax years 1991 through 1995. As a result of the audit, the IRS determined that the Medical Directors should have been treated as employees rather than as independent contractors for employment tax purposes. Western Neuro was assessed employment and unemployment taxes on the Medical Directors. (Compl. PP8-9, Ex. 1; Amend. Ans. and Counterclaim PP8-9, Ex. 2).

6. After an unsuccessful administrative appeal, Western Neuro filed twenty (20) amended employment tax returns (Form 941), one for each quarter of 1991 through 1995, and five (5) amended federal unemployment tax returns (Form 940), one for each year of the audit, [*5] paid a portion of the tax due, and filed a claim for refund and request for abatement for each of the amended returns (Form 843). (Compl. PP10-12, Ex. 1). After waiting the required six-month period without action by the IRS, Western Neuro filed this lawsuit seeking a refund of $ 14,011.64. paid on account of the taxes assessed. (Compl. P14, Ex. 1). The United States filed a counterclaim seeking $ 28,540.98, the total amount of the assessment. (Amend. Ans. and Counterclaim PP1-7, Ex. 2).

7. This case is one of ten cases filed by former subsidiaries of CMS concerning the treatment of Medical Directors and other medial personnel as independent contractors. Each former subsidiary was separately assessed by the IRS.

8. Each former subsidiary is a separate corporation with a separate tax identification number, and each former subsidiary filed separate employment tax returns. (Romberger Dep. at 47:1-13, Ex. 6 to Pl's Points & Auth.).

9. Western Neuro is currently a non-operating corporate entity which, after a

13: WESTERN NEURO V U.S.

series of acquisitions, is a subsidiary of HealthSouth Corporation, with its business located in Birmingham, Alabama. The hospital continues to operate in this judicial district [*6] through new ownership.

10. This action was transferred to this district from the Northern District of Alabama because many of the witnesses involved in this action reside in this district.

11. Western Neuro treated all Medical Directors as independent contractors and filed all required tax returns consistent with the treatment as independent contractors. (Def. Resp. to Pl's Req. for Admis. PP6, 7, Ex. 5).

12. The management personnel of Western Neuro and the management and legal personnel of CMS who provided guidance and advice to Western Neuro relied on their knowledge of the healthcare industry generally, and the specific for-profit rehabilitation hospital segment of the healthcare industry, in treating Medical Directors as independent contractors. (Pegler Aff. PP2-4, Ex. 7 to Pl's Points & Auth.; Ortenzio Dep. at 16:20-17:2, 34:20-36:15, 55:5-16, 60:1-22, Ex. 8 to Pl's Points & Auth.; Welsh Dep. at 12:7-14:1, 17:8-20:1, 41:1-4, 50:12-54:11, Ex. 3; Misitano Dep. at 38:21-39:8, 39:18-40:6, 40:14-41:7, 41:21-42:2, 44:2-45:9, Ex. 3; Rice Dep. at 51:8-54:1, 52:17-60:14, 63:19-64:4, Ex. 9 to Pl's Points & Auth.; Correa Dep. At 22:23-23:1, Ex. 10 to Pl's Points & Auth.). CMS executive [*7] personnel, including Robert Ortenzio, Anthony Misitano, Patricia Rice and legal counsel Deborah Myers Welsh determined that physicians should be treated as independent contractors rather than as employees because independent contractor treatment was consistent with general industry practice. (Ortenzio Dep. at 16:20-17:2, 34:20-36:15, 55:5-16, 60:1-22, Ex. 8; Welsh Dep. at 12:7-14:1, 17:8-19:3, 18:1-20:1, 41:1-4, 50:12-54:11, Ex. 3; Misitano Dep. 38:21-39:8, 39:18-40:6, 40:14-41:7, 41:21-42:2, 44:2-45:9, Ex. 3; Rice Dep. at 51:8-54:1, 52:17-60:14, 63:19-64:4, Ex. 9.)

[EDITOR'S NOTE: TEXT WITHIN THESE SYMBOLS [O> <O] IS OVER-STRUCK IN THE SOURCE.]

13. Western Neuro relied on the contracts with the Medical Directors being reviewed and approved by legal personnel from CMS. [O>In turn<O], Deborah Myers Welsh, legal counsel to CMS, believed it was appropriate to treat the Medical Directors as independent contractors [O>not only<O] because of the consistent practice of the industry and [O>also<O] upon the advice of both national and local counsel and on the advice of in-house tax and financial experts. (Welsh Dep. at 19:23-30:4, 30:20-31:21, Ex. 4).

14. Western Neuro exercised [*8] minimal direction or control over the means

13: WESTERN NEURO V U.S.

and manner by which the Medical Directors performed contractual services. Each individual signed an agreement outlining his or her goals and responsibilities and each person independently determined how to achieve the expected results. Western Neuro did not set hours, did not require a Medical Director's presence at any particular time, or [O>otherwise<O] control the day-to-day activities of the Medical Directors. (Misitano Dep. at 22:14-17, 104:22-105:22, Ex. 3; Ortenzio Dep. at 58:16-19, Ex. 8; Rice Dep. at 81:2-10, Ex. 9; Correa Dep. at 11:2-8, 23:6-11, Ex. 10; Kritz Dep. at 21:19-23, 27:21-28:8, Ex. 11). Western Neuro provided no employee benefits such as health or life insurance or pension plans. (Correa Dep. at 18:5-8, Ex. 10; Kritz Dep. at 19:25-20:9, 28:14-17, Ex. 11 to Pl's Points & Auth.). The Medical Directors were not provided secretaries, offices, or office supplies, and they were not reimbursed for travel or commuting expenses. (Kritz Dep. at 17:22-18:15, Ex. 11; Correa Dep. at 16:22-25, 17:1-3, Ex. 10.).

15. Western Neuro and the Medical Directors whose tax status is at issue in this case, and CMS were all concerned about [*9] state laws restricting the corporate practice of medicine. (Welsh Dep. at 22:19-24, 30:1-31:21, Ex. 4; Misitano Dep. at 103:1-15, Ex. 3.) California's prohibition on the corporate practice of medicine is strictly enforced and is applicable to the Medical Directors.

16. Deborah Myers Welsh, legal counsel to CMS, believed it was appropriate to treat Medical Directors as independent contractors not only because of the consistent practice in the industry but because of her general knowledge of Internal Revenue Service rulings, regulations and decisions learned through her research, her participation in continuing education programs, based on conversations with general counsel of other major for profit rehabilitation companies and her review of these companies' Medical Director contracts. [O>none of which raised concern over the treatment of physicians as independent contractors rather than an employees.<O] (Welsh Dep. at 17:8-19:3, 41:5-45:21, 50:12-54:11, Ex. 4).

17. Western Neuro exercised virtually no direction or control over the means and manner by which the Medical Directors performed contracted services. Each Medical Director signed an agreement outlining his or her goals and [*10] responsibilities, but each physician independently determined how to achieve the expected results. Western Neuro did not set hours, did not require a Medical Director's presence at any set time, or [O>otherwise<O] control the day to day activities of the Medical Directors. Western Neuro provided no employee benefits, such as health insurance or life insurance, and Western Neuro did not provide a pension plan. The administrative responsibilities of the Medical Directors were intertwined with their practice so that Western Neuro could not exercise direction or control over the manner in which services were delivered. (Misitano Dep. at

13: WESTERN NEURO V U.S.

22:14-17, 104:22-105:22, Ex. 3; Ortenzio Dep. at 58:16-21, Ex. 8; Rice Dep. at 81:2-10, Ex. 9; Correa Dep. at 11:2-8, 18:5-8, 23:6-11, Ex. 10; Kritz Dep. at 19:25-20:9, 21:19-23, 27:21-28:8, 28:14-17, Ex. 11).

CONCLUSIONS OF LAW

1. Western Neuro had a reasonable basis for treating the Medical Directors as independent contractors based on the long-standing practice of the for-profit rehabilitation industry. See H.R. Rep. No. 95-1748 (1978); General Inv. Corp. v. United States, 823 F.2d 337 (9th Cir. 1987); [O> In re Bentley, No. 93-30510, 1994 Bankr. LEXIS 261 [*11] (Bankr. E.D. Tenn. Feb. 25, 1994), aff'd, 175 B.R. 652 (Bankr. E.D. Tenn. 1994) (Attachment D to Pl's Points & Auth.);<O] Conrad v. Medical Board of California, 48 Cal. App. 4th 1038, 55 Cal. Rptr. 2d 901 (1996).

2. Western Neuro had a reasonable basis for treating the Medical Directors as independent contractors based on the advice of lawyers and accountants. See H.R. Rep. No. 95-1748 (1978); Critical Care Register Nursing, Inc. v. United States, 776 F. Supp. 1025 (E.D. Pa. 1991); [O> Queensgate Dental Family Practice, Inc. v. United States, 1991 U.S. Dist. LEXIS 13333, Civ. A. Nos. 1:CV-90-0918, 1:CV-90-1290, and 1: CV-90-1291,1991 WL 260452, at *1 (M.D. Pa. Sept. 5, 1991), aff'd, 970 F.2d 899 (3d Cir. 1992) (Attachment E to Pl's Points & Auth.);<O] Deja Vu Entm't Enter. Of Minnesota v. United States, 1 F. Supp. 2d 964 (D. Minn. 1998). [O> Taylor Blvd Theatre, Inc. v. United States, 1998 U.S. Dist. LEXIS 9355, No. Civ. A. 3:97- CV-63-H, 1998 WL 375291 (W.D. Ky. May 13, 1998) (Attachment F to Pl's Points & Auth<O]).

3. Western Neuro had a reasonable basis for treating the Medical Directors as independent contractors [*12] based on the corporate practice of medicine doctrine. [O> See Barry R. Furrow, et al., Health Law, § 5-10 (West 1995) (Attachment G to Pl's Points & Auth.); Patricia F. Jacobson, Prohibition Against Corporate Practice of Medicine: Dinosaur or Dynamic Doctrine, Health Law Handbook 67-77 (1993) and its accompanying chart (article and chart are attached as H to Pl's Points & Auth.);<O] See County of Los Angeles v. Ford, 121 Cal. App. 2d 407, 263 P.2d 638 (1953); Conrad v. Medical Board of California, 48 Cal. App. 4th 1038, 55 Cal. Rpt. 2d 901(1996); Sternsmith v. Medical Board of California, 85 Cal. App. 4th 458, 102 Cal. Rptr. 2d 115 (2000). [O> Farlow v. Wachovia Bank of North Carolina, No. 00-2251, 259 F.3d 309, 2001 U.S. App. LEXIS 17612, at *14-*15 (4th Cir. Aug. 6, 2001) (Attachment I to Pl's Points & Auth.); Queensgate Dental Family Practice, Inc., 1991 U.S. Dist. LEXIS 13333, WL 260452, at<O] *1.

13: WESTERN NEURO V U.S.

4. Western Neuro had a reasonable basis for treating its Medical Directors as independent contractors based on its reasonable treatment of these individuals under the traditional common law rules. See Critical Care Register Nursing, Inc., 776 F. Supp. at 1028; [*13] Hospital Res. Personnel, Inc. v. United States, 68 F.3d 421 (11th Cir. 1995). [O> Queensgate Dental Family Practice, Inc., 1991 U.S. Dist. LEXIS 13333, WL 260452, at *1.<O]

5. Western Neuro had a reasonable basis for treating the medical directors as independent contractors based on its continual efforts to properly classify these individuals. See General Inv. Corp., 823 F.2d at 340.

6. Western Neuro is entitled to recovery because the Medical Directors were properly treated as independent contractors cased on the applicable common law factors. See Critical Care Register Nursing, Inc., 776 F. Supp. at 1026-29; Hospital Res. Personnel, Inc., 68 F.3d at 427-28;Rev. Rul. 87-41, 1987-1 CB 296; Nationwide Mut. Ins. Co. v. Darden, 503 U.S. 318, 117 L. Ed. 2d 581, 112 S. Ct. 1344 (1992); [O> Mohamed v. United States, No. 97-15358, 1998 U.S. App. LEXIS 30485, at *4 (9th Cir. Nov. 27, 1998) (Attachment J)<O]; Empire StarMines Co., Ltd. v. California Employment Comm'n, 28 Cal.2d 33, 43, 168 P.2d 686, 692 (1946); Treasury Regulation § 31.3121(d)-1(c) [*14] ; [O> Queensgate Dental Family Prac, Inc., 1991 U.S. Dist. LEXIS 13333, 1991 WL 260452, at *4,<O] Professional & Executive Leasing, Inc. v. Commissioner, 89 T.C. 225 (1997), aff'd, 862 F.2d 751, 754 (9th Cir. 1988); United States v. Azad, 277 F. Supp. 258 (D. Minn. 1966), aff'd, Azad v. United States, 388 F.2d 74, 77-8 (8th Cir. 1968); 26 C.F.R. 31.3121(d)-1(c)(1).

Respectfully submitted,

Jeffrey Cooper (PA I.D. No. 21181)(Pro Hac Vice)

Alexander S. Helderman (PA. I.D. No. 84390)

SCHNADER HARRISON SEGAL & LEWIS
1600 Market Street
Suite 3600
Philadelphia, PA 19103-7286
(215) 751-2096
(215) 751-2205 (FAX)

Attorneys for Plaintiff

Western Neuro Residential Centers, Inc.

13: WESTERN NEURO V U.S.

Dated: December 10, 2001

IT IS SO ORDERED

DATE February 26, 2002

Alicemarie H. Stotler

U.S. DISTRICT COURT JUDGE

JUDGMENT FOR PLAINTIFF

[O>[PROPOSED] ORDER<O]

AND NOW, this 26th day of February, 2002, upon consideration of the Motion of Plaintiff Western Neuro Residential Centers, Inc. for Summary Judgment pursuant to Rule 56 of the Federal Rules of Civil Procedure, said [*15] Motion is hereby GRANTED.

Judgment in the amount of $ 14,011.64, together with interest and attorneys' fees as may be awarded after subsequent Motion, is here by entered in favor of plaintiff, Western Neuro Residential Centers, Inc. and against defendant, United States of America.

The clerk shall serve a copy of this Judgment on all counsel.

Stotler, J.

[O>[PROPOSED]<O] ORDER GRANTING PLAINTIFF'S MOTION FOR SUMMARY JUDGMENT

AND NOW, this 26th day of February, 2002, upon consideration of the Motion of Plaintiff Western Neuro Residential Centers, Inc. for Summary Judgment pursuant to Rule 56 of the Federal Rules of Civil Procedure, said Motion is hereby GRANTED.

Judgment in the amount of $ 14,011.64, together with interest and attorneys' fees as may be awarded after subsequent Motion, is hereby entered in favor of plaintiff Western Neuro Residential Centers, Inc. and against defendant, United States of America.

By

Stotler, J.

14: KM SYSTEMS V U.S.

KM SYSTEMS, INC., Plaintiff; Counter Defendant, v. UNITED STATES OF AMERICA, Defendant; Counter Claimant

Civil Action No. 02-4567 (FLW)

UNITED STATES DISTRICT COURT FOR THE DISTRICT OF NEW JERSEY

360 F. Supp. 2d 641; 2005 U.S. Dist. LEXIS 2958; 2005-1 U.S. Tax Cas. (CCH) P50,262; 95 A.F.T.R.2d (RIA) 1186

January 25, 2005, Decided

DISPOSITION: Motion denied.

COUNSEL: [**1] For KM SYSTEMS, INC., Plaintiff: PAUL R. FITZMAURICE, PELINO & LENTZ, P.C., PHILADELPHIA, PA.

For UNITED STATES OF AMERICA, Defendant: LINDSEY W. COOPER, U.S. DEPT. OF JUSTICE-CIVIL TAX DIV. EASTERN REGION, WASHINGTON, DC.

For UNITED STATES OF AMERICA, Counter Claimant: LINDSEY W. COOPER, U.S. DEPT. OF JUSTICE-CIVIL TAX DIV. EASTERN REGION, WASHINGTON, DC.

For KM SYSTEMS, INC., Counter Defendant: PAUL R. FITZMAURICE, PELINO & LENTZ, P.C., PHILADELPHIA, PA.

JUDGES: Honorable Freda L. Wolfson, United States District Judge.

OPINION BY: Freda L. Wolfson

OPINION

[*642] **ORDER**

This matter having been opened to the Court by Paul R. Fitzmaurice, counsel to KM Systems, Inc. ("Plaintiff" or "KM Systems"), seeking to recover a total of $ 58,129.41 in attorneys' fees and costs pursuant to 26 U.S.C. § 7430 ("§ 7430"), and the Court, having previously granted summary judgment on Plaintiff's claim that it had a reasonable basis for treating its cable installers as independent contractors in accordance with the safe harbor provision of Section 530(a)(2)(C) of the 1978 Internal Revenue Code ("Section 530"), and having considered the moving, opposition and reply papers, and having [**2] heard oral argument on January 21, 2005, and it appearing that:

14: KM SYSTEMS V U.S.

[*643] 1. § 7430 provides for the award of reasonable administrative and litigation costs, including attorneys' fees, under certain circumstances. See 26 U.S.C. § 7430. The Supreme Court has stated that a request for attorneys' fees should not result in a second major litigation. Pierce v. Underwood, 487 U.S. 552, 563, 101 L. Ed. 2d 490, 108 S. Ct. 2541 (1988). When deciding a request for such costs, the district court has considerable discretion in determining whether the government's position was substantially justified and in determining the amount of the award. See J&J Cab Serv. v. United States, 1998 U.S. Dist. LEXIS 5630, 1998 WL 264736, at *2 (W.D.N.C. Jun. 3, 1998) (citations omitted); see also United States v. Scheingold, 293 F. Supp.2d 447,450 (D.N.J. 2003). Thus, even if a plaintiff satisfies the statutory requirements, an award is not mandatory. See McClellan v. U.S., 900 F. Supp. 101, 104(E.D.Mich.Sept. 12, 1995); see also Zinniel v. Commissioner, 883 F.2d 1350, 1355 (7th Cir.1989) (noting that the statute "authorizes, rather than commands, the court to make an award [**3] ... for reasonable litigation costs.").

2. To be entitled to attorneys' fees, the moving party must also be a prevailing party. See 26 U.S.C. § 7430(a). In the instant matter, the Government concedes that Plaintiff is the prevailing party within the meaning of the statute. 1 See Def. Opp. at 4. The statute, however, provides that "a party shall not be treated as the prevailing party in a proceeding ... if the United States establishes that [its] ... position in the proceeding was substantially justified." 26 U.S.C. § 7430(c)(4)(B)(i). Under the statute, the United States has the burden of showing that its position was substantially justified. 2 See Pierce, 487 U.S. at 565 (interpreting phrase "substantially justified" for purposes of closely-related Equal Access to Justice Act, 28 U.S.C. § 2412(d) to mean justified to a degree that would satisfy a reasonable person). The fact that the government loses the underlying litigation is not dispositive of the determination that its position had no reasonable basis in law and fact. Rather, that fact remains a factor for the Court's consideration. [**4] See Pierce, 487 U.S. at 566 n.2; Gibbs v. U.S., 1998 U.S. Dist. LEXIS 1312, 1998 WL 226773 at *2 (D.N.J. Jan. 14, 1998); Bowles v. U.S., 947 F.2d 91,94 (4th Cir.1991); Phillips v. Commissioner, 851 F.2d 1492, 1499 (D.C.

14: KM SYSTEMS V U.S.

Cir. 1988); Snyder v. United States, 25 F. Supp.2d 777, 780 (E.D. Mich.1998) (finding that government's position was substantially justified even though its "position may not have been correct."); But see J&J Cab Service, 1998 U.S. Dist. LEXIS 5630, 1998 WL 264736 at *3 (stating that government's loss at summary judgment stage "does reveal something regarding the merits of the government's position."). The legislative history of § 7430 sets forth some factors a court may consider in determining whether the position of [*644] the government was unreasonable: (1) whether the government used the costs and expenses of litigation against its position to extract concessions from the taxpayer that were not justified under the circumstances of the case, (2) whether the government pursued the litigation against the taxpayer for purposes of harassment or embarrassment, or out of political motivation, and (3) such other factors [**5] as the court finds relevant. Bowles, 947 F.2d at 94; J&J Cab Service, 1998 U.S. Dist. LEXIS 5630, 1998 WL 264736 at *2. Thus, the court is permitted to "step back and take an overall view of the government's conduct in deciding an award under Section 7430." J&J Cab Service, 1998 U.S. Dist. LEXIS 5630, 1998 WL 264736 at *2.

1 Furthermore, the Government does not dispute the amount of attorneys' fees and costs requested by Plaintiff. According to the Government, the only issue is whether Plaintiff is entitled to such costs at all under § 7430. See Def. Opp. at 4 n. 2.

2 The Government concedes that the United States has this burden. See Def. Opp. at 1-2.

3. In this matter, the determination of whether the Government's position was substantially justified must be made at two stages: at the administrative stage when Plaintiff sought a refund of the taxes assessed against it for the 1992-1993 tax years, and at the litigation stage where Plaintiff asserted that it was entitled to Section 530 relief. [**6] See J&J Cab Service, 1998 U.S. Dist. LEXIS 5630, 1998 WL 264736, at *6 (finding that government's position was not substantially justified during both administrative proceeding and litigation stage); Nicholson v. Comm'r of Internal Revenue Service, 60 F.3d 1020, 1026 (3d Cir. 1995) (analyzing whether IRS's position substantially justified at time

14: KM SYSTEMS V U.S.

it assessed deficiency against taxpayers and also in underlying litigation); McClellan, 900 F. Supp. at 107 (finding that government's position not substantially justified because taxpayer provided surveys to IRS prior to its request for refund).

4. At the administrative proceeding and in connection with its attempt to obtain a refund in 2002, Plaintiff submitted to the Government a fourteen page submission, the majority of which dealt with an analysis of whether cable installers can be classified as employees under the common law. 3 See P1. Mot. Fees and Costs, Ex. B. However, with respect to Plaintiff's reasonable reliance argument under Section 530, this Court cannot find that the Government was not substantially justified in denying Plaintiff's request for a refund and proceeding with the case based on [**7] the information supplied by Plaintiff. For example, in its fourteen page submission to the IRS, Plaintiff stated that Francis Knoll ("Knoll"), one of Plaintiff's founders, worked as a cable installer at a company called CIS and performed services for "various systems in Pennsylvania, New Jersey, Maryland and Delaware." Id. at 1. Plaintiff claimed that Knoll was treated as a independent contractor during this time. Id. In addition, Plaintiff submitted that Pat Watson ("Watson"), Plaintiff's other founder, worked at NYT Cable Systems during the relevant time period and also had "experience in the cable industry in the four state area...." Id. However, neither CIS nor NYT Cable Systems existed in 2002, when Plaintiff sought the refund, and Plaintiff did not identify any specific cable installers in Pennsylvania, [*645] New Jersey, Maryland or Delaware who could attest to the practice of the cable installation industry treating installers as independent contractors. 4 Thus, the factual information provided to the Government at the administrative stage consisted merely of statements by the taxpayers about the practices of cable installation companies, which the Government could not [**8] contact to verify, along with Plaintiff's vague statement that it did not know of any other cable installation company that treated its cable installers as employees. See id. Based on these submissions, the Court finds that the Government had a reasonable basis for proceeding in this matter.

3 At the summary judgment stage, this Court did not reach Plaintiff's common law argument because it determined that Plaintiff had sufficiently demonstrated

14: KM SYSTEMS V U.S.

that it met the safe harbor provision of Section 530.

4 Plaintiff's counsel admitted as much during the oral argument. See Unoff. Tr. Oral Arg. dated Jan. 21, 2005, at 10-11.

> 5. Plaintiff's counsel asserted during oral argument that the Government could have sought out more information about the industry practice because shortly after 1993, Plaintiff provided the IRS with the identities of several of its cable installers in its 1099 tax forms. See Unoff.Tr. Oral Arg. dated Jan. 21, 2005,at 14. The Court finds this argument unpersuasive. First, Plaintiff [**9] did not identify that these cable installers worked for other cable installation companies and could testify about their experiences as independent contractors at such companies. Second, while Plaintiff states that the Government "had access to all of the cable installers" by virtue of the 1099 tax forms, it was not the Government's burden, at that stage, to conduct the investigative work on behalf of Plaintiff. While the Court recognizes that Section 530 is to be liberally construed in favor of the taxpayer, seeRev. Proc. 85-18 § 3.01(c); McClellan, 900 F. Supp. at 104-05; Overeen v. United States, 1991 U.S. Dist. LEXIS 13143, 1991 WL 338327, at *3 (W.D. Okla. Sept. 4, 1991), it still remains the taxpayer's burden to show reasonable reliance on a long-standing industry practice. See Section 530(a)(2)(C); 26 U.S.C. § 3401 note. Therefore, based on the information that Plaintiff provided to the Government in 2002, the Government had a reasonable basis, at least at the administrative stage, in pursuing this matter.

> 6. At the litigation stage of the case, the Government's main contention was that Plaintiff's reliance on its [**10] founders' past personal experiences was insufficient to satisfy the burden of proof under Section 530. During the litigation, several cable installers testified at depositions that they were treated as independent contractors at their previous places of employment. See KM Systems, Inc. v. U.S., 2004 WL 1386371, at *7 (D.N.J. May 10, 2004). The Court previously found that the testimony of these cable installers corroborated the founders' understanding of the industry practice and supported the inference that Plaintiff reasonably relied on the founders' and Plaintiff's cable installers' understanding of the practice of treating cable installers as inde-

14: KM SYSTEMS V U.S.

pendent contractors. See id. at 10. Despite this finding, however, for the Court to now find that Plaintiff is entitled to fees and costs under § 7430, it must determine that the Government had [*646] no reasonable basis in law or fact to pursue the matter at the litigation or summary judgment stages. After careful review of the record and hearing the parties' positions during oral argument, this Court finds that the Government was substantially justified in proceeding with the litigation.

7. The Government's main argument [**11] is that Plaintiff did not sufficiently demonstrate reasonable reliance on a long-standing industry practice. See Def. Opp. at 6-8; see also Unoff. Tr. Oral Arg. dated Jan. 21, 2005, at 19-21, 26-28. In support of this argument, the Government claims that it attempted to contact Starview, one of the two companies that Knoll claimed that he relied on when deciding to treat Plaintiff's cable installers as independent contractors. However, the Government was unable to find Starview, most likely because it was no longer in existence at the start of this litigation. See Unoff. Tr. Oral Arg. dated Jan. 21, 2005, at 19. Furthermore, while Knoll claimed that he also relied on the practices of Prince Cable, the Government asserts that Prince Cable was formed only a few months before KM Systems was formed in 1987. Thus, the Government contends that the practices of Prince Cable could not have constituted a long-standing industry practice as required by Section 530 and that Plaintiff's reliance on such practices was unreasonable. See id. at 20. Because Section 530 calls for "reliance" on a long-standing industry practice, the Court finds that it was reasonable, given these facts, [**12] for the Government to conclude that there was insufficient evidence of reliance and that Plaintiff did not meet the Section 530 requirements because it was relying merely on the personal experiences of Knoll and Watson.

8. Furthermore, the Court cannot find that the Government's interpretation of the applicable case law was unwarranted because the law was not directly on point with the facts of this case. For instance, several courts have considered a taxpayer's personal experience as insufficient evidence of the "long-standing recognized practice of a significant segment of the industry" within the meaning of Section 530. See Day v. Commissioner, T.C. Memo 2000-375, 80 T.C.M. (CCH)834 (2000); West

14: KM SYSTEMS V U.S.

Virginia Personnel Servs. v. United States, 1996 U.S. Dist. LEXIS 14450, 1996 WL 679643, at *9 (S.D. W.Va. 1996); Moore v. U.S., 1992 U.S. Dist. LEXIS 10316, 1992 WL 220913, at *8 (W.D. Mich. 1992). In this matter, however, the Court took a broader view of what constitutes "personal experience" for the purpose of Section 530 relief, particularly in light of the fact that the safe harbor provision of Section 530 is to be liberally construed in favor of the taxpayer. Plaintiff's [**13] founders had a breadth of personal knowledge based upon their experiences with other cable installation companies which was fleshed out during discovery. The Government may have taken a more limited view of what constitutes "personal experience" under Section 530; however, such a position did not ignore or run contrary to any well-settled proposition or law. Thus, based on the case law and the uncertainty surrounding when Plaintiff discovered that its cable installers worked at other companies that treated them as independent contractors, the Court finds [*647] that it was reasonable for the Government to pursue the litigation. It is a lawyer's responsibility to make certain decisions on how to interpret the law and balance the facts with the standards required by such law. Here, the Government's narrower, but not clearly erroneous, view on what constitutes "reasonable reliance" and "personal experience" under Section 530 does not mean that its position at the outset of this litigation was not substantially justified. Accordingly,

IT IS on this 25th day of January, 2005,

ORDERED that Plaintiff's motion for attorneys' fees and costs is **DENIED**.

/s/ Freda L. Wolfson

Honorable [**14] Freda L. Wolfson

United States District Judge

15: CA UNEMPLOYMENT INSURANCE CODE SECTION 656

"Employment" does not include professional services performed by a consultant

working as an independent contractor. For the purpose of this section, there shall be a rebuttable presumption that services provided by an individual engaged in work requiring specialized knowledge and skills attained through completion of recognized courses of instruction or experience are rendered as an independent contractor. These services shall be limited to those provided by attorneys, physicians, dentists, engineers, architects, accountants, chiropractors, and the various types of physical, chemical, natural, and biological scientists. Professional services shall not include services generally provided by persons who do not have a degree from a four-year institution of higher learning relating to the specialized knowledge and skills of the professional service being provided.

For the purposes of this section, the rebuttable presumption shall not apply to an individual who enters into a contract agreement with the recipient of the professional services which establishes an employer-employee relationship. However, the existence of a contract between a nonprofit, licensed, primary care clinic, as defined in subdivision (a) of Section 1204 of the Health and Safety Code, and a health care practitioner who is licensed as a physician and surgeon, osteopathic physician and surgeon, podiatrist, optometrist, chiropractor, or psychologist shall not constitute an employer-employee relationship if the contract stipulates that the professional services rendered to the clinic are by an independent contractor, not an employee. Independent contractors who conform to the provisions of this section or primary care clinics that contract with these individuals or organizations shall not be liable for any payments that may be required under an employer-employee relationship pursuant to this code.

16: GRUBB & ELLIS CO. V. SPENGLER (1983)

Grubb & Ellis Co. v. Spengler (1983) 143 Cal. App. 3d 890 [192 Cal.Rptr. 637]

[Civ. No. 68509. Court of Appeals of California, Second Appellate District, Division Five. June 14, 1983.]

GRUBB AND ELLIS COMPANY et al., Plaintiffs, Cross-defendants and Respondents, v. DANIEL S. SPENGLER, Defendant, Cross-complainant and Appellant.

Defendant, Daniel S. Spengler (Spengler), who appears here in pro. per., purports to appeal from the memorandum of decision and notice of intended judgment. [1] A memorandum of decision is not an appealable order. (Estate of Pieper (1964) 224 Cal. App. 2d 670, 675 [37 Cal.Rptr. 46].) [2] However, we construe the notice of appeal, filed November 26, 1980, as referring to the judgment entered August 4, 1980. (See Gregory v. Hamilton (1978) 77 Cal. App. 3d 213, 215, fn. 1.[142 Cal.Rptr. 563]; Channell v. Anthony (1976) 58 Cal. App. 3d 290, 302 [129 Cal.Rptr. 704].)

Suit was originally filed by Grubb and Ellis Commercial Brokerage Company (Grubb and Ellis) on certain promissory notes executed by Spengler in favor of Grubb and Ellis totaling $9,100, of which Grubb and Ellis claimed $6,574.84 remained due and payable by Spengler, plus interest at the rate of 7 percent per annum. Grubb and Ellis took the position that Spengler had been engaged by them on July 12, 1976, as a real estate salesman under what they termed an "independent contractor agreement" that provided for compensation based solely on commissions to be collected from parties to real estate transactions. Grubb and Ellis claimed that the promissory notes executed by Spengler represented loans made by Grubb and Ellis to Spengler in the form of a monthly [143 Cal. App. 3d 893] draw against commissions. The promissory notes were payable within six months or upon termination of Spengler's relationship with Grubb and Ellis. Spengler was terminated on July 29, 1977, and the plaintiffs claim the notes became due and payable at that time.

Spengler cross-complained for declaratory relief asserting that under the independent contractor agreement with Grubb and Ellis he was an employee and as such was entitled to an hourly minimum wage and social security benefits. Spengler also claimed moneys were due to him on the theory of quantum meruit, and he sought damages for breach of contract and fraud.

After a court trial, judgment was rendered in favor of Grubb and Ellis on its complaint in the amount of $5,694.42 plus interest from November 30, 1976, to date of judgment and $1,147.25 in attorneys' fees and costs. Judgment was rendered

16: GRUBB & ELLIS CO. V. SPENGLER (1983)

against Spengler on all counts of his cross-complaint. [3] Spengler contends that the fact that Grubb and Ellis failed to serve the proposed findings of fact and conclusions of law and judgment on him, as was then provided for in rule 232 of the California Rules of Court, is grounds for reversal on appeal. fn. 1

The trial court filed and served its memorandum of decision and notice of intended judgment on June 9, 1980. Spengler filed his request for findings of fact and conclusions of law on June 16, 1980. A notice to prepare findings was served by the court on June 17, 1980. The proposed findings of fact and conclusions of law and the proposed judgment are dated June 30, 1980, and were signed by the court and filed on August 4, 1980. The record indicates that the proposed findings of fact, conclusions of law and judgment were not served upon Spengler. Rule 232(c) provided at the time here pertinent that, "If the proposed findings, conclusions and judgment are not served and submitted within such time [15 days after service of a notice to prepare findings], or any additional time granted by the court as provided by subdivision (i), fn. 2 any other party who appeared at the trial may: (1) prepare, serve and submit to the court his proposed findings, conclusions and judgment, or (2) serve on all other parties [143 Cal. App. 3d 894] and file a notice of motion for an order that findings and conclusions be deemed waived." The record does not reveal that Spengler took advantage of the remedy provided by subdivision (c) of rule 232 by submitting his own findings when Grubb and Ellis failed to timely serve him with its findings. The record does not reveal that Spengler made any inquiry respecting the findings at any time after his request for findings was filed.

In Tsarnas v. Bailey (1962) 205 Cal. App. 2d 593 [23 Cal.Rptr. 336], the court, in construing former Code of Civil Procedure section 634 which provided for service of proposed findings upon all parties, stated at page 596: "The final contention on appeal is that the judgment is invalid since the findings of fact were not served on the defendant before the signing of the judgment in violation of section 634 of the Code of Civil Procedure. However, both the cases decided before and after the 1959 amendment to this section have uniformly held that failure to serve the findings is a mere irregularity and not grounds for reversal [citations]." (See Ball v. City Council (1967) 252 Cal. App. 2d 136 at pp. 146-147 [60 Cal.Rptr. 139].) The same reasoning is applicable with respect to the requirements of service of proposed findings contained in rule 232 of the California Rules of Court at the time here pertinent. (See Estate of Cooper (1970) 11 Cal. App. 3d 1114, 1121-1122 [90 Cal.Rptr. 283].) Spengler has made no showing of prejudice as a result of the failure to serve proposed findings and judgment upon him. He has not demonstrated cause for reversal of the judgment on this ground.

16: GRUBB & ELLIS CO. V. SPENGLER (1983)

In its findings of fact, the trial court found that Spengler executed various promissory notes while a real estate salesperson for Grubb and Ellis, and that, pursuant to stipulation of the parties, the amount outstanding on the notes was $5,694.42 with interest at the rate of 7 percent (7%) from November 30, 1976, to date of judgment. The trial court found that the relationship between Spengler and Grubb and Ellis was governed by the written independent contractor agreement, that Spengler's service with Grubb and Ellis was terminated in accordance with the agreement, and that Grubb and Ellis had not breached the agreement.

In its conclusions of law, the trial court stated, "Defendant Daniel S. Spengler at all times material to the above-entitled case, was not an employee of the Plaintiff, but rather an independent contractor and therefore, was not entitled to a minimum wage," and "was not subject to the Social Security System ... and was entitled only to compensation based on commissions earned according to the Independent Contractor Agreement. ..."

Spengler challenges the trial court's finding that he was an independent contractor. [143 Cal. App. 3d 895]

The answer to the question whether the relationship between a real estate broker and his real estate salesperson is one of employer and employee or one of principal and independent contractor depends upon the particular area of law one is examining.

It seems clear that for purposes of the administration of the real estate law, the salesperson is the employee and agent of the broker. (See Bus. & Prof. Code, Â§Â§ 10132, 10137, 10151, 10160, 10177, subd. (h); Grand v. Griesinger (1958) 160 Cal. App. 2d 397, 404-406 [325 P.2d 475].) For purposes of establishing tort liability, the California courts have held that a broker is liable under the doctrine of respondeat superior for the tortious acts of his salespeople during the course and scope of business because a salesperson is the agent of the broker. Thus, in Gipson v. Davis Realty Co. (1963) 215 Cal. App. 2d 190, at pages 206-207 [30 Cal.Rptr. 253], the court stated: "We are satisfied, accordingly, that while it may be a question of fact whether in each case a real estate salesman is an employee within the common law definition of master and servant, the Legislature has, by virtue of statutory enactment, made such a salesman an agent of the broker as a matter of law. A consideration of the several statutory provisions applicable to a real estate salesman impels the conclusion that such person can act only for, on behalf of, and in place of the broker under whom he is licensed, and that his acts are limited to those which he does and performs as an agent for such broker. [Citation.] We conclude, therefore, that a salesman, insofar

16: GRUBB & ELLIS CO. V. SPENGLER (1983)

as his relationship with the broker who employs him is concerned, cannot be classed as an independent contractor. Accordingly, any contract which purports to change that relationship from that of agent to independent contractor is invalid as being contrary to the provisions of the Real Estate Law. [Citation.]"

The status of a real estate salesman for purposes of workers' compensation insurance is less clear. In two early cases, prior to the enactment of the Real Estate Law (Bus. & Prof. Code, §§ 10000 et seq.), the courts found that an employer-employee relationship existed. In so concluding, the courts reviewed the circumstances surrounding the work relationship, considering the amount of control the broker exerted over his salesmen and weighing such factors as the method of compensation, who paid the salesman's expenses, how much time the salesman devoted to his work, and how much control the broker exerted over the salesman's movement and method of selling.

Payne v. White House Properties, Inc. (1980) 112 Cal. App. 3d 465 [169 Cal.Rptr. 373], considered the same question, but after the enactment of Business and Professions Code section 10177, subdivision (h), which provides that the commissioner may suspend or revoke the license of a broker who has failed to exercise reasonable supervision over the activities of his salesmen. The [143 Cal. App. 3d 896] court examined the question: "... whether or not the real estate broker is now required to exert that degree of supervision and control over real estate salespersons so that salespersons are employees for the purpose of worker's compensation as a matter of law." (112 Cal. App. 3d at p. 470.) The court concluded that, 'In most instances the real estate salesperson would be an employee for the purposes of worker's compensation, but that determination remains a question of fact." (112 Cal. App. 3d at p. 471.) fn. 3

In a related case, Resnik v. Anderson & Miles (1980) 109 Cal. App. 3d 569 [167 Cal.Rptr. 340], a real estate salesperson filed a claim with the California Labor Commission for commissions which he claimed his broker owed to him. The appellate court considered the question of whether the Labor Commissioner had jurisdiction over the salesperson's claim, his jurisdiction being limited to employee claims. (Lab. Code, §§ 96, 98, subd. (a).) The court concluded that the salesperson was an agent-employee as a matter of law. (109 Cal. App. 3d at pp. 572-573.)

In 1953 the issue of whether a real estate salesperson was an employee for purposes of unemployment insurance was clearly settled by the enactment of section 650 of the Unemployment Insurance Code. It provides in pertinent part, "'Employment' does not include services performed as a real estate ... broker or

16: GRUBB & ELLIS CO. V. SPENGLER (1983)

as a real estate ... salesman by an individual who is licensed in one of such classes by the state and who is remunerated solely by way of commission." Hence, for purposes of the unemployment insurance law a real estate salesperson who is compensated solely on a commission basis, as was Spengler in the case before us, is not an employee.

The status of real estate salespersons for purposes of federal employment taxes has been settled by the recent enactment of Internal Revenue Code section 3508 (26 U.S.C.A. § 3508, Pub.L. No. 97-248, 96 Stat. 551). That section provides in pertinent part, "(a) General Rule.--For purposes of this title, in the case of services performed as a qualified real estate agent ...--(1) the individual performing such services shall not be treated as an employee, and (2) the person for whom such services are performed shall not be treated as an employer." fn. 4 [143 Cal. App. 3d 897]

At the time pertinent in this case, the Internal Revenue Code and the applicable Treasury regulations embodied the usual common law rule for determining the existence of the relationship of employer and employee based generally on the amount of control exercised by the employer over the employee. (26 C.F.R. § 31.3121(d)-1(c), § 31.3401(c)-1.) In two reported cases in which the Internal Revenue Service has attempted to enforce the provisions of the Internal Revenue Code relating to social security and income tax withholding against the earnings of real estate salesmen, the federal court held, in each case, that the salesmen were not employees for such purposes. (See Dimmitt-Rickhoff-Bayer Real Estate Co. v. Finnegan (8th Cir. 1950) 179 F.2d 882; Henry Broderick, Inc. v. Squire (9th Cir. 1947) 163 F.2d 980.)

[4a] Insofar as our research reveals, no case or statutory enactment has specifically addressed itself to the question whether minimum wage laws are applicable to real estate salesmen. The federal legislation (29 U.S.C.A. § 206) applies only to employees engaged in interstate commerce. (29 U.S.C.A. § 203 (b).) Nothing in the record indicates that Grubb and Ellis was engaged in interstate commerce. In any case, in light of the fact that federal legislation excludes real estate salespersons from the definition of employees for purposes of federal employment taxes, it is unlikely that they would be considered employees for purposes of the minimum wage laws.

The state minimum wage laws specifically exclude outside salesmen from coverage. (Lab. Code, § 1171.) "The apparent reason for specifically providing that this chapter does not apply to individuals employed as outside salesmen is that such employees normally control their own hours and are paid on a commission

16: GRUBB & ELLIS CO. V. SPENGLER (1983)

basis." (Review of Selected 1972 Legislation (1973) 4 Pacific L.J. 213, pp. 482-483.) In title 8, California Administrative Code, section 11345, subdivision 2(J), "Outside salesperson" is defined as follows: "'Outside Salesperson' means any person, 18 years of age or over, who customarily and regularly works more than half the working time away from the employer's place of business selling tangible or intangible items or obtaining orders or contracts for products, services or use of facilities." Under Labor Code section 1171, there is a distinction between an independent contractor, who is not an employee, and an outside salesperson, who is an employee, but has been specifically excluded from the application of the minimum wage law. In the usual case, a real estate person would probably qualify as a non-employee either under the traditional common law "control" rule or as an outside salesperson as defined in Labor Code section 1171. In both circumstances, the minimum wage laws would not be applicable to real estate salespersons. [143 Cal. App. 3d 898]

In the case before us, minimal evidence was offered by Spengler in support of his claim that he was an employee under the traditional common law "control" test. In his first amended complaint, Spengler admitted that he entered into an independent contractor agreement with Grubb and Ellis. [5] The agreement was attached to his cross-complaint and incorporated by reference. fn. 5 The agreement provided in part, "This agreement does not constitute a hiring by either party. It is the parties' intention that, so far as shall be in conformity with law, the Salesperson [Spengler] shall be an independent contractor and not G & E's [Grubb and Ellis'] employee." Bill Puterbaugh, district manager of Grubb and Ellis at the time the company negotiated an agreement with Spengler, testified that Spengler worked for Grubb and Ellis as an independent contractor. The testimony pointed to by Spengler respecting the extent of company supervision was to the following effect: When a person first started with Grubb and Ellis, the company had "regular review sessions" with him. The salesmen also filled out a form called "transactions in progress" on a monthly basis. Mr. Puterbaugh testified, "we reviewed with them how they were doing on the transactions and tried to note[,] counsel and advise them." Mr. Puterbaugh testified that the purpose of the "transactions in progress" form was to provide a reason for the managers to talk to the salesmen "once a month." [4b] This evidence is insufficient to establish the kind of control over the manner in which Spengler performed his work that would indicate an employer-employee relationship. (S. A. Gerrard Co. v. Industrial Acc. Com. (1941) 17 Cal. 2d 411, 413-414 [110 P.2d 377]; Automatic Canteen Co. v. State Board of Equalization (1965) 238 Cal. App. 2d 372, 386-387 [47 Cal.Rptr. 848].)

While there may be some doubt as to whether a broker may hire a salesperson on

16: GRUBB & ELLIS CO. V. SPENGLER (1983)

an independent contractor basis (see Gipson v. Davis Realty Co., supra, 215 Cal. App. 2d 190 at p. 207), the evidence presented in this case was clearly sufficient to sustain the trial court's finding that Spengler was not an employee of Grubb and Ellis for the purpose of entitlement to minimum wages.

The judgment is affirmed.

Stephens, J., and Ashby, J., concurred.

FN 1. At the time of the trial in this case, Code of Civil Procedure section 632 required the trial court to render findings of fact and conclusions of law upon request of a party, and rule 232, California Rules of Court, specified the procedures and time limits for requesting and submitting proposed findings, making objections and counterfindings, etc. In 1981, Code of Civil Procedure section 632 was amended to delete the requirement of findings, and rule 232, California Rules of Court, was amended to reflect the changes in Code of Civil Procedure section 632.

FN 2. Subdivision (i) of rule 232 provided "The court may, by written order, extend any of the times prescribed herein and at any time prior to the entry of judgment, whether or not a signed judgment is filed, it may, for good cause shown and upon such terms as may be just, excuse a noncompliance with the time limits prescribed for doing any act required by this rule."

FN 3. Payne v. White House Properties Inc., supra, 112 Cal. App. 3d 465, 472, the court concluded that there was sufficient evidence to sustain the conclusion that the salesman was not an employee for purposes of worker's compensation insurance.

FN 4. The term "qualified real estate agent" is defined in Internal Revenue Code section 3508, subdivision (b)(1) as "any individual who is a sales person if [¶] (A) such individual is a licensed real estate agent, [¶] (B) substantially all of the remuneration (whether or not paid in cash) for the services performed by such individual as a real estate agent is directly related to sales or other output (including the performance of services) rather than to the number of hours worked, and [¶] (C) the services performed by the individual are performed pursuant to a written contract between such individual and the person for whom the services are performed and such contract provides that the individual will not be treated as an employee with respect to such services for Federal tax purposes."

FN 5. Matters admitted in pleadings do not require proof. (People v. Bestline Products, Inc. (1976) 61 Cal. App. 3d 879, 921 [132 Cal.Rptr. 767].)

17: RAMIREZ V YOSEMITE WATER CO.

85 Cal.Rptr.2d 844 (1999)
978 P.2d 2
20 Cal.4th 785

Peter RAMIREZ, Plaintiff and Appellant,

v.

YOSEMITE WATER COMPANY, INC., Defendant and Respondent.

No. S070114.

Supreme Court of California.

June 17, 1999.

846*846 Dennis F. Moss for Plaintiff and Appellant.

Sonnenschein, Nath & Rosenthal, Lee T. Paterson and Weston A. Edwards, Los Angeles, for Defendant and Respondent.

Sheppard, Mullin, Richter & Hampton, Richard J. Simmons, Los Angeles, and Kelly L. Hensley for the Employers Group as Amicus Curiae On behalf of Defendant and Respondent.

MOSK, J.

Generally, employees in the State of California who work more than 40 hours per week and 8 hours per day (at least, in the latter case, up until January 1, 1998) have had the right to receive premium pay for the hours worked over this limit. (See 1 Wilcox, Cal. Employment Law (rev. Mar. 1998) § 3.04, pp. 3-21 to 3-28.) Labor Code section 1171[1] expressly excludes from the overtime laws employees who are "outside salespersons,"[2] and the California Industrial 847*847 Welfare Commission (IWC), the agency charged with implementing section 1171, defined the term "outside salesperson" in Wage Order No. 7-80, as someone who "regularly works more than half the working time" engaged in sales activities outside the workplace. (Cal.Code Regs., tit. 8, § 11070, subd. 2(I) (hereinafter Wage Order No. 7-80, 2(I)).)[3] In this case we are called on to decide whether an employee who performs a mixture of sales and nonsales duties is an "outside salesperson" within the meaning of section 1171. The trial court and the Court of Appeal came to the conclusion that the employee, who delivered bottled water and was also expected to sell the water service to new customers, was an outside salesperson for purposes of section 1171. Their conclusion was based on a reading of federal regulations that differ substantially from the state regulations applicable in this ease: the former regulations define the term by determining the

17: RAMIREZ V YOSEMITE WATER CO.

employees'"primary purpose," rather than by calculating how they spend their time.

We conclude these courts may have erred in determining that the employee in this case was an outside salesperson because they incorrectly relied on the federal regulation and interpretation of that regulation when construing this state's distinct definition of "outside salesperson." Accordingly, we reverse the Court of Appeal's judgment and remand for further proceedings.

I. Factual and Procedural Background

Yosemite Water Company, Inc. (Yosemite) is in the business of selling bottled water and other products incidental to the bottled water business, such as cups, coffee, and other ingredients, and of renting water coolers. By 1995, the company had grown from 70 to 150 routes. A route is a defined territory over which a "route sales representative" is responsible for all delivery and sales activity.

Plaintiff Peter Ramirez was employed by Yosemite as a route sales representative between April 1989 and November 1992. From November 1992 to March 3, 1993, when he left the company, Ramirez served as a relief route sales representative.

After he left the company, Ramirez filed a complaint against Yosemite for unpaid overtime wages, unlawful wage deductions and employee charges, and unpaid wages. The company cross-complained against him for damages for interference with contractual relations and interference with prospective economic advantage as the result of his alleged attempt to solicit Yosemite's customers when he left the company. At a subsequent bench trial, much of the evidence presented concerned the matter of how Ramirez spent his average workday. Because the question whether Ramirez was an "outside salesperson," as we will see, turns on a detailed, fact-specific determination of this matter, we shall recount that evidence at some length.

Ramirez spent a substantial portion of his workday delivering bottled water to business and residential customers. Each five-gallon bottle of water Ramirez delivered weighed forty pounds. On an average business stop, Ramirez would deliver six to seven bottles; an average residential customer purchased one to two bottles. About 70 percent of his customers were presidential. When he began on route No. 15, it was an 800-bottle route serving about 400 customers. The route grew so that, at its height, he had 550 customers and averaged 1,500- 1,900 bottles delivered in a 10-day cycle, or an average of between 150 and 190 bottles per day. He averaged six delivery stops per hour, delivering one to two bottles on

17: RAMIREZ V YOSEMITE WATER CO.

average to residential customers and six to seven bottles for commercial ones. For established customers, he would carry the bottles into a business or place of residence, exchange full for empty bottles, and refill and replace other stock and supplies. He would also rotate bottles on his truck, check the bottles for leaks and foreign objects, and carry the bottles to the customer's house. For some customers, 848*848 he would also rotate the spare water bottles, wipe off the tops and place the bottles in the coolers. He would also do minor service on the coolers.

According to Ramirez's testimony, he engaged in very little solicitation of regular customers to persuade them to increase their service. He testified that once customers commenced service their purchasing habits became stable, and he generally did not "push" established customers into buying more or different products for fear of offending them. Moreover, he had little direct contact with residential customers, who were frequently not home when he delivered the water. He saw a customer only about 5 to 7 percent of the time, usually at the customer's request. He did not engage in selling to customers he did not see. Customers would communicate by leaving notes or calling, and he would leave bills and reminders of overdue payments under the bottles.

Yosemite employed several full-time employees as solicitors, whose principal task was to sign up new customers. Ramirez was also expected to engage in solicitation of new customers. He testified that he was expected to obtain at least 1 new customer per workday, and to do so, he made on average 10 contacts per day on his route, which took him a total of approximately 30 minutes. He was also generally responsible for "setting up" the new customers. Between once a month and once every two months, he spent six hours on Saturday with other route sales representatives going door-to-door soliciting new customers. He also attended sales meetings designed to improve sales techniques approximately twice a month. In a five-day workweek, he estimated he would spend about three to three and one-half hours trying to sell his service to potential new customers. Occasionally, he would pass out to old and new customers a list of the company's products.

If a potential customer called Yosemite to initiate service, Ramirez would receive a note to call that person back and set up a time to begin service. At the time he set up a new customer, if he met the customer face-to-face, he would explain the service rules and minimum purchases, and describe the additional products the company had to offer.

From the time Ramirez left the plant around 8 a.m., until he returned in the evening, he testified he worked anywhere from seven to nine hours not counting

17: RAMIREZ V YOSEMITE WATER CO.

the time he spent soliciting new customers. His average day lasted 11 hours and sometimes longer, such as when he had difficulty balancing his accounts. He worked Monday through Friday, more than 40 hours in a week, in addition to the occasional Saturday noted above. He was not paid for any overtime hours worked.

When he was a route sales representative, Ramirez was paid a minimum of $1,200-$1,400 per month, which Yosemite considered a "guaranteed draw" against future bottle sales. He would also receive an additional 22 percent per bottle and 10 percent for cups, tea, coffee and cooler rentals he delivered once he had exceeded the guaranteed draw. He was paid according to the number of bottles he delivered, whether or not he had originally solicited the customers to whom they were delivered. Thus, if a company solicitor sold water to a new resident located on route No. 15, Ramirez would deliver the water and get the credit for the bottles delivered even though he did not do the soliciting. In addition to his usual compensation, he received a small commission for each new customer he signed: He was paid nothing for the first 10 customers he signed, $5 per new customer for the 11th through 15th customers, $10 per customer for the next 10, and $20 for each new customer over 25.

Maya Soderstrom, Yosemite's president, testified that when a route sales representative made a delivery, he or she was expected to engage in selling activity. As Soderstrom explained, selling "is the main job of our route salespeople," who are in the field selling "constantly." The company's expectation is that the route sales representatives are selling 90 percent or more of their workday, although she later clarified that she was counting the time spent delivering bottles of water to the customer as part of the selling activity. She also explained that the route sales representatives are the primary contact between the company and the customer. 849*849 Daniel Ledbetter, Ramirez's route supervisor, also testified that over 80 percent of Ramirez's time at work was spent away from the Yosemite plant and over 90 percent of his working day was spent in selling activities, although it is unclear whether or not he had a similarly broad definition as Soderstrom of the term "sales." Ledbetter also confirmed that Ramirez was expected to obtain the equivalent of 1 new customer per day worked and to speak to 10-15 people a day to accomplish this goal.

Claude I. Niesen, special projects manager and a sales training manager at Yosemite, offered an opinion of the time Ramirez took to do various tasks. He purported to base his opinion on his longtime experience in the bottled water industry at Yosemite and other companies, on Ramirez's sales record and deposition, and discussions with Ledbetter and other supervisory personnel at Yosemite.

17: RAMIREZ V YOSEMITE WATER CO.

He opined that Ramirez spent 90 percent of his workweek in sales activity and that over 80 percent of his workweek was spent away from the company's premises. Niesen also opined that Ramirez must have spent 850 minutes a week engaged in face-to-face solicitation of prospective customers.

At the conclusion of the trial, the court found in favor of Yosemite that Ramirez was an "outside salesperson." In order to understand the basis of the trial court's decision, it is important to appreciate that there was a fundamental conflict between Ramirez's and Yosemite's interpretations of the meaning of the term "outside salesperson." As noted, IWC provides that an employee be considered an outside salesperson if he or she works more than half the working time away from the employer's place of business selling items or obtaining orders. (Wage Order No. 7-80, 2(I).) Ramirez claimed that the IWC wage order requires the court to tally the amount of time spent engaged in actual sales outside the workplace, as opposed to the time spent delivering products or performing services such as cooler maintenance. He claimed the evidence showed plainly that he spent more time delivering products and providing services than selling, and that therefore he was not an outside salesperson.

Yosemite contended, on the other hand, that the court should look to federal law. When a sales/delivery person is performing a dual function, the court must ascertain "the primary function" of the employee as determined by various factors discussed below. Yosemite argued that Ramirez's primary function was sales and therefore he was an outside salesperson. Yosemite also argued that inasmuch as the Wage Order No. 7-80, 2(1) could be construed to conflict with federal law, the IWC must have exceeded its authority, because Labor Code section 1171 intended to fully incorporate the federal definition of outside salesperson. The trial court appeared to agree with Yosemite both that the "primary function" analysis was applicable and that Ramirez was an outside salesperson.

The trial court also found that Ramirez was exempt from the overtime laws under another section of Wage Order No. 7-80 because he earned over 50 percent of his salary from commissions. (See Wage Order No. 7-80, subd. 3(c); see now Wage Order No. 7-98, set out at Cal.Code Regs., tit. 8, § 11070, subd. 3(B).)

The Court of Appeal affirmed, also accepting the federal "primary function" analysis. Although it acknowledged that the language of the IWC regulation defining outside salesperson differed from federal regulations, it nonetheless looked to the federal regulations "for guidance." After reviewing the pertinent federal regulations, which will be discussed more fully below, the court concluded that Ramirez's "prime function" was selling bottles of water and additional prod-

17: RAMIREZ V YOSEMITE WATER CO.

ucts, and that he therefore fit within the definition of "outside salesperson." It did not reach the question whether Ramirez was also exempt from the overtime' laws as a commissioned employee.

We granted review to determine the proper meaning of the term "outside salesperson."

II. Discussion

A. Standard of Review

The question whether Ramirez was an outside salesperson within the meaning of 850*850 applicable statutes and regulations is, like other questions involving the application of legal categories, a mixed question of law and fact. (See, e.g., Crocker National Bank v. City and County of San Francisco (1989) 49 Cal.3d 881, 888, 264 Cal.Rptr. 139, 782 P.2d 278.) In the present case, although there was some controversy as to the facts—i.e., as to what Ramirez did as an employee for Yosemite—the predominant controversy is the precise meaning of the term "outside salesperson," a question of law. It was this question on which we granted review. As such, we will review the Court of Appeal's and the trial court's judgment independently on the question of this term's meaning in this context. (Ibid.)

B. The Outside Salesperson Exemption

In interpreting the scope of an exemption from the state's overtime laws, we begin by reviewing certain basic principles. First, "past decisions ... teach that in light of the remedial nature of the legislative enactments authorizing the regulation of wages, hours and working conditions for the protection and benefit of employees, the statutory provisions are to be liberally construed with an eye to promoting such protection." (Industrial Welfare Com. v. Superior Court (1980) 27 Cal.3d 690, 702, 166 Cal.Rptr. 331, 613 P.2d 579.) Thus, under California law, exemptions from statutory mandatory overtime provisions are narrowly construed. (Nordquist v. McGraw-Hill Broadcasting Co. (1995) 32 Cal.App.4th 555, 562, 38 Cal. Rptr.2d 221; see also A H Phillips, Inc. v. Walling (1945) 324 U.S. 490, 493, 65 S.Ct. 807, 89 L.Ed. 1095.) Moreover, the assertion of an exemption from the overtime laws is considered to be an affirmative defense, and therefore the employer bears the burden of proving the employee's exemption. (Nordquist, supra, 32 Cal.App.4th at p. 562, 38 Cal.Rptr.2d 221; Corning Glass Works v. Brennan (1974) 417 U.S. 188, 196-197, 94 S.Ct. 2223, 41 L.Ed.2d 1.)

The IWC is the state agency empowered to formulate regulations (known as wage

17: RAMIREZ V YOSEMITE WATER CO.

orders) governing minimum wages, maximum hours, and overtime pay in the State of California. (Tidewater Marine Western, Inc. v. Bradshaw (1996) 14 Cal.4th 557, 561, 59 Cal.Rptr.2d 186, 927 P.2d 296.) The IWC's wage orders, although at times patterned after federal regulations, also sometimes provide greater protection than is provided under federal law in the Fair Labor Standards Act (FLSA) and accompanying federal regulations. (See, e.g., Tidewater, supra, 14 Cal.4th at pp. 566-567, 59 Cal. Rptr.2d 186, 927 P.2d 296 [seamen entitled to overtime under wage order despite exemption from FLSA]; Aguilar v. Association for Retarded Citizens (1991) 234 Cal.App.3d 21, 33-34, 285 Cal.Rptr. 515 [employees working shifts of less than 24 hours entitled to be paid for sleep time, notwithstanding contrary federal rule]; Skyline Homes, Inc. v. Department of Industrial Relations (1985) 165 Cal. App.3d 239, 247, 211 Cal.Rptr. 792, disapproved on other grounds in Tidewater, supra, 14 Cal.4th at p. 574, 59 Cal.Rptr.2d 186, 927 P.2d 296 [regular rate of pay for overtime purposes calculated by dividing salary by no more than 40 hours, notwithstanding federal rule authorizing use of fluctuating workweek].) The FLSA explicitly permits greater employee protection under state law. "The FLSA includes a `savings clause,' which provides: `No provision of this chapter or of any order thereunder shall excuse noncompliance with any ... State law or municipal ordinance establishing ... a maximum workweek lower than the maximum workweek established [hereunder]....' (29 U.S.C. § 218(a).) The federal courts that have addressed this question have interpreted this savings clause as expressly permitting states to regulate overtime wages. (See, e.g., ... Pacific Merchant Shipping Ass'n v. Aubry [(1990)] 918 F.2d [1409,] 1422 [`Congress has specifically allowed states to enforce overtime laws more generous than the FLSA,' citing the savings clause]....)." (Tidewater, supra, 14 Cal.4th at p. 567, 59 Cal.Rptr.2d 186, 927 P.2d 296.)

At issue in this case is an interpretation of section 1171 and Wage Order No. 7-80, 2(I). Section 1171, found in the chapter of the Labor Code pertaining to minimum wage, maximum hour, and overtime laws, states: "The provisions of this chapter shall 851*851 apply to and include men, women and minors employed in any occupation, trade, or industry, whether compensation is measured by time, piece, or otherwise, but shall not include any individual employed as an outside salesman."(Italics added.) Wage Order No. 7-80, 2(1), implementing section 1171, in turn defined "outside salesperson" as follows: "[A]ny person, 18 years of age or over, who customarily and regularly works more than half the working time away from the employer's place of business selling tangible or intangible items or obtaining orders or contracts for products, services or use of facilities." (Italics added.)

The Court of Appeal, finding no case law or other elucidation of this part of the

17: RAMIREZ V YOSEMITE WATER CO.

IWC wage order, turned, as noted, to federal regulations. These regulations explicate the meaning of the term "outside salesperson" in those employment situations in which the employee performs a mixture of delivery and sales work. The Court of Appeal purported to "synthesiz[e] the guidelines in federal regulations together with [Wage] Order No. 7-80" to arrive at the proper ruling in this case.

Those federal regulations to which the Court of Appeal looked for guidance differ substantially from the wage order. Section 541.5 of title 29 of the Code of Federal Regulations (1998) defines the term "outside salesman" as an "employee: [¶] (a) [w]ho is employed for the purpose of and who is customarily and regularly engaged away from his employer's place or places of business in: [¶] (1) [m]aking sales within the meaning of section 3(k) of the Act; or [¶] (2) [o]btaining orders or contracts for services or for the use of facilities for which a consideration will be paid by the client or customer; and [¶] (b) [w]hose hours of work of a nature other than that described in paragraph (a)(1) or (2) of this section do not exceed 20 percent of the hours worked in the workweek by nonexempt employees of the employer: Provided, [t]hat work performed incidental to and in conjunction with the employee's own outside sales or solicitations, including incidental deliveries and collections, shall not be regarded as nonexempt work." (First italics in original, other italics added.)

The operative effect of the federal exemption is concisely summarized at section 541.505(a) of title 29 of the Code of Federal Regulations (1998): "[I]n the case of outside salesmen ..., the employee's chief duty or primary function must be the making of sales or the taking of orders if he is to qualify under the definition in § 541.5. He must be a sales[person] by occupation. If he is, all work that he performs which is actually incidental to and in conjunction with his own sales effort is exempt work. All other work of such an employee is nonexempt work.... All of the duties performed by an employee must be considered. The time devoted to the various duties is an important, but not necessarily controlling, element." (Italics added.) In determining whether an employee's "primary function" is as a salesperson, such factors to be considered are the "presence or absence of customary or contractual prearrangements concerning amounts of products to be delivered; description of the employee's occupation in union contracts; the employer's specifications as to qualifications for hiring; sales training; attendance at sales conferences; method of payment; proportion of earnings directly attributable to sales effort; and other factors that may have a bearing on the relationship to sales of the employee's work." (29 C.F.R. § 541.505(e) (1998).)

Furthermore, 29 Code of Federal Regulations section 541.505(b) (1998), which appears to have the most direct bearing on the present case, states: "[T]here is lit-

17: RAMIREZ V YOSEMITE WATER CO.

tle question that a routeman who provides the only sales contact between the employer and the customers, who calls on customers and takes orders for products which he delivers from stock in his vehicle or procures and delivers to the customer on a later trip, and who receives compensation commensurate with a volume of products sold, is employed for the purpose of making sales."

Thus, the federal exemption focuses on defining the employee's "primary function," not on how much work time is spent selling. Although the federal exemption does place a 20 percent cap on nonexempt (i.e., nonsales) work, that cap does not apply to any nonsales activities that are "incidental" to outside 852*852 sales, including the making of deliveries. In other words, so long as it can be shown that the individual's chief duty or primary function is making sales, then every activity in any way incidental to sales may be funneled into the exempt category and excluded from the 20 percent cap on nonexempt work.

Wage Order No. 7-80, on the other hand, makes no mention of the primary function for which the person is employed. Rather, the state regulation takes a purely quantitative approach, focusing exclusively on whether the individual "works more than half the working time ... selling ... or obtaining orders or contracts." (Wage Order No. 7-80, 2(1).) State law also differs from the federal regulation in that it does not contain any provision that reclassifies intrinsically nonexempt nonsales work as exempt based on the fact that it is incidental to sales. The language of the state exemption only encompasses work directly involved in "selling ... items or obtaining orders or contracts." (Ibid.)

By choosing not to track the language of the federal-exemption and instead adopting its own distinct definition of "outside salespersons," the IWC evidently intended to depart from federal law and to provide, at least in some cases, greater protection for employees. Under the Court of Appeal's interpretation, on the other hand, a California employee is accorded significantly less, not more, protection than under the federal standard. This is so because the Court of Appeal imported the laxer federal criteria regarding what constitutes an exemption into a state standard that requires only more than 50 percent in exempt activities in order to qualify as an outside salesperson, as opposed to 80 percent under federal law. The Court of Appeal failed to recognize that the two numbers referred to two different types of classifications, with the former number measuring activities directly related to sales, and the latter, larger number measuring both those activities and activities "incidental to" sales, as that term has come to be broadly defined under federal regulations. (See 29 C.F.R. § 541.505(b), (e) (1998).) In confounding federal and state labor law, and thereby providing less protection to state employees, the Court of Appeal and the trial court departed from the teach-

17: RAMIREZ V YOSEMITE WATER CO.

ing that where the language or intent of state and federal labor laws substantially differ, reliance on federal regulations or interpretations to construe state regulations is misplaced. (See Aguilar v. Association for Retarded Citizens, supra, 234 Cal.App.3d 21, 34-35, 285 Cal. Rptr. 515; Skyline Homes, Inc. v. Department of Industrial Relations, supra, 165 Cal. App.3d at pp. 247-249, 211 Cal.Rptr. 792.)[4]

In sum, Wage Order No 7-80, 2(1), incorporates a quantitative method for determining whether an employee is an outside salesperson that differs in some respect from the qualitative method employed under federal law. The Court of Appeal and the trial court employed the federal method, or an improper hybrid of the state and federal methods, not fully acknowledging the differences between the two schemes and the consequently problematic nature of using interpretations of the federal regulation as a key to understanding the state regulation. These courts therefore erred in that respect.

Yosemite argues the IWC exceeded its regulatory authority in adopting a definition of "outside salesperson" at variance with the federal definition. Yosemite points to the fact that at the time the outside salesperson exemption contained in section 1171 was adopted in 1972 (Stats.1972, ch. 1122, § 2, p. 2153), the FLSA had already adopted the definition of that term and accompanying regulations reviewed above. Because the 853*853 term "outside salesperson" was used nowhere else in California law, Yosemite argues that it is logical to infer that the Legislature intended to fully incorporate the federal definition. Yosemite therefore concludes that the IWC exceeded its legislative mandate by adopting a regulation that is narrower than the federal one.

In assessing Yosemite's claim, we first consider the general framework of judicial review of administrative regulations. In Yamaha Corp. of America v. State Bd. of Equalization (1998) 19 Cal.4th 1, 78 Cal. Rptr.2d 1, 960 P.2d 1031 (Yamaha), we posited a dichotomy between "quasi-legislative" and "interpretive" rules. Quasilegislative regulations are those "adopted by an agency to which the Legislature has confided the power to `make law'" (id. at p. 7, 78 Cal.Rptr.2d 1, 960 P.2d 1031, italics omitted), and such rules "have the dignity of statutes" (id. at p. 10, 78 Cal.Rptr.2d 1, 960 P.2d 1031). On the other hand, interpretive regulations are those which involve "an agency's interpretation of a statute or regulation ..." (id. at p. 7, 78 Cal.Rptr.2d 1, 960 P.2d 1031), and are given variable deference according to a number of factors (id. at p. 12, 78 Cal. Rptr.2d 1, 960 P.2d 1031). As we acknowledged, "administrative rules do not always fall neatly into one category or the other; the terms designate opposite ends of an administrative continuum, depending on the breadth of the authority delegated by the

17: RAMIREZ V YOSEMITE WATER CO.

Legislature." (Id. at p. 6, fn. 3, 78 Cal.Rptr.2d 1, 960 P.2d 1031.)

Regulations that fall somewhere in the continuum may have both quasilegislative and interpretive characteristics, as when an administrative agency exercises a legislatively delegated power to interpret key statutory terms. In Moore v. California State Bd. of Accountancy (1992) 2 Cal.4th 999, 9 Cal.Rptr.2d 358, 831 P.2d 798 (Moore), for example, we reviewed a regulation by the Board of Accountancy, the agency statutorily chartered to regulate the accounting profession in this state, providing that those unlicensed by that board could not use the title "accountant." The agency was interpreting a statute, Business and Professions Code section 5058, that forbids use of titles "`likely to be confused with'" the titles of "`"certified public accountant"'" and `"public accountant." `" (2 Cal.4th at p. 1011, 9 Cal.Rptr.2d 358, 831 P.2d 798.) As we stated: "Inasmuch as enforcement of the provisions of the Accountancy Act, including section 5058, is entrusted to the Board, it seems apparent that the Legislature delegated to the Board the authority to determine whether a title or designation not identified in the statute is likely to confuse or mislead the public. Since the Board was also authorized to seek an injunction against the use of such terms, its authority to `adopt, repeal, or amend such regulations as may be reasonably necessary and expedient for the ... administration of [the Accountancy Act]' (§ 5010) includes the power to identify by regulation those terms which it finds are `likely to be confused with' "certified public accountant" or "public accountant," `the use of which may be enjoined under the broad prohibition of section 5058. To conclude otherwise would contravene the intent and purpose behind the statute." (2 Cal.4th at pp. 1013-1014, 9 Cal.Rptr.2d 358, 831 P.2d 798, italics added; see also Ford Dealers Assn. v. Department of Motor Vehicles (1982) 32 Cal.3d 347, 362, 185 Cal.Rptr. 453, 650 P.2d 328 [administrative agency with rulemaking power is authorized to "fill up the details" of a statutory scheme].))

The regulation at issue in the present case, as in Moore, has both quasilegislative and interpretive characteristics. The Legislature has expressly delegated to the IWC the authority to promulgate wage orders setting "minimum wages, maximum hours and standard conditions of labor for all employees." (§ 1185.) "Judicial authorities have repeatedly emphasized that in fulfilling its broad statutory mandate, the IWC engages in a quasi-legislative endeavor, a task which necessarily and properly requires the commission's exercise of a considerable degree of policy-making judgment and discretion. [Citations.] [¶] Because of the quasi-legislative nature of the IWC's authority, the judiciary has recognized that its review of the commission's wage orders is properly circumscribed." (Industrial Welfare Com. v. Superior Court, supra, 27 Cal.3d at p. 702, 166 Cal.Rptr. 331, 613 P.2d 579.) As in 854*854 Moore, this delegation of legislative authority

17: RAMIREZ V YOSEMITE WATER CO.

includes the power to elaborate the meaning of key statutory terms. On the other hand, since the IWC is engaged in construing the meaning of a portion of section 1171, its regulation is in some sense interpretive.

If Wage Order No. 7-80, 2(1) is considered quasi-legislative regulation, it is certainly valid. "`"[I]n reviewing the legality of a regulation adopted pursuant to a delegation of legislative power, the judicial function is limited to determining whether the regulation (1) is `within the scope of the authority conferred' [citation] and (2) is `reasonably necessary to effectuate the purpose of the statute' [citation]."'" (Yamaha, supra, 19 Cal.4th at p. 11, 78 Cal.Rptr.2d 1, 960 P.2d 1031.)

We conclude, first of all, that Wage Order No. 7-80, 2(1) is within the scope of the IWC's authority. Although the Legislature in 1972 adopted the outside salesperson exemption already found in federal law, nothing in either the language or the legislative history of the statute suggests that the Legislature thereby intended to incorporate, down to the last detail, all the federal regulations pertaining to that exemption. The only mention of the outside salesperson exemption we can uncover is a sentence in a Senate committee analysis noting that "opposition has also been expressed by the Vacuum Cleaner Manufacturers Association, who wish to examine the impact of outdoor salesman who work on a commission." (Sen. Com. on Industrial Relations, Analysis of Assem. Bill No. 30 (1971 Reg. Sess.) as amended Apr. 1, 1971, p. 1.) The next time the bill was amended, the outside salesperson exemption in its present form appeared for the first time. (Sen. Amend, to Assem. Bill No. 30 (1971 Reg. Sess.) July 27, 1971.) In the absence of statutory language or legislative history to the contrary, we have no reason to presume that the Legislature, in delegating broad regulatory authority to the IWC, obliged the agency to follow in each particular a federal regulatory agency's interpretation of a common term. And indeed, as cited above, and as the Legislature was presumably aware, there are numerous instances in which the IWC has chosen different methods of implementing laws pertaining to wages and hours. We therefore conclude that the IWC, in formulating a definition of "outside salesperson" that diverged from the federal definition, did not thereby exceed its statutory authority.

We also conclude that Wage Order No. 7-80, 2(1), was reasonably necessary to effectuate the purpose of section 1171. It was necessary for the IWC to establish some working definition of "outside salesperson" that takes into account the fact that some employees work in both sales and nonsales capacities. It was reasonable for the IWC, in formulating its definition, to take a quantitative approach, looking to the actual hours spent on sales activity to determine if an employee is

17: RAMIREZ V YOSEMITE WATER CO.

primarily a salesperson. Thus, we conclude that adoption of the IWC's definition of outside salesperson was not arbitrary or capricious, nor did it exceed the scope of the IWC's statutory mandate.

On the other hand, even if we considered Wage Order No. 7-80, 2(I) a purely interpretive regulation, it has two attributes which weigh in favor of considerable judicial deference to the agency's interpretation. First, the interpretation is contained in a regulation formally adopted pursuant to the Administrative Procedure Act. "`[A]n interpretation of a statute contained in a regulation adopted after public notice and comment is more deserving of deference than [one] contained in an advice letter prepared by a single staff member.'" (Yamaha, supra, 19 Cal.4th at p. 13, 78 Cal.Rptr.2d 1, 960 P.2d 1031.) Second, the regulation is entitled to greater deference because it embodies a statutory interpretation that the administrative agency "`has consistently maintained'" and "`is [of] long-standing'" (ibid.), i.e., for almost 20 years. For these reasons, the IWC's definition is entitled to deference regardless of whether it is deemed a quasi-legislative or interpretive regulation. We conclude that the IWC's interpretation of the term "outside salesperson" is reasonable and should not be invalidated.

Yosemite contends that the pertinent language of Wage Order No. 7-80, 2(I), strictly construed, will lead to an absurd result inasmuch as even those employed full time as salespeople often do not spend more than 855*855 half of their time directly selling to customers, but engage in other related activities such as preparation, travel time, and paperwork. There is, however, no need to interpret the wage order so strictly. If a salesperson must travel one hour to destination A in order to attempt a sale, then surely the most reasonable interpretation of the wage order is to count the hour of travel time as time spent "selling." But if, as in the present case, an employee travels to a destination to engage in both sales and nonsales activities, the travel time must be apportioned among the two types of activities for purposes of determining the total amount of time spent doing sales and nonsales work.

Having recognized California's distinctive quantitative approach to determining which employees are outside salespersons, we must then address an issue implicitly raised by the parties that caused some confusion in the trial court and the Court of Appeal: Is the number of hours worked in sales-related activities to be determined by the number of hours that the employer, according to its job description or its estimate, claims the employee should be working in sales, or should it be determined by the actual average hours the employee spent on sales activity? The logic inherent in the IWC's quantitative definition of outside salesperson dictates that neither alternative would be wholly satisfactory. On the one

17: RAMIREZ V YOSEMITE WATER CO.

hand, if hours worked on sales were determined through an employer's job description, then the employer could make an employee exempt from overtime laws solely by fashioning an idealized job description that had little basis in reality. On the other hand, an employee who is supposed to be engaged in sales activities during most of his working hours and falls below the 50 percent mark due to his own substandard performance should not thereby be able to evade a valid exemption. A trial court, in determining whether the employee is an outside salesperson, must steer clear of these two pitfalls by inquiring into the realistic requirements of the job. In so doing, the court should consider, first and foremost, how the employee actually spends his or her time. But the trial court should also consider whether the employee's practice diverges from the employer's realistic expectations, whether there was any concrete expression of employer displeasure over an employee's substandard performance, and whether these expressions were themselves realistic given the actual overall requirements of the job.

In the present case, the evidence is uncontroverted that Ramirez performed both sales and delivery functions for Yosemite. Delivery of preordered water bottles or the restocking of "empties" is not a sales activity in the conventional meaning of the word— one who only performed these delivery tasks could not be considered a salesperson. It is true, as Yosemite points out, that failure to properly deliver the product would lead to loss of the customer, but that does not make such delivery a sales activity, any more than an attorney's preparation of a legal brief in order to satisfy and thereby retain a client is a sales activity.

Although appellate courts normally defer to trial courts' resolution of conflicting evidence when there is substantial evidence to support the trial court's decision (see Gray v. Don Miller & Associates Inc. (1984) 35 Cal.3d 498, 503, 198 Cal.Rptr. 551, 674 P.2d 253), in the present case the record indicates that the trial court's review of the evidence of whether Ramirez was an outside salesperson was tainted by an interpretation of the term that was overly favorable to finding the exemption. In other words, the record suggests that the trial court would have found Ramirez to be an outside salesperson even if it believed all of Ramirez's testimony as to how he spent his time on the job to be true, whereas a plain reading of that testimony in light of Wage Order No. 7-80, 2(I) would yield the contrary conclusion. Thus, it is unclear from the record that the court ever saw the need to resolve inconsistent testimony presented at trial. (See Engalla v. Permanente Medical Group, Inc. (1997) 15 Cal.4th 951, 972-973, 64 Cal.Rptr.2d 843, 938 P.2d 903 [when trial court applies incorrect standard that keeps it from resolving factual disputes, remand for further factfinding appropriate]; see also Webster v. Trustees of Cal. State University (1993) 19 Cal.App.4th 1456, 1462- 1463, 24 Cal.Rptr.2d 150 [when 856*856 trial court in administrative writ proceedings

17: RAMIREZ V YOSEMITE WATER CO.

employs substantial evidence standard that makes resolution of conflicting evidence unnecessary, instead of the correct independent judgment test, remand is appropriate].) We therefore conclude that remand to the trial court is the most appropriate disposition. On remand the trial court may have to resolve significant factual discrepancies—for example, Ramirez's claim that he spent only 150 minutes a week on direct door-to-door sales versus Yosemite's claim that he spent 850 minutes a week.[5]

C. Ramirez as a Commissioned Employee

Wage Order No. 7-80, subdivision 3(c) and its successor, Wage Order No. 7-98, subdivision 3(B), state that "[p]rovisions of [overtime compensation] shall not apply to any employee whose earnings exceed one and one-half (1?) times the minimum wage, if more than half (?) of that employee's compensation represents commissions." As discussed above, the trial court found not only that Ramirez was an outside salesperson but also that he was compensated primarily through commissions within the meaning of this wage order. Therefore, for that independent reason, the court found he should be exempt from the overtime statute. There would be no need to remand this case if we agreed with the trial court that Ramirez was a commissioned employee.

The IWC wage order does not define the term "commission," but its meaning is set forth in Labor Code section 204.1 as follows: "Commission wages are compensation paid to any person for services rendered in the sale of such employer's property or services and based proportionately upon the amount or value thereof." Although section 204.1 applies specifically to employees of vehicle dealers, both parties contend, and we agree, that the statute's definition of "commission" is more generally applicable. In interpreting this language, the Court of Appeal in Keyes Motors, Inc. v. Division Labor Standards Enforcement (1987) 197 Cal.App.3d 557, 563, 242 Cal.Rptr. 873, stated: "We conclude Labor Code section 204.1 sets up two requirements, both of which must be met before a compensation scheme is deemed to constitute `commission wages.' First, the employees must be involved principally in selling a product or service, not making the product or rendering the service. Second, the amount of their compensation must be a percent of the price of the product or service." (Italics omitted.)

Ramirez was compensated at a flat rate of $1,200-$1400 per month, plus a percentage of the price of the bottles of water and related products sold when sales exceeded the flat rate. The parties dispute whether or not the $1,200- $1,400 sum represented a "draw" against future bottle sales, or was more in the nature of a salary. But regardless of which it was, and regardless of whether Ramirez's com-

17: RAMIREZ V YOSEMITE WATER CO.

pensation could be characterized as "a percentage of the price of the product or service," it is not at all clear that the first condition set forth by the Keyes court was met. As discussed above, it remains to be clarified on remand whether Ramirez was "involved principally in selling the product or service." Because our determination of whether Ramirez was a commissioned employee depends partly on matters to be decided by the trial court on remand, we believe this question is also best resolved on remand.

III. Disposition

For all of the foregoing reasons, we reverse the judgment of the Court of Appeal and remand for further proceedings consistent with this opinion.

GEORGE, C.J., and KENNARD, J., BAXTER, J., WERDEGAR, J., CHIN, J., and BROWN, J., concur.

[1] All statutory citations are to this code unless otherwise specified.

[2] The statute actually uses the term "outside salesman," as does the applicable federal regulation, but the regulation that is the primary focus of this opinion uses the term "outside salesperson." For the sake of consistency, we will use the term "outside salesperson."

[3] Wage Order No. 7-80 was superseded in 1998 by Wage Order No. 7-98, set forth at California Code of Regulations, title 8, section 11070. The present Wage Order does not change Wage Order No. 7-80 in any respect pertinent to the issues discussed herein. The definition of "outside salesperson" is unchanged.

[4] The IWC's distinct approach to defining categorical overtime exemptions can also be illustrated in its treatment of the exemption for administrative, executive, and professional employees. (Cal.Code Regs., tit. 8, § 11070, subd. 1(A).) The federal exemption for this category of employees adopts a core test which focuses on the employee's "primary duty"; if the "primary duty" test is met, then he or she is deemed exempt regardless of how much time the individual actually spends performing the primary duty. (29 C.F.R. §§ 541.1(f), 541.2(e)(2), and 541.3(e) (1998).) By contrast, the state law exemption, as in the case of "outside salespersons," adopts the requirement that the employee must be "engaged... primarily" in exempt work (Cal.Code Regs., tit. 8, § 11070, subd. 1(A)(1)); the term "primarily" is defined as "more than one-half the employee's work time." (Id., § 11070, subd. 2(J).)

[5] On remand, the trial court should, as Ramirez requested, itemize the types of

17: RAMIREZ V YOSEMITE WATER CO.

activities that it considers to be sales related, and the approximate average times that it finds the employee spent on each of these activities. Because the question whether a particular activity is sales related is a mixed one of law and fact, this itemization will enable an appellate court to review whether the trial court's legal classifications are correct, and whether its factual findings are supported by substantial evidence.

18: SECTION 1706 OF THE REFORM ACT

Section 530 (d) - Added by Section 1706 of the Revenue Act of 1978 Committee Reports

20. Study of treatment of certain technical services personnel

Present Law

In general, the determination of whether an employer-employee relationship exists for Federal tax purposes is made under a common law test. Under this test, an employer-employee relationship generally exists if the person contracting for services has the right to control not only the result of the services, but also the means by which that result is accomplished.

Section 530 of the Revenue Act of 1978 generally allows a taxpayer to treat a worker as not being an employee, regardless of the individual's actual status under the common law test, unless the taxpayer has no reasonable basis for such treatment. Although section 530 provides relief only with respect to the employment tax liability of the service recipient, it has been widely used to justify claims of independent contractor status for income tax purposes, both by the service recipients and by individuals with respect to whom a service recipient claims relief under section 530.

Section 1706 of the Reform Act provides that section 530 of the Revenue Act of 1978 does not apply in the case of an individual who, pursuant to an arrangement between the taxpayer and another person, provides services for such other person as an engineer, designer, drafter, computer programmer, systems analyst, or other similarly skilled worker engaged in a similar line of work.

House Bill

The House bill directs the Treasury Department to conduct a study of section 1706 and report to the House Ways and Means Committee and the Senate Finance Committee by September 1, 1989. The study is to include evaluation of the following issues: (a) the difficulty of administration of the provisions of section 1706, (b) whether there are any abuses in the reporting of income by independent contractors that justify the adoption of section 1706 (including any evidence of greater noncompliance by independent contractors when compared to employees), (c) the chilling effect that section 1706 has had on the ability of technical services personnel to get work, (d) the administrability of the present-law standards for determining whether an individual is an employee or an independent contractor, and (e) the equity of providing rules that distinguish between independent contractors who work through brokers and those who do not. The pro-

18: SECTION 1706 OF THE REFORM ACT

vision is effective on the date of enactment.

Senate Amendment
The Senate amendment is the same as the House bill.

Conference Agreement
The conference agreement follows the House bill and the Senate amendment

19: INTERNAL REVENUE CODE SECTION 3508

(a) General rule

For purposes of this title, in the case of services performed as a qualified real estate agent or as a direct seller –

(1) the individual performing such services shall not be treated as an employee, and

(2) the person for whom such services are performed shall not be treated as an employer.

(b) Definitions

For purposes of this section –

(1) Qualified real estate agent

The term "qualified real estate agent" means any individual who is a sales person if –

(A) such individual is a licensed real estate agent,

(B) substantially all of the remuneration (whether or not paid in cash) for the services performed by such individual as a real estate agent is directly related to sales or other output (including the performance of services) rather than to the number of hours worked, and

(C) the services performed by the individual are performed pursuant to a written contract between such individual and the person for whom the services are per-formed and such contract provides that the individual will not be treated as an employee with respect to such services for Federal tax purposes.

(2) Direct seller

The term "direct seller" means any person if –

(A) such person –

> (i) is engaged in the trade or business of selling (or soliciting the sale of) consumer products to any buyer on a buy-sell basis, a depositcommission basis, or any similar basis which the Secretary prescribes by regulations, for resale (by the buyer or any other person) in the home or otherwise than in a permanent retail establishment,

19: INTERNAL REVENUE CODE SECTION 3508

      (ii) is engaged in the trade or business of selling (or soliciting the sale of) consumer products in the home or otherwise than in a permanent retail establishment, or (iii) is engaged in the trade or business of the delivering or distribution of newspapers or shopping news (including any services directly related to such trade or business),

(B) substantially all the remuneration (whether or not paid in cash) for the performance of the services described in subparagraph (A) is directly related to sales or other output (including the performance of services) rather than to the number of hours worked, and

(C) the services performed by the person are performed pursuant to a written contract between such person and the person for whom the services are performed and such contract provides that the person will not be treated as an employee with respect to such services for Federal tax purposes.

(3) Coordination with retirement plans for self employed This section shall not apply for purposes of subtitle A to the extent that the individual is treated as an employee under section 401(c)(1) (relating to self-employed individuals).

20: CLEVELAND INSTITUTE V U.S.

CLEVELAND INSTITUTE OF ELECTRONICS, INC., Plaintiff, vs. UNITED STATES OF AMERICA, Defendant.

Case No. 1:91CV0325

UNITED STATES DISTRICT COURT FOR THE NORTHERN DISTRICT OF OHIO, EASTERN DIVISION

787 F. Supp. 741; 1992 U.S. Dist. LEXIS 3602; 92-1 U.S. Tax Cas. (CCH) P50,182; 69 A.F.T.R.2d (RIA) 1015; Unemployment Ins. Rep. (CCH) P16,583A

March 12, 1992, Filed

COUNSEL: [**1] For plaintiff: Richard Katcher, Esq., Christopher J. Swift, Esq., Baker & Hostetler, 3200 National City Center, Cleveland, OH 44114-3401, 216-621-0200.

For defendant: Stephen T. Lyons, Esq., 202-307-6546, Box 55, Department of Justice, Tax Division, Ben Franklin Station, P.O. Box 55, Washington, DC 20044. Annette G. Butler, 216-363-3928, Office of the U.S. Attorney, 1404 East Ninth Street, Ste. 500, Cleveland, OH 44114, 216-363-3900.

JUDGES: ALDRICH

OPINION BY: ANN ALDRICH

OPINION

[*742] MEMORANDUM AND ORDER

ALDRICH, J.

Plaintiff Cleveland Institute of Electronics ("CIE") brings this action for a refund of taxes, interest, and penalties that were assessed against, and collected from, CIE by the United States. The government claims that CIE's sales persons are employees from whom CIE must withhold federal income taxes. CIE counters that its sales persons are independent contractors, and that therefore CIE need not withhold any federal income tax from its sales persons' compensation. At stake is approximately $ 474,000 in employment taxes, penalties, and interest, which the Internal Revenue Service ("IRS") has assessed against CIE for the years 1986, 1987, and 1988. [1]

> 1 CIE has not contested whether the IRS properly computed the amount of taxes, interest, and penalties owed under 26 U.S.C. § 3509.

20: CLEVELAND INSTITUTE V U.S.

[**2] CIE has paid to the IRS the taxes, penalties, and interest assessed against it with respect to one of its sales persons. Now, CIE seeks to recover those amounts from the IRS through this suit for a refund. There is no genuine issue of material fact, and both parties have moved for summary judgment on the issue of whether CIE sales persons are independent contractors as defined by statute. Because the Court finds that CIE is entitled to judgment as a matter of law, CIE's motion for summary judgment is granted, and the IRS's motion ford partial summary judgment is denied.

I.

The relevant material facts are not in dispute. In 1986, 1987, and 1988, CIE sold home study educational courses to students worldwide. These educational courses instruct students in several disciplines within the field of electronics, such as industrial electronics or broadcast engineering. When a student buys a CIE course, he receives course-specific lesson books and equipment by mail. Students study at home at their own pace, completing lessons in the lesson book and experimenting with or repairing the equipment. Students take open-book examinations and send them by mail to CIE, where the examinations are [*743] normally [**3] graded the same day and returned by mail. Students must achieve a minimum of 70% to pass an examination. Students may also take a closed-book, practical examination, which is supervised by an individual of the student's own choosing.

CIE mandates that certain courses must be successfully completed by a student as a prerequisite to that student's taking further courses. At the end of a chosen curriculum, a successful student receives from CIE a diploma and letters of recommendation. While pursuing their studies, students are eligible for Pell grants, guaranteed student loans, and veterans' benefits.

CIE advertises and sells its educational courses through direct mail. In addition, CIE sells its courses through the use of commissioned sales persons. CIE's sales persons are compensated solely on the basis of their sales performance. The sales persons solicit sales of the CIE educational courses by meeting with prospective students in homes, in shopping malls, at military posts, and at other locations that are not permanent retail establishments. The functions of CIE sales persons include only selling -- they do not serve as educational instructors for CIE.

As previously mentioned, CIE's [**4] sales persons sign a contract with CIE which states that the sales persons will be paid solely on a commission basis. The contract also states that the sales person is an independent contractor and that he

20: CLEVELAND INSTITUTE V U.S.

will not be treated as an employee for federal tax purposes. Accordingly, CIE did not withhold any federal taxes from its compensation payments to its sales persons during the years in question. The sales persons reported to the IRS that their compensation from CIE was income from self-employment, and they paid appropriate amounts of self-employment tax.

Nonetheless, the IRS took the position that the CIE sales persons were not independent contractors, but were instead CIE employees. As such, the IRS assessed Federal Insurance Contributions Act ("FICA") taxes, Federal Unemployment Tax Act ("FUTA") taxes, federal withholding taxes, and non-payment penalties against CIE. The total assessment exceeded $ 474,000. This suit is to determine whether the assessment of those taxes was appropriate.

II.

For many years, the question of whether a taxpayer was an independent contractor or an employee was a question to be answered exclusively by the common law. Borrowing principles from agency [**5] law, courts would weigh up to twenty factors in determining whether a worker was an independent contractor or an employee. See, e.g., American Bicycle Service, Inc. v. United States, 128 Bankr. 436, 451-57 (Bankr. N.D. Ind. 1990) (citing factors outlined in other cases and in the Restatement (Second) of Agency). Because the common law approach used so many factors to determine employment tax status, however, employers often found themselves guessing about whether they had to pay employment taxes.

In response to the "problems arising from increased employment tax status controversies," Congress enacted 26 U.S.C. § 3508. Staff of Joint Comm. on Taxation, 97th Cong., 2d Sess., General Explanation of the Revenue Provisions of the Tax Equity and Fiscal Responsibility Act of 1982, p. 382 (Comm. Print 1982) [hereinafter, "Joint Committee Report"]. The purpose of 26 U.S.C. § 3508 was to create a shelter for taxpayers who met certain criteria. By meeting the statutory requirements, an individual was automatically given the status of an independent contractor, and was therefore not an employee for employment tax purposes:

The Act establishes two categories of statutory [**6] nonemployees: (1) qualified real estate agents and (2) direct sellers. If certain conditions are satisfied, sales persons who are licensed real estate agents and individuals who are direct sellers will be treated, for Federal income and employment tax purposes, as self-employed persons.

Id.

20: CLEVELAND INSTITUTE V U.S.

The new statute did not supplant the common law; rather, it merely guaranteed [*744] independent contractor status for those taxpayers who met its conditions. If a taxpayer did not meet the criteria set forth in the statute, he could still qualify as an independent contractor under the established common law tests. But Congress created a shelter exclusively for "certain direct sellers and real estate sales persons" because it "believed that it was these workers who were most in need of an immediate solution to the problem of proper employment tax status." *Id.*

In the instant case, the government takes the position that CIE sales persons do not meet the test for independent contractor status under either 26 U.S.C. § 3508 or the common law. However, the motions for summary judgment before this Court are limited to the issue whether CIE sales persons are protected by the shelter of 26 U.S.C. § 3508. [**7] As acknowledged earlier by both parties, summary judgment for CIE on this issue would end the case -- if CIE sales persons are independent contractors under the statute, CIE would be entitled to a refund. Summary judgment for the government, on the other hand, would lead to extended discovery to determine whether CIE sales persons pass the common law test for independent contractor status. Therefore, both parties agreed to submit motions for summary judgment on the sole issue of whether CIE employees are independent contractors under 26 U.S.C. § 3508. Through its holding that summary judgment should be granted to CIE, the Court enters a final appealable order and finds that further discovery is unnecessary.

III.

26 U.S.C. § 3508 begins with the general rule that "in the case of services performed as a . . . direct seller -- (1) the individual performing such services shall not be treated as an employee, and (2) the person for whom such services are performed shall not be treated as an employer" for employment tax purposes. The statute then sets forth three conditions that must be satisfied in order for a taxpayer to qualify as a direct seller:

The term "direct seller" means any [**8] person if --

(A) such person --

i) is engaged in the trade or business of selling (or soliciting the sale of) consumer products to any buyer on a buy-sell basis, a deposit-commission basis, or any similar basis which the Secretary prescribes by regulations, for resale (by the buyer or any other person) in the home or otherwise than in a permanent retail establishment, or

20: CLEVELAND INSTITUTE V U.S.

(ii) is engaged in the trade or business of selling (or soliciting the sale of) consumer products in the home or otherwise than in a permanent retail establishment,

(B) substantially all the remuneration (whether or not paid in cash) for the performance of the [direct selling] services . . . is directly related to sales or other output (including the performance of services) rather than to the number of hours worked, and

(C) the services performed by the person are performed pursuant to a written contract between such person and the person for whom services are performed and such contract provides that the person will not be treated as an employee with respect to such services for Federal tax purposes.

26 U.S.C. § 3508(b)(2).

CIE argues that its sales persons qualify as "direct sellers" because they meet all [**9] three of the conditions set forth under 26 U.S.C. § 3508. CIE asserts that: 1) CIE sales persons sell consumer products directly to buyers in locations that are not permanent retail establishments; 2) CIE sales persons are compensated on a commission basis only; and 3) the agreements between CIE and its sales persons explicitly state that, for federal tax purposes, the sales person is an independent contractor and not a CIE employee.

The government concedes that CIE sales persons meet the second of the three conditions listed in the statute, since CIE sales persons are compensated based exclusively upon their sales performance and not upon hours worked. The government also admits [*745] that CIE sales persons meet the third condition of the statute, since CIE and its sales persons have entered into written agreements that clearly outline the sales persons' tax employment status. However, the government argues that CIE sales persons do not meet the first condition set forth in the statute.

The first condition listed in the statute states that to qualify as a "direct seller," a person must sell "consumer products in the home or otherwise than in a permanent retail establishment." 26 U.S.C. [**10] § 3508(A)(1). The government acknowledges that CIE sales persons sell the CIE educational courses in "homes or otherwise than in permanent retail establishments." However, the government contends that the educational courses which the sales persons are selling are not "consumer products."

Because CIE sales persons sell something other than "consumer products," the

20: CLEVELAND INSTITUTE V U.S.

government argues, the sales persons do not meet the first condition of the statute and therefore cannot claim its shelter. Thus, the sole issue raised by the cross-motions for summary judgment is whether the educational courses sold by CIE sales persons are "consumer products" within the context of 26 U.S.C. § 3508.

IV.

The government argues that the educational courses sold by CIE are not consumer products, because CIE is really selling a course of education and not merely books and equipment. The government asserts that by selling a course of education, CIE sales persons are selling an intangible service and not tangible goods, and that only tangible goods can be consumer products.

CIE responds by arguing that Congress did not mean to limit the term "consumer products" to encompass only tangible goods, and that the CIE [**11] educational courses are properly deemed "consumer products" as contemplated by Congress. CIE also argues that its sales persons are indeed selling tangible goods -- books and equipment -- so that even under the government's definition of consumer product:, CIE sales persons may find shelter under the statute.

The term "consumer products" is not defined in 26 U.S.C. § 3508 itself. However, there are three other sources that can inform the Court on the meaning of this term: 1) the statute's legislative history; 2) uses of the same term as found in other federal statutes; and 3) federal regulations construing the statute. These sources are examined separately below.

A. *Legislative History*

The legislative history behind 26 U.S.C. § 3508 begins with a House Bill, H.R. 4961, 97th Cong., 1st Sess., § 271 (1981) [hereinafter "House Bill 4961"]. House Bill 4961 proposed enactment of a statute that would provide a safe harbor for sales persons that met certain requirements. If the following five criteria were met, a sales person would be treated as an independent contractor for tax purposes and his employer would not have to pay employment taxes: 1) the sales person, not the employer, [**12] controlled the hours the sales person worked; 2) the sales person provided or paid for his own office space; 3) the sales person's income was based on his own sales output, not on hours worked; or, the sales person had invested substantially in assets necessary to work for the employer; 4) the sales person and employer entered into a written contract stating that the sales person was an independent contractor for federal tax purposes and that he was responsible for paying self-employment taxes; and 5) the employer filed the necessary tax returns. Absent from House Hill 4961 is any use of the terms

20: CLEVELAND INSTITUTE V U.S.

"direct sellers" or "consumer products."

House Bill 4961 was passed and sent to the Senate, which produced its own Bill. S. Rep. No. 494 (Vol. 1), 97th Cong., 2d Sess. 91, 358-70 (1982), reprinted in 1982 U.S. Code Cong. & Admin. News 861, 1091-1102 [hereinafter "Senate Bill 494"]. While Senate Bill 494 modified many provisions of the proposed legislation, it did not modify § 271 of House Bill 4961. Senate Bill 494 did, however, provide a lengthy [*746] discussion of the then-present common law applicable to employment tax status and an explanatory section titled "Reasons for Change." Senate [**13] Bill 494 at 363. The primary reasons cited for the proposed change in the law were that a statutory 'safe-harbor' test for determining . . . whether an individual should be classified as an employee or an independent contractor will reduce the number of tax status controversies . . ., and will provide greater certainty and simplification in this area of the tax law. In addition, . . . the formal requirements of the safe-harbor will improve tax compliance on the part of independent contractors qualifying under its provisions.

Id. Senate Bill 494 stressed this last reason, adding that other provisions in the Bill would also "greatly improve tax compliance among independent contractors." Id. Again, however, Senate Bill 494 makes no mention of the terms "direct sellers" or "consumer products."

The "consumer products" phrase appeared in the Bill that came out of conference between the two houses of Congress. H.R. Conf. Rep. No. 760, 97th Cong., 2d Sess. 467, 650-51 (1982), reprinted in 1982 U.S. Code Cong. & Admin. News 1190, 1420-21 [hereinafter "Conference Report 760"]. Conference Report 760 explained that the safe-harbor test proposed in House Bill 4961 and Senate Bill [**14] 494 had been abandoned in conference. Instead of a broad safe-harbor test, the new proposal was given a much narrower focus. The legislation that came out of conference merely created "two categories of statutory nonemployees." Conference Report 760 at 651. Under the conference version, only qualifying real estate agents and direct sellers were afforded independent contractor status. Conference Report 760 contains no discussion of the "Reasons for Change" from the common law, or any reasons for change from the proposals contained in the House and Senate Bills. Nor does the Conference Report make any mention of exactly what is meant by the term "consumer products." [2] The Congressional Record is similarly unrevealing of what Congress meant by the phrase "consumer products" in the context of 26 U.S.C. § 3508.

> 2 The Senate Conference Report did not discuss the meaning of consumer products, either. See Senate Conf. Rep. No. 530, 97th

20: CLEVELAND INSTITUTE V U.S.

Cong., 2d Sess. (1982).

In sum, the legislative history behind 26 U.S.C. § 3508 provides [**15] no clue as to exactly what Congress meant when it used the term "consumer products," and certainly gives no indication whether CIE's educational courses qualify as consumer products. At best, the legislative history demonstrates that the purposes behind the statute are to reduce the number of controversies regarding employment tax status and to improve tax compliance on the part of independent contractors. Before relying on the statutory purpose alone to decide this case, other sources of meaning for the phrase "consumer products" must be examined.

B. *"Consumer Products" In Other Legislation*

There exist four other statutes passed by Congress that employ the term "consumer products." They include the Consumer Product Safety Act, the Magnuson-Moss Warranty Act, the Federal Anti-Tampering Act, and the Energy Policy and Conservation Act. The definitions of the term "consumer products" employed by these Acts are as follows:

1. *The Consumer Product Safety Act*

The Consumer Product Safety Act defines a "consumer product" as

any article, or component part thereof, produced or distributed (i) for sale to a consumer for use in or around a permanent or temporary household or residence, [**16] a school, in recreation, or otherwise, or (ii) for the personal use, consumption or enjoyment of a consumer in or around a permanent or temporary household or residence, a school, in recreation, or otherwise . . . .

15 U.S.C. § 2052(a)(1).

2. *The Magnuson-Moss Warranty Act*

The Magnuson-Moss Warranty Act defines a consumer product as

[*747] any tangible personal property which is distributed in commerce and which is normally used for personal, family, or household purposes . . . .

15 U.S.C. § 2301(1).

3. *The Federal Anti-Tampering Act*

The Federal Anti-Tampering Act defines a consumer product as

20: CLEVELAND INSTITUTE V U.S.

(A) any "food," "drug," "device," or "cosmetic," as those terms are respectively defined in . . . the Federal Food, Drug, and Cosmetic Act (21 U.S.C. 321); or

(B) any article, product or commodity which is customarily produced or distributed for consumption by individuals or use by individuals for purposes of personal care or in the performance of services ordinarily rendered within the household, and which is designed to be consumed or expended in the course of such consumption or use.

18 U.S.C. § 1365(g)(1).

4. The Energy Policy and Conservation Act

Finally, the Energy [**17] Policy and Conservation Act defines a consumer product as

any article (other than an automobile . . .) of a type --

(A) which in operation consumes, or is designed to consume, energy; and

(B) which, to any significant extent, is distributed in commerce for personal use or consumption by individuals;

without regard to whether such article of such type is in fact distributed in commerce for personal use or consumption by an individual.

42 U.S.C. § 6291(a)(1).

The government correctly notes that under the Federal Anti-Tampering Act and the Energy Policy and Conservation Act, CIE's educational courses would not qualify as consumer products. The government also insists that all of these Acts have in common the limitation that "consumer products" means only tangible goods, like toothpaste or books, and not services or other intangibles, like haircuts, insurance policies, or CIE's educational courses.

The government, of course, is right -- under any of these other statutes, CIE's educational courses probably would not qualify as consumer products. [3] However, the Court is not interpreting these other statutes, and indeed, they are inapposite. These statutes address, respectively, [**18] ensuring the safety of consumer products, ensuring the adequacy of warranties on consumer products, preventing criminal tampering with consumer products, and improving the energy efficiency of consumer products. These statutes have nothing to do with tax employment status or direct selling activity.

20: CLEVELAND INSTITUTE V U.S.

3 On the other hand, the books and especially the equipment that CIE sends to its students may well have to meet the standards set forth in these statutes regarding safety, energy efficiency, and adequacy of warranties.

Moreover, the fact that each statute has a different definition for the same term argues against using any one of these definitions in the context of 26 U.S.C. § 3508. It is clear that Congress has treated the meaning of the phrase "consumer products" as malleable, changing its significance to meet the purpose of the statute in which the term is employed. In fact, Congress has defined "consumer products" differently every time it has used the term -- except once. The exception is 26 U.S.C. § 3508, when [**19] Congress failed to provide any definition at all. Thus, searching for the meaning of "consumer products" as used in 26 U.S.C. § 3508 by examining other federal legislation is fruitless. Congress's past use of this term does not provide the Court with any meaningful guidance. 4

4 Moreover, Congress appears disinclined to provide the guidance that the Court seeks. Not only has Congress failed to specifically authorize any regulations construing the statute, but observers noted nine years ago that "either additional legislation in [this] area will be forthcoming soon or Congress is signaling its intent to dodge the issue entirely." Sally M. Jones and Robert L. Black, TEFRA clarifies independent contractor status but area still remains unsettled, 58 J. Tax'n. 148 (Mar. 1983).

C. Federal Regulations

The IRS has published proposed regulations construing 26 U.S.C. § 3508. These [*748] regulations provide the following definition for the term "consumer product:"

The term "consumer product" means any tangible [**20] personal property which is distributed in commerce and which is normally used for personal, family, or household purposes (including any such property intended to be attached to or installed in any real property without regard to whether it is so attached or installed). The term "consumer product" does not include any product used in the manufacture of another product to be distributed in commerce or any product used only incidentally in provding [sic] a service (e.g. insecticide used in a pest control service, materials used in an appliance repair business).

Treatment of Qualified Real Estate Agents and Direct Sellers as Nonemployees, 51 Fed. Reg. 619, 624 (proposed Jan. 7, 1986) (proposed as 26 C.F.R. § 31.3508-1(g)(3)).

20: CLEVELAND INSTITUTE V U.S.

These regulations, if accepted by the Court as controlling, would settle the issue at hand. The CIE "educational courses" sold by CIE's sales persons include books and equipment, which of course are tangible goods. However, these tangible goods are only sold incidentally to the provision of a service -- the education of CIE customers. [5] Under the regulations, therefore, CIE's sales persons are not selling consumer products.

> 5 CIE argues that the books and equipment are not "incidental" to the educational courses because the books and equipment are not "nonessential." However, CIE misconstrues the meaning of "incidental" in this context; in these regulations, incidental means "secondary", not "nonessential." Pesticide is not "nonessential" to pest control services. Rather, pesticide is "secondary" to the primary service of pest control, and books and equipment are "secondary" to the gaining of an education.

[**21] Because the regulations are merely proposed and not adopted, however, they must be construed as having been published for the limited purpose of giving the public notice that the regulations are under consideration. Id at 622; 10 Bender's Federal Tax Service § P:10.41[3] (1991). In fact, at public hearings on these proposed regulations, testimony was heard criticizing the suggested definition of consumer products. Sam Goodley, IRS Hears Testimony on Qualified Real Estate Agents and Direct Sellers Regulations, 31 Tax Notes 1164 (June 23, 1986) (Neil H. Offen, testifying on behalf of the Direct Selling Association, stated that the distinction drawn in the proposed regulations between sellers of tangible goods and intangible services was "without support in the statute or relevant legislative history.").

Furthermore, there are other factors that give the Court reason not to adopt the definition of "consumer products" as set forth in the proposed regulations. The proposed regulations were published in 1986. Six years later, they have still not been adopted in final form. This delay might indicate that the IRS itself has not determined whether the [**22] proposed regulations should be ratified. See Garvey, Inc. v. United States, 1 Cl. Ct. 108, 118-19 (Cl. Ct. 1983), aff'd, 726 F.2d 1569 (Fed. Cir. 1984), cert. denied, 469 U.S. 823, 105 S. Ct. 99, 83 L. Ed. 2d 44 (1984) (passage of five years from publication of proposed regulations without final adoption could logically give rise to inference that IRS had reason to doubt wisdom of proposals). In addition, the proposed regulations were not issued until nearly four years after 26 U.S.C. § 3508 was enacted. Regulations not promulgated contemporaneously with or shortly after enactment of a statute should be given less deference, since the congressional intent is no longer presumed to have

20: CLEVELAND INSTITUTE V U.S.

been known. Rowan Cos. v. United States, 452 U.S. 247, 253, 68 L. Ed. 2d 814, 101 S. Ct. 2288 (1981) (quoting National Muffler Dealers Assn. v. United States, 440 U.S. 472, 477, 59 L. Ed. 2d 519, 99 S. Ct. 1304 (1979)); see generally Michael I. Saltzman, IRS Practice and Procedure 3.02[4][b] (2d ed. 1991) (discussing interpretive regulations).

Thus, the Court is not persuaded by the proposed federal regulations that CIE's educational courses fail to qualify as "consumer products." The proposed [**23] regulations define the term "consumer products" by drawing a distinction between tangible and intangible products. Introductory remarks [*749] to the proposed regulations rely on this distinction to state that a door-to-door sales person selling vacuum cleaners may be considered a direct seller of consumer products, but that a door-to-door sales person selling cable television subscriptions may not. The Court does not find support for this distinction in the statute itself, nor in the statute's legislative history, nor in language used in other federal statutes. The meaning of the term "consumer products," as Congress used this term in 26 U.S.C. § 3508, must come from another source.

V.

Faced with a decision concerning the meaning of a disputed term in a statute, and without other convincing guidelines, a Court must rely on two things: the plain meaning of the term and the underlying purpose of the statute. See, e.g., Moskal v. United States, 112 L. Ed. 2d 449, 111 S. Ct. 461, 468 (1990) (finding the meaning of a statute "both in the plain meaning of [the statute's] words and in the legislative purpose underlying them"). Unfortunately, there seems not to be a plain meaning of the term "consumer [**24] products." The Court is aware of the terms "consumer goods" and "consumer services;" does the term "consumer products" contemplate both of these? If Congress meant to limit the meaning of "consumer products" to denote only tangible consumer goods and not consumer services, as the proposed regulations suggest, then why did Congress not use the term "consumer goods?" As shown by Congress's use of the term "consumer products" in different pieces of legislation, this phrase does not have an exact, plain meaning.

This leaves, as a guide for the Court, the underlying purpose of the statute. As stated in Senate Bill 494, the purposes originally behind the statute were to reduce the number of controversies regarding employment tax status and to improve tax compliance on the part of independent contractors. It is clear that the purposes behind the statute are best advanced if the term "consumer products" is construed to include both tangible consumer products and intangible consumer services.

20: CLEVELAND INSTITUTE V U.S.

The number of controversies regarding employment tax status will be decreased by allowing direct sellers of goods and services, who meet the other statutory requirements, to be considered independent [**25] contractors. To find that this statute applies only to direct sellers of tangible goods will inevitably lead to disputes over whether a direct seller is selling goods or services.

This suit is a prime example. The regulations attempt to address this issue with examples of goods sold "incidentally" to the provision of services, but disputes over the meaning of "incidental" are also sure to appear. And what to make of a sales person who sells both household cleaning products and subscriptions to a long distance telephone carrier? 6 The task of resolving these disputes is avoided if "consumer products" is given a different meaning than the one proposed in the regulations. If the statute is instead construed to confer independent contractor status on all direct sellers who meet the statute's other criteria, regardless of what it is the direct sellers are selling, then fewer employment tax status controversies will result.

> 6 Individuals selling for Amway Corporation, for example, sell both Amway household products as well as subscriptions to MCI Telecommunications Corporation's long distance telephone service.

[**26] The other purpose behind the statute is to improve the tax compliance of independent contractors. Giving effect to this statutory purpose has no correlation with whether "direct sellers of consumer products" is construed to mean "direct sellers of tangible consumer goods only" or "direct sellers of tangible consumer goods or intangible consumer services." Either way, the direct sellers have to meet the other criteria in the statute before they are considered independent contractors. And it is these other criteria that go to the issue of tax compliance -- that is, the sales persons must enter into an agreement with the employer which explicitly states that the [*750] sales person is an independent contractor and not an employee for federal tax purposes. Indeed, in this case, even though the IRS insists that CIE sales persons were not selling consumer products, the IRS does not contest CIE's assertion that its sales persons paid all appropriate self-employment taxes.

Accordingly, the Court holds that the underlying purposes of 26 U.S.C. § 3508 are best served by interpreting the term "consumer products," as used in that statute, to include both tangible consumer goods and intangible consumer [**27] services. The Court does not make a finding as to whether CIE's sales persons are selling tangible goods incidental to providing a service, or are selling consumer

20: CLEVELAND INSTITUTE V U.S.

goods alone, or are selling consumer services alone, since such a finding is unnecessary. Under the Court's reading of 26 U.S.C § 3508, CIE's sales persons are selling "consumer products." Hence, CIE's sales persons are statutory nonemployees. Therefore, CIE's motion for summary judgment is granted, and judgment is entered accordingly.

IT IS SO ORDERED.

ANN ALDRICH

UNITED STATES DISTRICT JUDGE

[*n] one

EDITOR'S NOTE: The following court-provided text does not appear at this cite 787 F. Supp. 741.

ORDER - March 12, 1992, Filed

ALDRICH, J.

The Court has filed its memorandum and order granting plaintiff's motion for summary judgment, and denying defendant's motion for partial summary judgment; therefore,

IT IS ORDERED that plaintiff's motion for summary judgment is granted; defendant's motion for partial summary judgment is denied; and the case is dismissed.

IT IS FURTHER ORDERED that this judgment is final and appealable.

ANN ALDRICH

UNITED STATES [**28] DISTRICT JUDGE

21: THE R CORP. V U.S.

THE R CORPORATION, a Florida corporation, Plaintiff, v. UNITED STATES OF AMERICA, Defendant. UNITED STATES, Counter-Plaintiff, v. THE R COR-PORATION, a Florida corporation, Counter-Defendant.

Case No. 92-1368-CIV-T-24B

UNITED STATES DISTRICT COURT FOR THE MIDDLE DISTRICT OF FLORIDA, TAMPA DIVISION

1994 U.S. Dist. LEXIS 20314; 94-2 U.S. Tax Cas. (CCH) P50,380; 74 A.F.T.R.2d (RIA) 5620; Unemployment Ins. Rep. (CCH) P14,033B

July 15, 1994, Decided

COUNSEL: [*1] For R CORPORATION, a Florida corporation, plaintiff, counter-defendant: William G. Lambrecht, Mark Alan Schwartz, Williams, Parker, Harrison, Dietz & Getzen, Sarasota, FL.

For USA, defendant, counter-claimant: Bruce T. Russell, U.S. Dept. of Justice, Tax Division, Washington, DC.

JUDGES: SUSAN C. BUCKLEW, United States District Judge

OPINION BY: SUSAN C. BUCKLEW

OPINION

ORDER

This matter is presently before the Court on cross-motions for summary judgment filed on behalf of The R Corporation (Doc. No. 10, filed February 24, 1994) and the United States (Doc. No. 24, filed April 12, 1994). The plaintiff instituted this action alleging that the United States erroneously assessed FICA and FUTA taxes, along with interest and penalties, against The R Corporation with regard to certain salespersons performing door-to-door sales services during tax years 1987 and 1988. The United States disagrees and is seeking unpaid taxes relating to the assessment of the FICA and FUTA taxes against The R Corporation. For the reasons set forth below, this Court grants the plaintiff's motion for summary judgment and denies the government's motion for partial summary judgment.

I.

The focal point of this dispute lies [*2] in 26 U.S.C. § 3508. The question raised is whether intangible services are encompassed within the meaning of "consumer

21: THE R CORP. V U.S.

products" as defined in § 3508. If they are, The R Corporation will recover whatever federal payroll taxes it paid in 1987 and 1988. If they are not, the United States will recover the remaining taxes owed by Plaintiff for the same time period.

This issue begins with The R Corporation's direct sales division. This division is engaged solely in the business of door-to-door sales of cable television subscriptions and equipment such as stereos and home computers. The R Corporation claims that its salespersons are independent contractors. In support of this contention, The R Corporation's employment contract states that the salespersons are independent contractors and would not be treated as employees. Furthermore, the salespersons are compensated solely in proportion to the sales they generate. Believing its salespersons to be independent contractors, The R Corporation did not pay any federal payroll taxes in 1987 and 1988 for these individuals/salespersons. The United States, however, believed that The R Corporation salespersons were employees and not independent [*3] contractors and levied taxes, interest, and penalties against The R Corporation for the years in question.

II.

A court shall render summary judgment upon a showing that there is no genuine issue of material fact and that the movant is entitled to judgment as a matter of law. Fed. R. Civ. P. 56(c). The rule provides that "the mere existence of some alleged factual dispute between the parties will not defeat an otherwise properly supported motion for summary judgment; the requirement is that there be no genuine issue of material fact." Anderson v. Liberty Lobby, Inc., 477 U.S. 242, 247-48, 91 L. Ed. 2d 202, 106 S. Ct. 2505 (1986). The United States claims that Plaintiff's motion for summary judgment must fail because there exists a genuine issue of material fact. However, "only disputes over facts that might affect the outcome of the suit under the governing law will properly preclude the entry of summary judgment." Id. at 248. The issue in dispute according to the United States is whether The R Corporation salespersons sold tangible goods as well as cable subscriptions. Yet, this disputed fact is not material, since the Court finds that "consumer products" within § [*4] 3508 encompasses intangible services. Therefore, the outcome of the suit is in no way affected by the disputed fact's determination.

III.

The issue giving rise to this case arises from the statutory definition of an independent contractor under 26 U.S.C. § 3508. The purpose of this section "was to create a shelter for taxpayers who met certain criteria." Cleveland Inst. of Elec.,

21: THE R CORP. V U.S.

Inc. v. United States, 787 F. Supp. 741, 743 (N.D. Ohio 1992). "By meeting the statutory requirements [of a direct seller], an individual was automatically given the status of an independent contractor. . . ." Id. A "direct seller" is defined under 26 U.S.C. § 3508 as follows:

> (A) such person --
>
> (i) is engaged in the trade or business of selling (or soliciting the sale of) consumer products to any buyer on a buy-sell basis, a deposit-commission basis, or any similar basis which the Secretary prescribes by regulations, for resale (by the buyer or any other person) in the home or otherwise than in a permanent retail establishment, or
>
> (ii) is engaged in the trade or business of selling (or soliciting the sale of) consumer products in the home or otherwise than in a permanent retail establishment,
>
> (B) [*5] substantially all the remuneration (whether or not paid in cash) for the performance of the services described in subparagraph (A) is directly related to sales or other output (including the performance of service) rather than to the number of hours worked, and
>
> (C) the services performed by the person are performed pursuant to a written contract between such person and the person for whom the services are performed and such contract provides that the person will not be treated as an employee with respect to such services for federal tax purposes.

26 U.S.C. § 3508(b)(2).

IV.

The R Corporation contends that cable television subscriptions fall under § 3508's definition of "consumer product" because: (1) the plain meaning of "consumer product" encompasses both tangible and intangible property and (2) the Cleveland Institute court held that intangible services qualify as "consumer products" as the term is used in § 3508. The United States argues that this Court should follow the guidance set forth by the Treasury in the proposed regulations for 26 U.S.C. § 3508 that expressly conclude that "consumer products" include only tangible goods. Furthermore, the United States [*6] suggests that this Court

21: THE R CORP. V U.S.

should not adopt the analysis set forth in Cleveland Institute to the effect that the definition in the proposed regulations is unduly narrow and not reflective of congressional intent concerning § 3508.

V.

Cleveland Institute is the only reported case construing § 3508. The United States District Court for the Northern District of Ohio ruled that the term "consumer products" includes intangible consumer services. In Cleveland Institute, the salespersons performing services for the taxpayer were engaged in the business of selling educational courses in electronics, which included a sale of books, equipment for the student to practice, and the service of grading examinations. The salespersons were paid only on a commission basis and had signed a contract stating that the salesperson is an independent contractor and that the taxpayer would not treat the salesperson as an employee for federal income tax purposes.

After analyzing the legislative history of § 3508, the plain meaning of the term "consumer products," and its use in other federal statutes, the Cleveland Institute court granted the taxpayer's motion for summary judgment holding [*7] that as a matter of law intangible consumer services such as educational courses are consumer products for purposes of § 3508. In analyzing the term "consumer products," the Cleveland institute court examined the legislative history of § 3508, which reflects that Congress enacted § 3508 as a means of reducing the controversies surrounding the employment status of salespersons by providing a clear test for independent contractor status. Cleveland Inst., 787 F. Supp. at 745-46, citing S. Rep. No. 494 (Vol. 1), 97th Cong., 2d Sess. 358-70 (1982), reprinted in 1982 U.S.C.C.A.N. 1091-102. The court determined that the legislative history provided no clue as to exactly what Congress meant when it used the term "consumer products."

The Cleveland Institute court then reviewed the term "consumer product" as used in four other federal statutes, including the Consumer Product Safety Act, the Magnuson-Moss Warranty Act, the Federal Anti-Tampering Act, and the Energy Policy and Conservation Act. The court found no meaningful guidance from theses statutes because each statute had a different definition for the term.

The court then examined regulation section 31.3508-1(g)(3), [*8] which was proposed by the Treasury in 1986, but had not been adopted. 51 Fed. Reg. 619, 624 (proposed Jan. 7, 1986). This regulation proposed to limit the definition of "consumer products" to include only tangible personal property. 26 C.F.R. § 31-3508-1(g)(3). The Cleveland Institute court noted that it was not bound by the pro-

21: THE R CORP. V U.S.

posed regulation and refused to apply it on the basis that the regulation drew an unreasonable distinction between tangible personal property and intangible personal property that was not supported by the statute or the underlying legislative history of § 3508. Furthermore, since the regulations have not been adopted in final form after more that eight years, the "delay might indicate that the IRS itself has not determined whether the proposed regulations should be ratified." Cleveland Inst., 787 F. Supp. at 748.

The Cleveland Institute court then looked to the plain meaning of the term "consumer products" and found that the term was clearly broad enough to include intangible consumer services such as educational courses or cable television subscriptions. In keeping the legislature's intention to reduce controversies surrounding the employment [*9] status of door-to-door salespersons, the Cleveland Institute court concluded that the term "consumer products" includes both intangible consumer services as well as tangible personal property. The court recognized that because the salespersons were hired to sell both tangible goods and intangible services, a determination of independent contractor status under the Internal Revenue Code based on whether the salesperson was selling tangible or intangible goods at any given time would undercut the purpose of having a clear statutory test. The court concluded that the "purposes behind the statute are best advanced if the term 'consumer products' is construed to include both tangible consumer products and intangible consumer services." Id. at 749. Accordingly, the court held that the taxpayer's sellers of educational courses are statutory non-employees as a matter of law and granted the taxpayer's motion for summary judgment.

VI.

The facts in Cleveland Institute are strikingly similar to the facts in the present case. The only issue to resolve is whether cable subscriptions are considered intangible services. In Satellite T Associate v. Continental Cablevision of Virginia, Inc., [*10] 586 F. Supp. 973 (E.D. Va. 1982), aff'd, 714 F.2d 351 (4th Cir. 1983), the court analyzed the nature of cable television to determine whether cable was a commodity. The court concluded that

> the equipment and machinery necessary to provide cable television is merely incidental to providing the entertainment service. The subscriber contracts for this intangible service, not for the tangible equipment required to receive the service. If he could have the service without the equipment he would be just as happy--or happier.

21: THE R CORP. V U.S.

586 F. Supp. at 976. Therefore, there is no question that the cable subscriptions sold by The R Corporation salespersons were intangible services, which are deemed "consumer products" under § 3508 as a matter of law.

The United States further argues that the meaning of consumer products" is clear from the face of the statue. The government claims that since 3508(b)(2)(a)(i) refers to the selling (or soliciting the sale of) consumer products for resale, and that intangible consumer services cannot be resold, § 3508, therefore, can only be referring to tangible goods. This argument is based on a very narrow reading of § 3508(b)(2)(a)(i), so narrow [*11] that the government fails to look at the "language and design of the statute as a whole," because it overlooks § 3508(b)(2)(a)(ii) that allows non-resale type sales. Sullivan v. Everhart, 494 U.S. 83, 89, 108 L. Ed. 2d 72, 110 S. Ct. 960 (1990); Georgia v. Shalala, 8 F.3d 1565 (11th Cir. 1993).

VII.

This Court agrees and adopts the Cleveland Institute court's analysis of § 3508 and finds that the salespersons of The R Corporation are "direct sellers" within the meaning of § 3508. Therefore, according to § 3508(a)(2), The R Corporation is not an employer for purposes of the Internal Revenue Code and are not liable for FICA and FUTA taxes for its salespersons for 1987 and 1988.

Accordingly, it is ORDERED and ADJUDGED that:

(1) Plaintiff's motion for summary judgment (Doc. No. 10) is GRANTED.

(2) Government's motion for partial summary judgment (Doc. No. 24) is DENIED.

(3) Government's motion to stay discovery and continue trial setting (Doc. No. 29, filed June 2, 1994) is MOOT.

(4) Plaintiff's motion to stay discovery and continue trial setting (Doc. No. 33, filed July 13, 1994) is MOOT.

DONE AND ORDERED in Chambers in Tampa, Florida, this 15 day of July, 1994.

[*12] SUSAN C. BUCKLEW

United States District Judge

22: REVENUE PROCEDURE 85-18

Revenue Procedure 85-18

Rev. Proc. 85-18; 1985-1 C.B. 518; 1985 IRB LEXIS 317; 1985-13 I.R.B. 27

January 1985

[*1]

APPLICABLE SECTIONS:

26 CFR 601.401: Employment taxes. (Also Part 1, Sections 3102, 3111, 3301, 3403; 31.3102-1, 31.3111-4,

31.3301-1, 31.3403-1.)

TEXT:

SECTION 1. PURPOSE

The purpose of this revenue procedure is to amplify and supersede Rev. Proc. 81-43, 1981-2 C.B. 616, which provides instructions for implementing the provisions of section 530 of the Revenue Act of 1978, 1978-3 (Vol. 1) C.B. xi, 119 (the Act), relating to the employment tax status of independent contractors and employees.

SEC. 2. BACKGROUND

.01 Rev. Proc. 81-43 is superseded to reflect changes made to section 530 of the Act by section 269 (c) of the Tax Equity and Fiscal Responsibility Act of 1982, 1982-2 C.B. 462, 536, which extends the provisions of section 530 indefinitely.

Section 530 (a) (1) of the Act, as amended, provides that if, for purposes of the employment taxes under subtitle C of the Internal Revenue Code, a taxpayer did not treat an individual as an employee for any period, then the individual will be deemed not to be an employee for that period, unless the taxpayer had no reasonable basis for not treating the individual as an employee. For any period after December 31, 1978, the relief applies only if (1) all federal tax returns

[*2] (including information returns) required to be filed by the taxpayer with respect to the individual for the period are filed on a basis consistent with the taxpayer's treatment of the individual as not being an employee, and (2) the treatment is consistent with the treatment for periods beginning after December 31, 1977.

.02 A new section 3.02 titled "Filing of Returns" has been added stating that

22: REVENUE PROCEDURE 85-18

relief under section 530 (a) (1) of the Act will not be granted if a Form 1099 has not been timely filed for each worker for any period after December 31, 1978.

.03 Section 3.05 (relating to refunds, credits, and abatements) is clarified to state that it does not apply to periods in which a taxpayer "treated" an individual as an employee.

SEC. 3. APPLICATION

.01 "Safe Haven" Rules

There are several alternative standards that constitute "safe havens" in determining whether a taxpayer has a "reasonable basis" for not treating an individual as an employee. Reasonable reliance on any one of the following "safe havens" is sufficient:

> (A) judicial precedent or published rulings, whether or not relating to the particular industry or business in which the taxpayer is engaged, or technical advice, a letter [*3] ruling, or a determination letter pertaining to the taxpayer; or

> (B) a past Internal Revenue Service audit (not necessarily for employment tax purposes) of the taxpayer, if the audit entailed no assessment attributable to the taxpayer's employment tax treatment of individuals holding positions substantially similar to the position held by the individual whose status is at is- sue (a taxpayer does not meet this test if, in the conduct of a prior audit, an assessment attributable to the taxpayer's treatment of the individual was offset by other claims asserted by the taxpayer); or

> (C) long-standing recognized practice of a significant segment of the industry in which the individual was engaged (the practice need not be uniform throughout an entire industry).

A taxpayer who fails to meet any of the three "safe havens" may nevertheless be entitled to relief if the taxpayer can demonstrate, in some other manner, a reasonable basis for not treating the individual as an employee. In H.R. Rep. No. 95-1748, 95th Cong., 2d Sess. 5 (1978), 1978-3 (Vol. 1) C.B. 629, 633, it is indicated that "reasonable basis" should be construed liberally in favor of the taxpayer.

.02 Filing of Returns.

22: REVENUE PROCEDURE 85-18

For any period [*4] after December 31, 1978, the relief under section 530 (a) (1) will not apply, even if the taxpayer has met the "safe haven" rules of paragraph 3.01 of this revenue procedure, if the appropriate Form 1099 has not been timely filed with respect to the workers involved. See Rev. Rul. 81-224, 1981-2 C.B. 197.

.03 Interpreting the Word "Treat" In determining whether a taxpayer did not "treat" an individual as an employee for any period within the meaning of section 530 (a) (1) of the Act, the following guidelines should be followed:

(A) The withholding of income tax or the Federal Insurance Contributions Act (FICA) tax from an individual's wages is "treatment" of the individual as an employee, whether or not the tax is paid over to the Government.

(B) Except as provided in paragraph (C) and (E) below, the filing of an employment tax return (including Forms 940 (Employer's Annual Federal Unemployment Tax Return), 941 (Employer's Quarterly Federal Tax Return), 942 (Employer's Quarterly Tax Return for Household Employees), 943 (Employer's Annual Tax Return for Agricultural Employees), and W-2 (Wage and Tax Statement)) for a period with respect to an individual, whether or not tax was withheld from [*5] the individual, is "treatment" of the individual as an employee for that period.

(C) The Filing of a delinquent or amended employment tax return for a particular tax period with respect to an individual as a result of Service compliance procedures is not "treatment" of the individual as an employee for that period. For this purpose, Collection or Examination activities constitute compliance procedures. For example, if the Service determines as a result of an audit that a taxpayer's workers are common law employees, that determination is not "treatment" of the workers as employees for the period under audit. However, if the taxpayer withholds employment taxes or files employment tax returns with respect to those workers for the periods following the period under audit, the action is "treatment" of the workers as employees for those later periods.

(D) Internal Revenue Service Center notices that merely advise the taxpayer that no return has been filed and request information from the taxpayer are not compliance procedures.

(E) A return prepared by the Service under section 6020 (b) of the Code is not "treatment" of an individual as an employee; nor is the signing of an audit Form 2504 (Agreement [*6] to Assessment and Collection of Additional Tax and Acceptance of Overassessment).

22: REVENUE PROCEDURE 85-18

.04 Consistency in prior periods The relief under section 530 (a) (1) of the Act, as amended, does not apply to the employment tax treatment of any individual for any period ending after December 31, 1978, if the taxpayer (or a predecessor) treated any individual holding a substantially similar position as an employee for employment tax purposes for any period beginning after December 31, 1977. However, relief will not be denied under the consistency provision for any periods prior to the period in which the individuals were treated as employees. For example, a taxpayer did not treat an individual as an employee in 1978 and 1979. In 1980, the taxpayer began treating individuals holding substantially similar positions as employees. This subsequent treatment does not prevent the taxpayer from receiving relief under section 530 (a) (1) for 1978 and 1979. The application of the consistency rule prevents taxpayers from changing the way they treat workers solely to take advantage of the relief provisions. The application of this provision to predecessors is intended to prevent evasion of this rule, for example, [*7] by reincorporations.

.05 Refunds, Credits, and Abatements

Relief under section 530 (a) (1) of the Act is available to taxpayers who are under audit by the Service or who are involved in administrative (including Appellate) or judicial processes with respect to assessments based on employment status reclassifications. Relief also is extended to any claim for a refund or credit of any overpayment of an employment tax resulting from the termination of liability under section 530 (a) (1), provided the claim is not barred on the date of enactment of this provision (November 6, 1978) by any law or rule of law.

Taxpayers who have entered into final closing agreements under section 7121 of the Code or compromises under section 7122 with respect to employment status controversies are ineligible for relief under the Act, unless they have not completely paid their liability. Thus, for example, a taxpayer who has agreed to or compromised a liability for an amount which is to be paid in installments, but who still has one or more installments to pay, is relieved of liability for such outstanding installments. Taxpayers who settled employment status controversies administratively with the Service on [*8] any basis other than section 7121 or 7122 of the Code or who unsuccessfully litigated such cases also are eligible for relief, provided their claims are not barred by the statute of limitations or by the application of the doctrine of res judicata. However, unpaid judgments will be abated if section 530 (a) (1) of the Act applies. Thus, an unsuccessful litigant in an employment status case who fulfills the Act's requirements can avoid collection of any unpaid employment tax liabilities, regardless of the doctrine of res judicata.

22: REVENUE PROCEDURE 85-18

The application of the doctrine of res judicata will prevent a refund based on section 530 (a) (1) of the Act if a taxpayer paid a judgment in an action relating to the same issue as to the same taxpayer. Thus, if the specific matter was judicially decided and the judgment paid, relief under section 530 (a) (1) is not available.

This subsection will not apply to those periods in which a taxpayer "treated" an individual as an employee within the meaning of subsection .03 of this section.

.06 Handling of Claims

Relief under section 530 (a) (1) of the Act applies to the taxes imposed on an employer by sections 3111 or 3301 of the Code. [*9] It also applies to an employer's liability under section 3102 and 3403 to withhold and pay the taxes imposed by sections 3101 and 3402. Therefore, an unpaid assessment of those taxes against an employer who qualifies for relief under section 530 (a) (1) of the Act should be abated. Timely claims for refund of such taxes paid by a taxpayer who qualifies for relief will be honored.

.07 Interest and Penalties

If a taxpayer is relieved of liability under section 530 (a) (1) of the Act, any liability for interest or penalties attributable to that liability is forgiven automatically. This relief from interest and penalties applies whether charged directly against the taxpayer or personally against a corporate taxpayer's officers.

.08 Status of Workers

Section 530 of the Act does not change in any way the status, liabilities, and rights of the worker whose status is at issue. Section 530 (a) (1) terminates the liability of the employer for the employment taxes but has no effect on the workers. It does not convert individuals from the status of employee to the status of self-employed.

Section 31.3102-1 (c) of the regulations provides, with respect to the collection and payment of the employee's share [*10] of the FICA tax, that "until collected from him [by the employer] the employee is also liable for the employee tax with respect to all wages received by him." Therefore, if an employer's liability under section 3102 of the Code for the employee's share of the tax imposed by section 3101 is terminated under section 530 (a) (1) of the Act, the employee remains liable for that tax. Employees who incorrectly paid the self-employment tax (section 1401 of the Code) may file a claim for refund; however, the amount of the self-employment tax refund will be offset by the amount of the employee's share

22: REVENUE PROCEDURE 85-18

of the tax imposed on the employee as a result of the application of section 31.3102-1 (c) of the regulations.

.09 Definition of Employee For purposes of section 530 (a) of the Act, the term employee means employees under sections 3121 (d), 3306 (i), and 3401 (c) of the Code.

SEC. 4. EFFECT ON OTHER DOCUMENTS

Rev. Proc. 81-43 is amplified and superseded.

23: SARGENT V CM

Gary A. Sargent and Janice B. Sargent, Appellants, v. Commissioner of Internal Revenue, Appellee. Steven M. Christoff and Tami Jo Christoff, Appellants, v. Commissioner of Internal Revenue, Appellee. Steven M. Christoff, Appellant, v. Commissioner of Internal Revenue, Appellee

No. 90-1782

UNITED STATES COURT OF APPEALS FOR THE EIGHTH CIRCUIT

929 F.2d 1252; 1991 U.S. App. LEXIS 5311; 91-1 U.S. Tax Cas. (CCH) P50,168; 67 A.F.T.R.2d (RIA) 718; 13 Employee Benefits Cas. (BNA) 2058

December 13, 1990, Submitted
April 2, 1991, Filed

PRIOR HISTORY: [**1] Appeal from the United States Tax Court; Honorable Theodore Tannenwald, Judge.

COUNSEL: Counsel who presented argument on behalf of the Appellants was John W. Hughes of New York, New York.

Counsel who presented argument on behalf of the Appellee was Bruce R. Ellisen of Washington, District of Columbia.

JUDGES: Arnold and Beam, Circuit Judges, and Andrew W. Bogue, * Senior District Judge. Arnold, Circuit Judge, dissenting.

> * The Hon. Andrew W. Bogue, Senior United States District Judge for the District of South Dakota, sitting by designation.

OPINION BY: BOGUE

OPINION

[*1253] BOGUE, Senior District Judge

This case, on appeal from the United States Tax Court, is one of first impression for this Court. Initially, the Commissioner of Internal Revenue issued Notices of Deficiency with respect to the federal income [*1254] taxes of Gary A. Sargent [1] for the years 1978 through 1981; and for Steven M. Christoff [2] for the years 1980 through 1982.

23: SARGENT V CM

1 The Commissioner determined the following deficiencies in Gary A. Sargent's Federal Income taxes: 1978 - $ 14,577.74; 1979 - $ 18,041.24; 1980 - $ 18,852.04; 1981 - $ 27,882.96. In each year, Sargent's Federal Income taxes were paid jointly with his wife, Janice B. Sargent.

[**2]

2 The Commissioner determined the following deficiencies in Steven M. Christoff's Federal Income taxes: 1980 - $ 21,798; 1981 - $ 23,118.35; 1982 - $ 519. In 1981 and 1982, Christoff paid his taxes jointly with his wife, Tami Jo Christoff.

Sargent and Christoff (hereinafter "Appellants") were hockey players with the Minnesota North Stars Hockey Club (hereinafter the "Club"). Appellants' personal service corporations (PSC), created to represent the business associations of each Appellant, contracted with the Club to provide each Appellant's services to the Club as a hockey player and, in the case of Sargent, also as a consultant. The North Stars paid each PSC for the use of each Appellant's services; each PSC, in turn, paid each Appellant a salary and contributed the remainder to each PSC's qualified pension plan. The Commissioner proposed to disallow these pension deductions and elected to tax Appellants on the entire amount paid by the Club to the PSC.

Appellant Sargent filed a Petition with the Tax Court on March 11, 1986, contesting the deficiencies. Appellant Christoff did likewise on May [**3] 17, 1988, and May 18, 1988. 3 The case was tried in the United States Tax Court, New York, New York, on November 16, 1988; and on November 13, 1988, Judge Tannenwald, Jr., writing for the majority, 4 issued an opinion upholding the deficiencies proposed by the Commissioner. We reverse the decision of the Tax Court and hold that Appellants were employees of their respective personal service corporations; and, therefore, Appellants should not be taxed on the pension deductions of their PSCs.

3 These cases were consolidated for trial and five other taxpayers who received similar Notices of Deficiency have agreed to be bound by the outcome of this case. See Petitioners docket numbers 8821-87, 10976-87, 7131-88, 8490-88, and 17373-88.

4 Twelve judges concurred in Judge Tannenwald's opinion, while six judges dissented, with Judge Wells writing for the dissenters.

23: SARGENT V CM

STANDARD OF REVIEW

We review decisions of the United States Tax Court on the same basis as decisions in civil bench trials in United States District [**4] Courts. Commissioner v. Duberstein, 363 U.S. 278, 290-91, 80 S. Ct. 1190, 1199, 4 L. Ed. 2d 1218 (1960). The trial judge's findings of fact will not be set aside unless clearly erroneous. Id.; Fed. R. Civ. P. 52(a). Mixed questions of law and fact that require the consideration of legal concepts and involve the exercise of judgment about the values underlying legal principles are reviewable de novo. United States v. McConney, 728 F.2d 1195, 1199-1204 (9th Cir. 1984) (en banc), cert. denied, 469 U.S. 824, 105 S. Ct. 101, 83 L. Ed. 2d 46 (1984).

The determination of an employer-employee relationship involves a mixed question of law and fact. Because, however, the decision is predominantly one of determining whether the established facts [5] fall within the relevant legal definition, and does not involve constitutional issues, we apply a clearly erroneous standard of review. Id. at 1202-03. The Tenth Circuit has similarly concluded that the determination of an employer-employee relationship is a question of fact. Marvel v. United States, 719 F.2d 1507, 1515 (10th Cir. 1983). [**5]

> [5] Prior to trial, the parties entered into a Stipulation of Facts, a Second Stipulation of Facts, a Third Stipulation of Facts, and a Supplemental Stipulation of Facts. Typically, "we review de novo the applicability of tax benefit principles to the stipulated facts." Schwartz Rojas v. Commissioner, 901 F.2d 810, 812 (9th Cir. 1984). In this case, however, we are doing more than simply applying tax benefit principles to the stipulated facts; we are also defining the nature of the employer-employee relationship within the rubric of personal service corporations.

BACKGROUND

The facts are set forth in detail in the Tax Court's opinion, and we shall state [*1255] only the essentials: Appellants were both professional hockey players with the Minnesota North Stars Hockey Club. Prior to signing with the North Stars, Appellant Sargent sought out the assistance of Attorney Arthur Kaminsky concerning the benefits of incorporation. Kaminsky advised Sargent that incorporation provided two primary benefits: increased [**6] bargaining power and the possibility of placing money into a pension plan.

Based upon his consultations with Kaminsky, Sargent incorporated Chiefy-Cat, Inc. (Chiefy-Cat) on July 20, 1978. Sargent was the sole shareholder, president,

23: SARGENT V CM

and sole director of this personal service corporation. On July 20, 1978, Sargent entered into an Employment Contract with Chiefy-Cat wherein he agreed to provide his services as a professional hockey player and consultant exclusively for Chiefy-Cat for the period July 1, 1978, to June 30, 1984. At the same time, Chiefy-Cat agreed to furnish the services of Sargent as both a hockey player and consultant to the Club. In exchange, the Club agreed to pay Chiefy-Cat a set salary during each respective playing season. [6] Further, Sargent's employment agreement with Chiefy-Cat provided that Chiefy-Cat agreed to pay Sargent a set salary during each respective season. [7]

> 6 In exchange for Sargent's services as both hockey player and consultant, the Club paid to Chiefy-Cat the following: 1978 - $ 85,000; 1979 - $ 115,000; 1980 - $ 120,000; 1981 - $ 130,000.
> 7 The employment contract between Chiefy-Cat and Sargent provided that Chiefy-Cat agreed to pay Sargent $ 60,000 during the first year and $ 95,000 for each succeeding year.

[**7] Chiefy-Cat withheld and paid the applicable federal and state income taxes and timely filed Employers Quarterly Federal Tax Returns and Forms W-2 and W-3. On March 5, 1980, the Commissioner of the Internal Revenue Service issued a letter whereby the pension plan established by Chiefy-Cat and covering Sargent was determined to be a qualified pension plan. [8] That favorable determination is still in effect and is not an issue before this Court.

> 8 Apparently, not only has the IRS recognized the viability of each PSC's pension plan, in two separate Stipulations of Settled Issues (November 23, 1988 and February 2, 1989), the Commissioner agreed that interest and dividends earned on the amounts contributed to each PSC's qualified pension plan (both Chiefy-Cat and RIF), are not taxable to Sargent and Christoff individually. Chiefy-Cat made the following contributions to the plan: 1978-79 -- $ 20,893; 1979-80 -- $ 24,675; 1980-81 -- $ 27,099; 1981-82 - $ 27,749.

[**8] Christoff followed substantially the same route toward incorporation. He employed the services of Attorney Kaminsky, and sought the same benefits as those sought by Sargent. Thus, on August 11, 1980, Christoff incorporated RIF Enterprises, Inc. (RIF), and entered into an employment agreement with RIF identical -- for the most part -- to that between Sargent and Chiefy-Cat. Likewise, RIF contracted with the North Stars and agreed to provide Christoff's services as a hockey player to the Club. In exchange, the Club agreed to pay RIF a salary dur-

23: SARGENT V CM

ing each respective hockey season. [9] From this salary, RIF directed contributions to the PSC's qualified pension plan. [10]

> 9 The Club paid RIF the following during each respective season: 1980 - $ 63,500; 1981 - $ 71,500. In turn, RIF paid Christoff $ 45,000 during 1980, and $ 50,000 during 1981.
>
> 10 On September 1, 1981, the Commissioner issued a letter whereby RIF's pension plan covering Christoff was determined to be a qualified pension plan. RIF made the following contributions to the plan: 1980-81 -- $ 7,200; 1981-82 -- $ 17,750; 1982-83 -- $ 1,625.

[**9] During the years at issue, neither Sargent nor Christoff were considered employees of the Club for purposes of the National Hockey League Players' Pension Plan. In each case, the Club paid Chiefy-Cat and RIF, respectively, the amounts that it would otherwise have contributed to the Players' Pension Plan on their behalf. The sole issue before this Court is whether Sargent and Christoff should be taxed now on those amounts contributed by their respective PSC's to each PSC's qualified pension plan. [11]

> 11 It is interesting to note that Robert Smith and Michael Fidler, also hockey players with the Minnesota North Stars, established similar personal service corporations at the same time as Appellants -- and with the same attorney. Following an audit, the Commissioner determined that the income paid by the North Stars to Smith's and Fidler's PSCs was taxable directly to Smith and Fidler, respectively, and issued Notices of Deficiency to each. After the cases were docketed, the Commissioner conceded that the amounts paid by the Club to the PSCs was taxable to the PSCs, and not to Smith and Fidler individually. The Stipulation of Settlement in the Smith case stated: "The Petitioner does not have additional wages of $ 26,050, $ 41,186, or $ 50,098 for the years 1978, 1979, and 1980, respectively; this income was properly reported as the income of Denlate Ice, Inc."

[**10] [*1256] I.

The Tax Court takes the position that because Sargent and Christoff were members of a hockey "team," the requisite control over them -- for purposes of taxation -- was lodged in the hockey Club, and not in their respective PSCs, with which they had a contractual employment relationship. We reject this contention.

23: SARGENT V CM

With respect to the "control" factor, which is heavily relied upon by the Tax Court, the Regulations state:

> In this connection, it is not necessary that the employer actually direct or control the manner in which the services are performed; it is sufficient if he has the right to do so.

Treasury Regulation § 31.3121(d)-1(c)(2) (1980).

It seems to this Court that legal analysis is forgotten if we simply measure the control element of an employment relationship by whether the employee is or is not a member of a superficially defined "team." Eventually, the issue becomes mired in a game of definitions: If the organizational structure is itself mislabeled a "team," a personal service corporation, as a matter of law, is a forbidden tax deferment tool for each and every person providing his or her services to that organization. On the other hand, if the organization to which [**11] the services are provided is not defined as a "team," then those same service-providers are free to create a PSC and subject that PSC's legitimacy to traditional common law and tax code analysis, regardless of the level of control exerted over those persons by the organization. Such an arbitrary approach is specious at best.

Accordingly, within Regulation § 31.3121(d)-(1)(c)(2), two necessary elements must be met before the corporation, rather than the service-recipient, in this case the North Stars Hockey Club, may be considered the true controller of the service-provider. First, the service-provider must be just that -- an employee of the corporation whom the corporation has the right to direct or control in some meaningful sense. See Vnuk v. Commissioner, 621 F.2d 1318, 1320-21 (8th Cir. 1980); Johnson v. Commissioner, 78 T.C. 882 (1982). Second, there must exist between the corporation and the person or entity (Club) using the services a contract or similar indicium recognizing the corporation's controlling position. See Pacella v. Commissioner, 78 T.C. 604 (1982); Keller v. Commissioner, 77 T.C. 1014 (1981), [**12] aff'd 723 F.2d 58 (10th Cir. 1983); Johnson, supra.

These two elements were applied in a case strikingly similar to the one before us. In Johnson, supra, Charles Johnson, a professional basketball player with the San Francisco Warriors, created a PSC and the IRS sought to tax Johnson for the entire amount paid to his PSC by the Warriors. Without ever addressing whether Johnson was or was not a member of a "team," the Tax Court ultimately held the contracts to be dispositive of the issue of control:

> In the case before us, we accept arguendo that the [PSC-Johnson] agreement was a valid contract which required the payments

23: SARGENT V CM

with respect to [Johnson's] performance as a basketball player ultimately to be made to the [PSC]. We also accept arguendo that the [PSC-Johnson] agreement gave [the PSC] a right of control over [Johnson's] services, . . . Thus, the first element [of control] is satisfied. [emphasis added]

Johnson, 78 T.C. at 883.

Ultimately, Johnson was required to pay individual income tax on the entire amount paid to his PSC, but only because his PSC had no contractual arrangement with the Warriors [**13] basketball team. Said the Tax [*1257] Court regarding the second prong of the "control" test: "crucial is the fact that there was no contract or agreement between the Warriors and [the PSC]." Id. at 884. We are not faced with such a dilemma in this case. Not only did Appellants have a contractual arrangement with their respective PSCs, thereby passing the first prong of the analysis, each PSC also had a contractual relationship with the North Stars Hockey Club. Consistent with its analysis in the past, the Tax Court in Johnson concluded that the existence of bona fide contracts between the parties satisfied the requisite elements of control. Indeed, the Tax Court at no time concerned itself with whether Johnson was or was not a member of a "team."

The Tax Court's "team" analysis further breaks down when one looks at a decision handed down by the Tax Court just one day after the case before us. In Pflug v. Commissioner, 1989 Tax Ct. Memo LEXIS 615, 58 T.C.M. (CCH) 685, 1989 T.C. Memo 615 (1989), an actress entered into an exclusive employment contract with her husband's corporation, Charwool Production, Inc. ("Charwool"), of which she was an officer. Subsequently, Charwool entered into a contract with [**14] 20th Century Fox Studios, agreeing to provide the services of Ms. Pflug for a new TV series. Although the ultimate issue was whether Ms. Pflug was subject to self-employment taxes on income received from Charwool, the Court was first required to decide whether Ms. Pflug was an employee of Charwool. In holding that Ms. Pflug was an employee of Charwool, and not an employee of 20th Century Fox Studios, the Tax Court held the contracts between the respective parties to be dispositive and stated:

> The fundamental question is whether Charwool had the right to exercise dominion and control over the activities of [Pflug], not only as to results but also as to the means and methods used to accomplish the result. We find, by virtue of the contract [Pflug] entered with Charwool, Charwool had the requisite right to control [Pflug].

23: SARGENT V CM

Id. at 688.

This Court is perplexed to find that those same contractual arrangements which were dispositive of the issue of "control" in Pflug were summarily discarded in the case before us. By the same token, those same "team" factors which were dispositive of the issue of control in the case before us were not even discussed in Pflug.

[**15] Was not Joanne Pflug a part of a team every bit as "controlled" as Sargent and Christoff? Like a hockey team in which different players assume different roles to insure success, the members of Pflug's team included the cast, writers, directors, and producers all working toward the common goal of producing a successful TV series. More importantly, just as a hockey player has a generalized set of plays tailored to fit his talents and the talents of his teammates, so, too, Ms. Pflug's "plays" included movements carefully choreographed to mesh with other cast members, a script prepared for her to follow, cue cards to insure that little or no deviation from the designed "play" occurred, and numerous retakes to guarantee that ultimate control vested in the hands of the studio, not Ms. Pflug's PSC. Nevertheless, the Tax Court concluded that Ms. Pflug was an employee of her PSC.

There can be little question that Ms. Pflug was part of a team under more stringent production controls than those placed on either Sargent or Christoff by the Club. But, as the Tax Court concluded, ". . . by virtue of the contract [Pflug] entered with Charwool, Charwool had the requisite right to control [Pflug]." [**16] Id. Appellants' contractual arrangements, which were every bit as bona fide as those entered into by Ms. Pflug, 12 should and do provide the requisite control for Appellants to be considered employees of their respective PSCs.

> 12 Actually, the contracts in this case were of a more bona fide nature because they were in writing. A written contract between Ms. Pflug and Charwool was never produced, and the only evidence of the existence of a contract was Ms. Pflug's oral testimony. Pflug v. Commissioner, 58 T.C.M. at 688.

Once the "team" analysis of control is disregarded, this Court is able to fall back [*1258] on ample Tax Court precedent which upholds the sanctity of contractual relations between taxpayers and their respective personal service corporations. In Haag v. Commissioner, 88 T.C. 604 (1987), the contractual arrangements between a doctor and his PSC again dictated the Courts' disposition of the case. The Tax Court stated:

23: SARGENT V CM

> We find that the employment agreement effectively [**17] gave
> the [PSC] the right to control petitioner's medical practice. Id. at
> 612.

Although the Commissioner argues that in each of these cases the employer-
employee relationship was never addressed, this Court thinks otherwise. Each
time the legitimacy of the employee's relationship with the corporation was
raised, the Tax Court pointed to the existence of a contractual relationship
between the corporation and the employee/service-provider as the rationale for
upholding the legal significance of the PSC. In Keller, supra, for example, the Tax
Court respected the contractual arrangements entered into by the taxpayer and
the PSC, and held them out as the basis for distinguishing its decision in Roubik
v. Commissioner, 53 T.C. 365 (1969), stating:

> The corporation (in Roubik) did not enter into any arrangements
> to provide the services of its purported employees; personal con-
> tractual obligations between the taxpayers and the parties for
> whom they provided services persisted.

77 T.C. at 1032.

The Commissioner's position (in Keller) -- that the existence of the
employer/employee relationship was never addressed [**18] -- is further eroded
when one realizes that Dr. Keller was required to pay individual income taxes for
the single year in which he had no contractual relationship with the PSC. One
year later, when contractual arrangements were entered into between Keller, Inc.
and MAL, Inc., the payments from MAL to Keller were not taxed to Dr. Keller
individually, but instead were taxed to his PSC.

Quite simply, we agree with the position taken by the Tax Court in Keller, supra,
when it stated: "we find that an employment relationship was created in this case
by the employment agreement and that it was maintained by the parties to the
agreement after execution." 77 T.C. at 1032. Appellants in this case entered into
bona fide arms lengths agreements with their respective PSCs. For this reason,
each is considered to be an employee of that PSC, and not an employee of the
North Stars Hockey Club.

II.

By rejecting the Tax Court's "team" test, and embracing the viability of the contractual relations between Appellants and their personal service corporations, we
have effectively decided the only issue presented for our deliberation: By whom

23: SARGENT V CM

were Appellants employed? [**19] Thus, because Appellants were employees of their respective PSCs, they were improperly taxed on the entire amount paid by the North Stars Hockey Club to the PSCs.

Furthermore, by embracing the "contract" theory of this case, we are at the same time discarding the Tax Court's conclusion that this case involves the "assignment of income" doctrine, as articulated in Lucas v. Earl, 281 U.S. 111, 50 S. Ct. 241, 74 L. Ed. 731 (1930), [13] and its progeny, and Section 61 of the Tax Code. The Tax Court's contention that Appellants were attempting to employ a corporate "assignment of income" scheme to evade their income tax responsibility is without merit.

> 13 Lucas v. Earl involved a contract between husband and wife which declared all property which they were to receive to be taken by them as joint tenants. The husband received salary and attorneys' fees and was the only party to the contracts by which the salary and fees were earned. The Supreme Court held that half the husband's personal service income could not by the contract be assigned to the wife for tax purposes. Mr. Justice Holmes noted that the arrangement was one by which "the fruits are attributed to a different tree from that on which they grew." 281 U.S. 111, 115, 50 S. Ct. 241, 74 L. Ed. 731. In the case before us, Appellants' PSCs have a contract with an unrelated third party [the Club] which requires payments directly to the PSC. The situation in Lucas v. Earl is clearly inapposite.

[**20] [*1259] We do not doubt that the "assignment of income" doctrine serves a useful tax purpose. For example, as the Tax Court observed in Keller: "The assignment of income doctrine * * * constitutes an essential tool * * * where the corporation is not respected by the taxpayer/shareholder as a separate entity which carries on business activities." 77 T.C. at 1033. Overuse of the assignment of income doctrine, however, has met with stiff resistance.

In Foglesong v. Commissioner, T.C. Memo 1976-294, 1976 T.C. Memo 294, 35 T.C.M. (CCH) 1309 (1976), rev'd and remanded at 621 F.2d 865 (7th Cir. 1980), the IRS attempted to set aside the transactions entered into by a corporation without ever looking at the validity of the corporation itself. Said the Seventh Circuit:

> We believe that, where the issue is application of the assignment of income doctrine to effectively set aside the corporation, under

23: SARGENT V CM

the particular circumstances of this case * * *, an attempt to strike a balance between tax avoidance motives and "legitimate" business purposes is an unproductive and inappropriate exercise. Such an approach places too low a value on the policy of the law to recognize corporations as economic [**21] actors except in exceptional circumstances.

Id. at 872.

In Johnson, supra, a case whose facts run parallel to the facts of this case, the Tax Court also observed, regarding the blind application of Lucas v. Earl:

However, the realities of the business world present an overly simplistic application of the Lucas v. Earl rule whereby the true earner may be identified by pointing to the one actually turning the spade or dribbling the ball. Recognition must be given to corporations as taxable entities which, to a great extent, rely upon the personal services of their employees to produce corporate income. Where a corporate employee performs labors which give rise to income, it solves little merely to identify the actual laborer. Thus, a tension has evolved between the basic tenets of Lucas v. Earl and recognition of the nature of the corporation business form.

Id. at 890.

As long as a corporation carries on some form of business, the Supreme Court has concluded that the tax advantages which properly flow from incorporation should not be questioned. The Supreme Court reasoned:

The doctrine of corporate entity fills a useful purpose [**22] in business life. Whether the purpose be to gain an advantage under the law of the state of incorporation or to avoid or to comply with the demands of creditors or to serve the creator's personal or undisclosed convenience, so long as that purpose is the equivalent of business activity or is followed by the carrying on of business by the corporation, the corporation remains a separate taxable entity.

Moline Prop. Inc. v. Commissioner, 319 U.S. 436, 438-39, 63 S. Ct. 1132, 87 L. Ed. 1499 (1943).

23: SARGENT V CM

The Tax Court voiced this same conclusion almost forty years later, when it stated that "the policy favoring the recognition of corporations as entities independent of their shareholders requires that we not ignore the corporate form so long as the corporation actually conducts business." Keller, 77 T.C. at 1031. Indeed, at no time has the Commissioner questioned the legitimacy of Appellants' corporate business activities. According to the record, both RIF and Chiefy-Cat withheld income and employment taxes from the salary payments to Appellants; paid contributions to the Chiefy-Cat Pension Plan and the RIF Pension Plan on account of their employment of Sargent and Christoff, [14] respectively; [**23] filed forms 940 and 941 with respect to the withholding taxes; and filed corporate tax returns and paid corporate income taxes. Such obvious business activity by Appellants' [*1260] PSCs is far removed from that conduct which is forbidden under the "assignment of income" doctrine.

> 14 Chiefy-Cat adopted the Chiefy-Cat, Inc. Money Purchase Pension Plan, effective July 1, 1978; and, on March 5, 1980, the Commissioner issued a favorable determination letter to Chiefy-Cat, confirming the Plan to be qualified under Section 401 of the Code. Accordingly, RIF adopted the RIF Enterprises, Inc. Money Purchase Pension Plan and received a similar favorable determination letter on September 1, 1981, confirming the Plan's Section 401 qualification.

Neither will this Court question the motivation behind Appellants' desire to incorporate. That each Appellant has taken steps to enhance his retirement through a richer corporate sponsored pension plan is of no consequence to this court. The Code provisions relating to qualified retirement plans are a deliberate congressional bestowal of benefits upon employers and employees; efforts to obtain the advantages of these benefits, by way of conducting business in the corporate form, are not to be deemed to render the taxpayer culpable of illegal tax avoidance or evasion. See Keller, 77 T.C. at 1030. Thus, "once a corporation is formed and all organizational and operational requirements are met, it should be recognized for tax purposes [**24] regardless of the fact that it was formed to take advantage of richer corporate retirement plans." Achiro v. Commissioner of Internal Revenue, 77 T.C. 881, 895-96 (1981).

Unfortunately, taxpayers will often go to great lengths to evade unlawfully the payment of income taxes.

Whether it simply be lying on their tax forms, assigning income to those who have not earned it, or sheltering income in non-existent or improper tax-avoid-

23: SARGENT V CM

ance investments, each is destructive to the often painful revenue-production responsibility of the IRS. In this case, however, we are presented with taxpayers who [**25] have fulfilled each and every task required of them in order to become properly incorporated. More importantly, for purposes of this case, Appellants took steps to insure that each was a contractually-bound employee of his respective PSC. That these contracts of employment were recognized and respected by the North Stars Hockey Club, the National Hockey League and the Minnesota Office of Administrative Hearings [15] lends substantial credibility to the fact that Appellants were employees of their respective PSCs -- and not the North Stars Hockey Club.

> 15 As the employer of Christoff, RIF was required under Minnesota law to obtain worker's compensation insurance for Christoff. When Employer's Insurance of Wausau, RIF's worker's compensation insurer, was required to pay claims on behalf of Christoff, it refused, arguing that it was not responsible for these claims because Christoff was an employee of the Club and not RIF. Thus, Employer's Insurance of Wausau claimed that the Club's insurer, Great American Insurance Company, was required to pay Christoff's claim. After a hearing and testimony, Judge Otto of the State of Minnesota Office of Administrative Hearings determined that "Mr. Steven Christoff was an employee of RIF Enterprises, Inc., at all times material to this proceeding for injuries sustained by him while playing hockey for the North Stars Hockey Partnership subsequent to August 11, 1980."

[**26] III.

This Court agrees with the Tax Court that our result is unaffected by application of Section 482 of the Code. [16] Section 482 allows the Commissioner to "distribute, apportion or allocate gross income, deductions, credits or allowances" between or among "two or more organizations, trades or businesses * * * owned or controlled directly or indirectly by the same interests" if he determines that such action is "necessary in order to prevent evasion of taxes or clearly to reflect the income of any of such organizations, trades or businesses." [17]

> 16 Section 482 of the Tax Code provides: In any case of two or more organizations, trades, or businesses (whether or not incorporated, whether or not organized in the United States, and whether or not affiliated) owned or controlled directly or indi-

23: SARGENT V CM

rectly by the same interests, the Secretary may distribute, apportion, or allocate gross income, deductions, credits, or allowances
between or among such organizations, trades, or businesses, if he
determines that such distribution, apportionment, or allocation
is necessary in order to prevent evasion of taxes or clearly to
reflect the income of any of such organizations, trades, or businesses. In the case of any transfer (or license) of intangible property (within the meaning of section 936(h)(3)(B)), the income
with respect to such transfer or license shall be commensurate
with the income attributable to the intangible.

(Aug. 16, 1954, c. 736, 68A Stat. 162; Oct. 4, 1976, Pub.L. 94-
455, Title XIX, § 1906(b)(13)(A), 90 Stat. 1834; Oct. 22, 1986,
Pub.L. 99-514, Title XII, § 1231(e)(1), 100 Stat. 2562.)

[**27]

17 Congress enacted Section 269A of the Code in 1982 to specifically address personal service corporations. Generally, section
269A provides that the commissioner may apportion a PSCs
income taxes if it appears that the PSC was formed: (1) to provide its services to one other corporation, partnership, or entity;
and (2) the principal purpose behind formation was the avoidance or evasion of income taxes by reducing the income for any
employee-owner which would not otherwise be available. We
have already concluded, however, that Appellants' PSCs were
established for a legitimate purpose, and Appellants had bona
fide employment contracts with their respective PSCs.

[*1261] Our result is unchanged because, as we stated earlier, Appellants created
their respective PSCs for a legitimate business purpose. An apportionment by the
Commission would result in Appellants being taxed only on those amounts paid
to them by their respective PSCs. Accordingly, those amounts transferred into corporate pension funds are the legitimate by-product of each PSC's corporate existence.

IV.

In conclusion, this Court finds that [**28] Appellants were, at all times relevant
to this case, employees of their respective personal service corporations.
Furthermore, the PSCs established by Appellants are legitimate corporate entities,
created to conduct Appellants' business. Appellants, therefore, are obligated to

23: SARGENT V CM

pay income tax only on those amounts paid to them as salary by their respective PSC. For all of the reasons articulated above, the decision of the United States Tax Court is

Reversed.

DISSENT BY: ARNOLD

DISSENT

ARNOLD, Circuit Judge, dissenting.

I would affirm, essentially for the reasons given in Judge Tannenwald's thorough opinion for the Tax Court, 93 T.C. 572 (1989). In my view, the finding that the taxpayers were employed by the Minnesota North Stars Hockey Club, rather than by their respective personal-service corporations, is not clearly erroneous. The coach of the North Stars had the right to control, and actually did control, the conduct of Sargent and Christoff on the ice. The idea that the coach issued orders to Sargent and Christoff in their capacity as corporate officers, which orders they then relayed to themselves as corporate employees, is fanciful.

24: LEAVELL V CM

Allen Leavell, Petitioner v. Commissioner of Internal Revenue, Respondent

Docket No. 29996-91

UNITED STATES TAX COURT

104 T.C. 140; 1995 U.S. Tax Ct. LEXIS 8; 104 T.C. No. 6

January 30, 1995, Filed

DISPOSITION: [**1] Decision will be entered under Rule 155.

SYLLABUS

P, a professional basketball player, formed a personal service corporation. P agreed to furnish his services to his personal service corporation; the personal service corporation, in turn, executed an NBA Uniform Player Contract with the Rockets to furnish P's services. As a condition to executing the player contract, the Rockets required P to execute a written agreement with the Rockets wherein P personally agreed to perform the individual services called for by the terms and conditions of the player contract. Held: The Rockets had the right to control the manner and means by which P's personal services were performed; accordingly, with respect to P's services as a player for the Rockets, P was an employee of the Rockets. It follows that the $ 204,333.35 paid by the Rockets to P's personal service corporation constitutes income allocable to P. Sargent v. Commissioner, 93 T.C. 572 (1989), revd. 929 F.2d 1252 (8th Cir. 1991), followed.

COUNSEL: Bennett G. Fisher and Ian Cain, for petitioner.

Victoria Sherlock and Susan Sample, for respondent.

JUDGES: Ruwe, Chabot, Parker, Cohen, Gerber, Parr, Halpern, [**2] Beghe, Chiechi, Swift, Laro, Hamblen, Jacobs, Wells

OPINION BY: RUWE

OPINION

[*140] RUWE, Judge: * This case is before the Court pursuant to a petition filed by Allen Leavell for redetermination of respondent's determination of a deficiency of $ 66,897 in petitioner's 1985 Federal income tax. Unless otherwise [*141] indicated, section references are to the Internal Revenue Code in effect for 1985, the taxable year in issue. Rule references are to the Tax Court Rules of Practice and Procedure.

24: LEAVELL V CM

* This case was reassigned to Judge Robert P. Ruwe by order of
the Chief Judge.

After concessions by the parties, the sole issue for decision is whether $
204,333.35 paid to petitioner's wholly owned personal service corporation, Allen
Leavell, Inc. (corporation), is includable in his gross income. The Houston
Rockets (Rockets), a basketball team in the National Basketball Association
(NBA or association), paid this amount to corporation in exchange for petition-
er's services as a professional basketball player.

FINDINGS OF FACT

Many of the [**3] facts have been stipulated and are so found. The stipulation of
facts, first supplemental stipulation of facts, and attached exhibits are incorporated herein by this reference. For the taxable year in issue, petitioner filed a 1985
Form 1040, U.S. Individual Income Tax Return, with the Austin Service Center of
the Internal Revenue Service. When he filed his petition in this Court, petitioner
resided in Houston, Texas.

Petitioner began playing professional basketball for the Rockets in 1979. On July
1, 1980, upon advice of counsel, petitioner formed corporation to serve as his
representative/employer for his services as a professional basketball player and to
market his personal appearances and endorsement opportunities. [1] Corporation
observed all corporate formalities as required by the laws of Texas, its State of
incorporation, and was in good standing throughout the taxable year in issue.
Corporation had a fiscal year that ended on June 30.

> 1 In addition to their salary from playing basketball, well-known
> players in the NBA can earn money through endorsements.

[**4] Petitioner was the sole shareholder of corporation during its existence and
served as corporation's president and treasurer; petitioner also served as one of
corporation's two directors. Petitioner's attorney and agent, Lance Luchnick,
served as corporation's vice president and secretary; Mr. Luchnick also served as
corporation's other director. Mr. Luchnick was actively involved in the day-to-day
operation of corporation; his duties and responsibilities included opening corporation's [*142] mail and paying its bills, maintaining and controlling its checking
account, depositing and writing its checks, paying its payroll, preparing (or caus-
ing to be prepared) its tax returns, and negotiating all contracts on its behalf.
Petitioner met routinely with Mr. Luchnick to review the business of corporation.

In his individual capacity, petitioner entered into an employment agreement with

24: LEAVELL V CM

corporation under which petitioner agreed to provide his basketball and promotional services exclusively for corporation. This agreement gave corporation the right to determine the professional basketball team for which petitioner would perform and also the right and authority to contract with any professional [**5] basketball team. [2] With respect to his promotional services, corporation generated income opportunities for petitioner based on his endorsements of consumer products (e.g., Nike shoes, athletic equipment, and clothing) and by promoting petitioner's appearances at selected events. For each of these income opportunities, corporation had the right to dictate to petitioner the time and place of the endorsement or the event.

> [2] Respondent argues that petitioner has failed to prove that an agreement between petitioner and corporation actually existed. Petitioner testified that such an agreement existed but admitted that it was never put into writing. There was no evidence regarding the date of the agreement or whether it was for a specific period of time or terminable at the will of either party. There was also no evidence regarding the method or means by which such nonwritten agreement was entered into. The trial judge, based upon the evidence, concluded that there was an agreement between petitioner and corporation, and we will follow his finding that the agreement existed.

[**6] On December 11, 1984, the Rockets and corporation executed a contract entitled "Uniform Player Contract". The Uniform Player Contract was a form contract drafted by the NBA; the individual teams in the NBA were required to use the Uniform Player Contract to bind a player to their team, and could not omit or reject any of the provisions therein. The 1984 Uniform Player Contract executed by corporation and the Rockets was for a term of 2 years starting on September 1, 1984, and covered the Rockets' 1984-85 and 1985-86 basketball seasons. [3]

> [3] Basketball seasons for teams in the NBA begin in one calendar year and end in the following calendar year.

The 1984 Uniform Player Contract designated Allen Frazier Leavell, Inc., as the "player". There is nothing in the written terms of the 1984 Uniform Player Contract that specifically calls for petitioner to personally perform the services [*143] required to be provided by the "player". [4] The contract required that the "player": Attend each training camp; play the scheduled [**7] games during each season; play all scheduled exhibition games during and prior to the season; when

24: LEAVELL V CM

invited, play in the All-Star Games and attend every event associated with the All-Star Games; play in the playoff games subsequent to each regular season; report at the time and place fixed by the Rockets in good physical condition; keep in good physical condition throughout each season; give his best services and loyalty to the Rockets; agree to give immediate notice of any injury suffered by him, including the time, place, cause, and nature of such injury, and submit himself to a medical examination and treatment by a physician designated by the Rockets; play only for the Rockets or its assignees; report to the club to whom his contract has been assigned within 48 hours after receiving notice of the assignment or within such longer time for reporting as may be specified in the notice; and refrain from, directly or indirectly, enticing any player or coach to enter into negotiations for or relating to his services as a basketball player.

> 4 The entire Dec. 11, 1984, Uniform Player Contract is attached as the appendix.

[**8] The contract also required that the "player": Observe and comply, at all times whether on or off the playing floor, with all requirements of the Rockets respecting conduct of its team and its players; be neatly and fully attired in public and always conduct himself according to the highest standards of honesty, morality, fair play, and sportsmanship, on and off the court; not do anything which is detrimental to the best interests of the Rockets or the association; not engage in sports endangering his health or safety (including, but not limited to, professional boxing or wrestling, motorcycling, moped riding, auto racing, sky diving, and hang gliding); except with written consent of the Rockets, not engage in any game or exhibition of basketball, football, baseball, hockey, lacrosse, or other athletic sport; allow the Rockets or the association to take pictures of the "player", alone or together with others, at such times as the Rockets or association may designate; refrain from public appearances, participating in radio or television programs, permitting his picture to be taken or writing or sponsoring newspaper or magazine articles or commercial products without the written consent [**9] of [*144] the Rockets, which shall not be withheld except in the reasonable interests of the Rockets or professional basketball; make himself available for interviews by representatives of the media conducted at reasonable times; agree to participate in all other reasonable promotional activities of the Rockets and the association; and conform his personal conduct to standards of good citizenship, good moral character, and good sportsmanship.

Under the contract, the Rockets could impose fines, sanctions, and other disciplinary measures for "player" violations. For example, the "player" could be: Fined, suspended, and have his compensation reduced for violating the requirements of

24: LEAVELL V CM

the Rockets respecting conduct of its team and players; suspended and have his compensation reduced for not arriving in good physical condition for the first game of the season, or if he fails to remain in good physical condition throughout the season (unless the condition results from any injury sustained as a direct result of participating in any practice or game played for the Rockets); suspended and have his compensation reduced for failing to report to a club to whom his contract has been assigned; [**10] and fined and suspended for engaging in sports that may endanger his health or safety.

The contract also provides that the association could impose fines, sanctions, and other disciplinary measures. For example, the "player" could be: Suspended or indefinitely expelled by the commissioner if he bet, or offered or attempted to bet, money on the outcome of any game participated in by any club which is a member of the association; subject to a fine not exceeding $ 1,000 by the association for giving, authorizing, or endorsing any statement having or designed to have, an effect that is prejudicial or detrimental to the best interests of basketball or of the association; subject to a fine not exceeding $ 10,000 and suspended by the association for engaging in an act or conduct during a preseason, championship, playoff, or exhibition game that is prejudicial to or against the best interests of the association or the game of basketball; and subject to a fine not exceeding $ 1,000 and be suspended for a definite or indefinite period for engaging in conduct that, in the opinion of the commissioner, is prejudicial or detrimental to the association.

[*145] The 1984 Uniform Player Contract [**11] was negotiated primarily by Mr. Luchnick on behalf of corporation and by Ray Patterson on behalf of the Rockets. Petitioner signed the contract for corporation in his capacity as its officer, 5 and Mr. Patterson signed the contract for the Rockets in his capacity as the Rockets' president and general manager. Mr. Patterson signed the 1984 Uniform Player Contract with the understanding that it was not a contract with petitioner, but rather, was a contract between the Rockets and corporation in order to acquire petitioner's services. The Rockets wanted to obtain petitioner's services and did not care if his services were obtained through corporation. However, as a condition to entering into the 1984 Uniform Player Contract, the Rockets required petitioner, in his individual capacity, to enter into a written agreement with the Rockets entitled "Personal Guarantee by Player". This "Personal Guarantee", which was also signed on December 11, 1984, provided as follows:

> 5 Petitioner's signature on the 1984 Uniform Player Contract appears immediately above the designation "Allen Leavell Player" and his home address. While petitioner's signature does

24: LEAVELL V CM

not explicitly indicate that he was signing in the capacity of a corporate representative or agent, petitioner testified that he intended to sign in his capacity as a corporate officer. The trial judge accepted petitioner's testimony on this point, and we will follow his finding.

[**12] PERSONAL GUARANTEE BY PLAYER

(For Use When Player Contract Is Entered Into By Player Corporation)

I, /s/ Allen Leavell, in order to induce ___ (hereinafter called the "Club") to enter into the annexed Player Contract with ALLEN LEAVELL, INC. (hereinafter called the "Company"), and intending the Club to rely hereon, do hereby make the following representations, warranties, and agreements:

1. I have read the annexed Player Contract (and any amendments, riders, and addenda thereto), and understand that it calls for the Company to provide my services as a professional basketball player. In consideration of the promises, conditions, and provisions contained in said Player Contract, I hereby expressly accept and agree to be bound by all the terms and conditions thereof.

2. The Company has the right to enter into the annexed Player Contract, to grant all the rights therein granted, and to supply my services to the Club pursuant to the terms thereof. I will cause the Company to perform all of its obligations pursuant to the terms of the annexed Player Contract.

3. I will perform and supply all of the services which the Company has agreed to perform and supply to the Club pursuant [**13] to the terms of the annexed Player Contract.

[*146] IN WITNESS WHEREOF, I have executed this personal guarantee this 11 day of DECEMBER, 1984.

/s/ Allen Leavell

WITNESS:

/s/ Ray A. Patterson

As a member in the NBA, the Rockets played games at the times and places scheduled by the NBA. The Rockets had the right to require petitioner to provide his services at the times and places of scheduled games. The facilities in which games were played were provided by the respective team organizations. The

24: LEAVELL V CM

Rockets provided the arena in which its home games were played. The Rockets, through its coach, scheduled the time and place where petitioner was required to attend training camp and practice sessions and provided for the facilities in which they were conducted. The coach determined the type of drills that would be performed by players during training camp and practice sessions.

NBA teams like the Rockets generally have 12 players on their active team roster. During a game, only five players from each team are actually playing at any one time. Coaches regularly substitute players during games. The primary object of the team having possession of the ball is to score. [**14] This generally requires the five individual players on the basketball court to coordinate their actions. The primary object of the team that does not have possession of the ball is to prevent the offensive team from scoring and to gain possession of the ball. This also generally requires the individual players to coordinate their defensive actions.

The coach of the Rockets determined the general game strategy that was to be utilized by the players during games. The coach also had the authority to direct players as to game tactics and the use of specific plays. Because of the fast pace of the game, the players were expected to exercise discretion to adjust their play to meet the immediate circumstances, even if this sometimes required deviation from the coach's directives. The coach had the authority to determine who would play in a game, how much time a player would play, and who would be cut from the team. This authority provided the coach with leverage over players in order to induce them to conform to his directions and expectations.

[*147] During the year in issue, petitioner's regular position on the Rocket's basketball team was "point guard". That position required petitioner [**15] to take a leadership role during games. The point guard would generally bring the ball up the court and generally provide direction to other team members.

When the Rockets paid corporation the compensation required by the 1984 Uniform Player Contract, the Rockets did not withhold income taxes or pay or withhold payroll taxes. For the 1985 calendar year, the Rockets issued corporation a 1985 Form 1099-MISC, Miscellaneous Income, reporting that the Rockets paid corporation $ 204,333.35 in nonemployee compensation during that calendar year. For its fiscal year ended June 30, 1985, corporation filed a Form 1120, U.S. Corporation Income Tax Return, and reported in its gross income all amounts that the Rockets paid corporation during that fiscal year pursuant to the 1984 Uniform Player Contract. Corporation also included in its gross income all compensation that it received during that fiscal year for petitioner's endorsement and promotional services. Corporation's Form 1120 further reported that corpo-

24: LEAVELL V CM

ration paid petitioner $ 135,600 during corporation's fiscal year ended June 30, 1985. Corporation withheld both Federal income taxes and Social Security taxes from this amount.

For its fiscal [**16] year ended June 30, 1986, corporation filed a Form 1120 and reported in its gross income all amounts that the Rockets paid corporation during that fiscal year pursuant to the 1984 Uniform Player Contract. Corporation's Form 1120 also reported that corporation paid petitioner $ 100,400 during corporation's fiscal year ended June 30, 1986, and that corporation contributed $ 27,663 to a pension plan.

Corporation issued petitioner a 1985 Form W-2, Wage and Tax Statement, reporting that corporation paid petitioner wages of $ 111,400 during the 1985 calendar year and that, with respect to these wages, corporation withheld: (1) Federal income taxes of $ 10,560.37, and (2) Social Security taxes of $ 2,791.80. On petitioner's 1985 Form 1040, he included the wages on line 7, wages, salaries, tips, etc., and included the withheld Federal income taxes on line 57, Federal income taxes withheld.

[*148] Corporation did not pay any expenses incurred for petitioner's travel as a member of the Rockets. These travel expenses were paid directly by the Rockets.

Respondent determined that the entire amount paid by the Rockets to corporation during the 1985 calendar year should be included in the income [**17] of petitioner and, accordingly, increased petitioner's income by $ 92,933 (the difference between (1) the $ 204,333 that the Rockets paid corporation during the 1985 calendar year, and (2) the $ 111,400 that petitioner included in his 1985 gross income as paid to him by corporation during that calendar year). Respondent did not determine any reassignment of income received by corporation for services performed by petitioner other than with respect to the payments from the Rockets. Respondent does not contest the fact that corporation was a separate, legal entity for some purposes; respondent argues that corporation should be disregarded for purposes of the compensation paid to it by the Rockets.

OPINION

The issue before us is whether compensation paid by the Houston Rockets in return for the performance of personal services by petitioner is income to him or to his personal service corporation. [6] Whether a personal service corporation should be recognized as the recipient of income for tax purposes has been the subject of numerous cases. We recently had occasion to analyze this issue in the context of professional athletes. See Sargent v. Commissioner, 93 T.C. 572 (1989),

24: LEAVELL V CM

[**18] revd. 929 F.2d 1252 (8th Cir. 1991).

> 6 Respondent has not argued and has disavowed reliance on sec. 269A.

The facts in Sargent are analogous to those presented here. The taxpayers in Sargent were professional hockey players who formed personal service corporations and entered into contracts to furnish their services to their personal service corporations. The personal service corporations, in turn, contracted with the professional hockey club (the club) to furnish the services of the individual taxpayers to the club. The individual taxpayers also guaranteed that they would perform these services for the club.

In Sargent v. Commissioner, supra, we applied the assignment of income doctrine articulated in Lucas v. Earl, 281 U.S. 111, 114-115 [*149] (1930), in which the Supreme Court held that the predecessor to section 61 taxed salaries, fees, and compensation "to those who earned them", "that the tax could not be escaped by anticipatory arrangements [**19] and contracts however skilfully devised to prevent the salary when paid from vesting even for a second in the man who earned it", and that "no distinction can be taken according to the motives leading to the arrangement by which the fruits are attributed to a different tree from that on which they grew." This was reaffirmed in United States v. Basye, 410 U.S. 441, 450 (1973):

The principle of Lucas v. Earl, that he who earns income may not avoid taxation through anticipatory arrangements no matter how clever or subtle, has been repeatedly invoked by this Court and stands today as a cornerstone of our graduated income tax system. * * *

See also Commissioner v. Culbertson, 337 U.S. 733, 739-740 (1949) ("the first principle of income taxation * * * [is] that income must be taxed to him who earns it").

In deciding whether the compensation paid by the club was income of the individual hockey players, as opposed to income of their personal service corporations, we used the test for determining whether the individual players were "employees" of the club, as opposed to being employees of their personal service corporations. [**20] The criteria for making this determination are comparable to those used to determine whether an individual is an employee or an independent contractor. Sargent v. Commissioner, 93 T.C. at 578. [7] In the employee versus independent contractor analysis, the issue turns on whether the service recipient has the right to control the manner and means by which the services are performed. [8] Weber v.

24: LEAVELL V CM

Commissioner, 103 T.C. 378, 387 (1994). If the answer is yes, the service provider is an employee. If the [*150] answer is no, the service provider is an independent contractor. As an independent contractor, the individual service provider retains control over his activities. This control generally includes the right to grant an intermediate entity the right to control his services. Thus, individual persons who are independent contractors generally retain the right to choose to do business as a corporation. This same flexibility, however, does not exist where there is an employer-employee relationship between the individual service provider and the service recipient. [9] If the service provider's relationship with the service recipient [**21] gives the recipient the actual right to control the manner and means by which services are provided, the service provider cannot, with respect to those same services, simultaneously be an employee of his personal service corporation. Put simply, the individual service provider who is an employee of the recipient of his services cannot transfer control over his activities to his personal service corporation, because he cannot transfer something which he does not have.

7 As we have previously stated:

While the cases which deal with the common law factors usually involve a determination of whether a person is an employee or an independent contractor, the principles are equally applicable to determine by whom an individual is employed. [Professional & Executive Leasing, Inc. v. Commissioner, 89 T.C. 225, 232 (1987), affd. 862 F.2d 751 (9th Cir. 1988); fn. ref. and citation omitted.]

8 Throughout this opinion, we describe the test as the right to control the "manner and means" by which the services are performed. This test is also often described as control over the "method and means", "details and means", and various other formulations. See Weber v. Commissioner, 103 T.C. 378, 388-389 (1994); Professional & Executive Leasing, Inc. v. Commissioner, 89 T.C. at 231-232; sec. 31.3121(d)-1(c)(2), Employment Tax Regs.

[**22]

9 Whether an individual taxpayer is classified as an independent contractor or as an employee has important income and employment tax consequences, many of which would be nullified if

24: LEAVELL V CM

employees were able to alter their tax status simply by forming a personal service corporation.

Sargent was the first case involving a personal service corporation in which we applied the assignment of income doctrine by reference to the common law test for determining whether an employer-employee relationship existed between the service recipient and the individual service provider. The primary consideration for determining whether an individual is an employee of one organization or another is which of the two has the right to control the activities of the individual person whose status is in issue. Sargent v. Commissioner, 93 T.C. at 578. Whenever this issue arises in a setting involving a personal service corporation, there are three parties: The individual service provider, the recipient of the service, and the personal service corporation that has been formed as a legal entity [**23] through which the individual seeks to offer his services. In this context, it is critical to examine the reality of the relationship between the individual service provider and the recipient of those services.

In Sargent, we found that the taxpayers were employees of the club because the activities of the hockey players in question were subject to the control of the club. We, therefore, [*151] held that the compensation paid by the club was earned by the taxpayers as individual employees of the club and taxable to them individually. In Sargent, we distinguished previously decided cases that involved the issue of whether compensation paid by the recipient of personal services was income to the individual workers or their personal service corporations, because the issue of whether the service provider was an employee of the service recipient had not been examined. As a result, we found those previous cases inapplicable to our analysis. Sargent v. Commissioner, 93 T.C. at 580-583. [10]

> 10 In both Haag v. Commissioner, 88 T.C. 604 (1987), affd. without published opinion 855 F.2d 855 (8th Cir. 1988), and Keller v. Commissioner, 77 T.C. 1014 (1981), affd. 723 F.2d 58 (10th Cir. 1983), the individual taxpayers, prior to the formation of their personal service corporations, were partners in medical partnerships. As partners, the manner and means by which the services were performed were not controlled by the patients or clients of the taxpayers. Similarly, in Pacella v. Commissioner, 78 T.C. 604 (1982), the taxpayer was a medical professional who provided services to patients who had no right to control the manner and means by which the services were performed. In Johnson v. Commissioner, 78 T.C. 882 (1982), affd. without published opinion 734 F.2d 20 (9th Cir. 1984), there was no con-

24: LEAVELL V CM

tractual relationship between the personal service corporation and the team. Therefore, it was not necessary that we address the issue of whether the team or the personal service corporation had the right to control the manner and means by which the taxpayer provided his basketball services to the team. See infra note 11.

[**24] Because our decision in Sargent was reversed by the Court of Appeals for the Eighth Circuit, we will reconsider the legal principles upon which we relied in Sargent. We will begin our analysis by identifying the issues upon which we and the Court of

Appeals agree.

First, the Court of Appeals accepted our use of the employer-employee analysis as the proper focus for determining whether or not to apply the assignment of income doctrine. Sargent v. Commissioner, 929 F.2d at 1254. Second, the Court of Appeals accepted the principle that the most important single factor for determining the identity of the employer is answered by identifying who has the right to control the manner and means by which the individual's services are performed. Id. at 1256. In this respect, the Court of Appeals held that in order for a personal service corporation to be recognized as the employer: (1) It must have "the right to direct and control" the activities of the individual service provider "in some meaningful sense", and (2) "there must exist between the corporation and the person or entity (club) using the services a contract or [**25] similar indicium recognizing [*152] the corporation's controlling position." [11] Id. at 1256. In this respect, we also agree with the Court of Appeals.

> 11 In Johnson v. Commissioner, supra at 893, we found that this second prong of the two-part test had not been met. We found that there was no contract between the taxpayer's personal service corporation and the service recipient. Accordingly, for purposes of argument, we assumed, without deciding, that the first prong of the two-part test had been satisfied--i.e., that the personal service corporation had the right to direct and control the taxpayer's activities in "some meaningful sense." Id. at 891-892. In Johnson, we stated:
>
> We accept arguendo that the * * * [personal service corporation] agreement [with the taxpayer] was a valid contract * * *. We also accept arguendo that the * * * agreement gave * * * [the

24: LEAVELL V CM

personal service corporation] a right of control over [the taxpayer's] services * * * [Id.]

[**26] The Court of Appeals' reversal was based on its holding that the taxpayers were employees of their respective personal service corporations rather than employees of the professional hockey club. Id. at 1254. This holding was based on two points. First, the Court of Appeals concluded that we had used a doctrinaire approach requiring that any individual who provides services as a member of a "team" should be automatically considered an employee of the team organization. Thus, the Court of Appeals stated:

It seems to this Court that legal analysis is forgotten if we simply measure the control element of an employment relationship by whether the employee is or is not a member of a superficially defined "team." Eventually, the issue becomes mired in a game of definitions: If the organizational structure is itself mislabeled a "team," a personal service corporation, as a matter of law, is a forbidden tax deferment tool for each and every person providing his or her services to that organization. On the other hand, if the organization to which the services are provided is not defined as a "team," then those same service-providers are free to create a PSC and subject that PSC's legitimacy [**27] to traditional common law and tax code analysis, regardless of the level of control exerted over those persons by the organization. Such an arbitrary approach is specious at best. [Sargent v. Commissioner, 929 F.2d at 1256.]

We agree with the Court of Appeals that the mere use of the word "team" to describe the organization that is the recipient of personal services is not determinative of employer status. However, we do not believe that we applied such a superficial standard in Sargent.

In Sargent, we dealt with a specific professional sports organization that owned and operated a professional hockey team in the National Hockey League. In deciding that the taxpayers were employees of the organization that owned and operated the team, we relied on specific facts regarding the taxpayers' relationships with the professional hockey [*153] club. [12] The taxpayers in Sargent argued that, by virtue of their individual personal talents, they retained control of their own playing activities despite the specific elements of control that were retained and exercised by the club over when, where, how, and how much they would play. It was in this [**28] factual context that we said that the nature of team sports "must be taken into account in determining the existence of an employer-employee relationship in accordance with common law principles." Sargent v. Commissioner, 93 T.C. at 579. Nowhere in Sargent did we state or

24: LEAVELL V CM

imply that the mere description of the service recipient as a "team" would be determinative. [13] In light of our findings of fact in Sargent regarding the reality of the relationships between the individual players and the club, we discerned nothing to indicate that the personal service corporations had any "meaningful" control over the performance of the individual hockey players' activities as members of the hockey team.

12 Included in our findings of fact was that:

Each memorandum of agreement gave the club the right to sell, transfer or assign, or loan out the services of Sargent and Christoff, respectively. Each memorandum of agreement provided that Sargent and Christoff, respectively, would not, without the club's consent, engage in any other athletic sport nor make any public appearances, sponsorships, etc., relating to the services performed for the club. The club provided Sargent and Christoff with uniforms and hockey equipment during the years in issue. As between the club and petitioners, the club controlled the scheduling of the games in which the Minnesota North Stars team would play. During a game, the coach of the club had the responsibility of deciding which players would play and for how long and the strategy of play. The coach was also responsible for conducting the practices which the players were required to attend. Training camps were held by the club and were run by the coach with the assistance of the general manager. If a player with a contract failed to show up at training camp, he could be fined pursuant to the NHL rules. [Sargent v. Commissioner, 93 T.C. 572, 577 (1989), revd. 929 F.2d 1252 (8th Cir. 1991).] We also found that each of the individual taxpayers guaranteed to the club that he would personally render the services called for in the contracts between their personal service corporations and the club. Id. at 574, 576.

[**29]

13 As we have stated:

Whether or not an employer-employee relationship exists is a question which must be determined on the basis of the specific facts and circumstances involved. Simpson v. Commissioner, 64 T.C. 974, 984 (1975); Ellison v. Commissioner, 55 T.C. 142, 152

24: LEAVELL V CM

(1970); Hand v. Commissioner, 16 T.C. 1410, 1414 (1951). Sec. 31.3121(d)-1(c)(3), Employment Tax Regs. * * * [Professional & Executive Leasing, Inc. v. Commissioner, 89 T.C. 225, 232 (1987), affd. 862 F.2d 751 (9th Cir. 1988).] See also Weber v. Commissioner, 103 T.C. 378, 386-387 (1994).

The Court of Appeals' apparent reason for holding that the taxpayers in Sargent were employees of their personal service corporations, as opposed to the club, was the language of the written agreements between the individual taxpayers and their personal service corporations, and between the personal [*154] service corporations and the club, whose literal terms [**30] appeared to recognize the personal service corporations' controlling position as employers. Sargent v. Commissioner, 929 F.2d at 1256-1258. [14] The Court of Appeals did not refer to any other facts that would indicate that the personal service corporations in Sargent had a right to direct and control the activities of the individual taxpayers "in some meaningful sense." While we agree that contract terms are important in determining whether a personal service corporation is to be recognized as the true employer of the individual service provider, we do not believe that the mere existence of such terms in a contract is sufficient when the reality of the relationship is otherwise. As we have previously held:

A contract purporting to create an employer-employee relationship will not control where the common law factors (as applied to the facts and circumstances) establish that the relationship does not exist. In Bartels v. Birmingham, * * * [332 U.S. 126 (1947)], the Supreme Court was asked to determine whether certain orchestra members were employees of the orchestra leader or of the operators of various dance halls [**31] where they performed. After applying the common law rules to the facts of the case, the Court held that the orchestra leader was the employer (and therefore responsible for the employment tax) despite the formal contractual agreement designating the proprietors of the dance halls as the employers. * * * [Professional & Executive Leasing, Inc. v. Commissioner, 89 T.C. 225, 233 (1987), affd. 862 F.2d 751 (9th Cir. 1988).]

In Professional & Executive Leasing, the contracts literally purported to give control over the individual service providers to the taxpayer-corporation. Nevertheless, as the Court of Appeals for the Ninth Circuit observed: "The right to control, however, was at best illusory." Professional & Executive Leasing, Inc. v. Commissioner, 862 F.2d at 754.

14 The Court of Appeals for the Eighth Circuit's opinion perceives an inconsistency between our opinions in Sargent and

24: LEAVELL V CM

Pflug v. Commissioner, T.C. Memo. 1989-615. Sargent v. Commissioner, 929 F.2d 1252, 1257 (8th Cir. 1991). The issue before the Court in Pflug was whether the taxpayer (an actress) was an employee of her husband's wholly owned production corporation, as the taxpayer contended, or whether the taxpayer was an independent contractor subject to self-employment tax, as the Government contended. Considering only those arguments, on that narrow issue, in light of the particular facts presented, the Court in Pflug held that the taxpayer was an employee of her husband's wholly owned corporation. The assignment of income doctrine was not an issue in Pflug and neither party argued that the ultimate recipient of the taxpayer's personal services, as opposed to her husband's corporation, was her employer. The opinion in Pflug does not even cite Sargent. However, if one were to still perceive any inconsistency between Sargent and Pflug, it should be clear that our holding in Sargent, which was reviewed by the full Court, embodies this Court's position as opposed to any perceived inconsistent statement in a memorandum opinion.

[**32]

[*155] We will continue to examine all the facts and circumstances in order to determine the reality of who has control over the manner and means by which the individual service provider delivers services. Any other approach would simply elevate form over substance so as to thwart the assignment of income doctrine that requires compensation to be taxed to the person who earns it, regardless of "anticipatory arrangements and contracts however skilfully devised". Lucas v. Earl, 281 U.S. 111, 114-115 (1930). In this respect, we believe that Judge Arnold's dissent in Sargent captured the essence of that case when he wrote: "The idea that the coach issued orders to Sargent and Christoff in their capacity as corporate officers, which orders they then relayed to themselves as corporate employees, is fanciful." Sargent v. Commissioner, 929 F.2d at 1261. After carefully reconsidering our position in Sargent v. Commissioner, supra, in light of its reversal by the Court of Appeals for the Eighth Circuit, we conclude that our approach in Sargent was correct. [15] We now turn to an analysis of the facts in the instant [**33] case.

15 In Golsen v Commissioner, 54 T.C. 742, 757 (1970), affd. 445 F.2d 985 (10th Cir. 1971), we stated that we will follow a Court of Appeals' decision that is squarely in point where appeal

24: LEAVELL V CM

lies to that court. In the instant case, venue for appeal lies to the Court of Appeals for the Fifth Circuit.

We first look to what is clearly the most important factor--the right to control the manner and means by which the individual service provider renders the services for which compensation is being paid. [16] The Rockets wanted to acquire the professional basketball services of petitioner for a term of 2 years beginning in the fall of 1984. Being a member of the NBA, the Rockets were required to use the Uniform Player Contract drafted by the NBA. The variable terms of [*156] the contract for petitioner's services were negotiated between petitioner's attorney and the Rockets' general manager. Petitioner wanted the NBA Uniform Player Contract to be between his [**34] personal service corporation and the Rockets. The Rockets wanted to obtain petitioner's services and did not care if his services were obtained by way of a contract with petitioner's corporation, so long as they were able to secure petitioner's services under the terms and conditions required by the standard NBA Uniform Player Contract. Satisfied that this was possible, they were willing to, and did, enter into a standard player contract with petitioner's corporation. The contract was executed on December 11, 1984. The preprinted terms of the 1984 Uniform Player Contract are identical to player contracts entered into with individual players. However, the first paragraph identifies Allen Frazier Leavell, Inc., [17] as the party who is referred to thereafter as the "Player".

16 Factors commonly considered by courts in determining the existence of the employer-employee relationship are: (1) The right to control the details of the work; (2) furnishing the tools and the workplace; (3) withholding taxes, workmen's compensation, and unemployment insurance funds; (4) right to discharge; and (5) permanency of the relationship. Professional & Executive Leasing, Inc. v. Commissioner, 862 F.2d at 753 (citing United States v. Silk, 331 U.S. 704, 714-716 (1947); Simpson v. Commissioner, 64 T.C. 974, 984-985 (1975)).

Although each factor is important, the test usually considered fundamental is set out in a Treasury regulation:

"Generally, such relationship exists when the person for whom services are performed has the right to control and direct the individual who performs the services, not only as to the result to be accomplished by the work but also as to the details and means by which that result is accomplished. That is, an employee is subject to the will and control of the employer not only as to what

24: LEAVELL V CM

shall be done but how it shall be done. In this connection, it is not necessary that the employer actually direct or control the manner in which the services are performed; it is sufficient if he has the right to do so." [Id. (quoting sec. 31.3121(d)-1(c)(2), Employment Tax Regs.).]

[**35]

17 On the written contract, the term "Inc." was inserted by handwriting.

The remaining portions of the contract refer to the obligations of the "player" in a way that clearly indicates that the language of the contract contemplated binding a specific individual person with basketball playing skills to perform services for and under the specific supervision of the Rockets. The first numbered paragraph begins by stating that "The Club hereby employs the Player as a skilled basketball player for a term of two year(s)", and paragraph 9 states that

The Player represents and agrees that he has extraordinary and unique skill and ability as a basketball player, that the services to be rendered by him hereunder cannot be replaced or the loss thereof adequately compensated for in money damages, and that any breach by the Player of this contract will cause irreparable injury to the Club and to its assignees. * * *

The contract requires the "player" to render services under conditions that give the Rockets a great degree of control over his basketball services and many of his personal activities to [**36] the extent that they might affect his playing ability or reflect on the Rockets or the NBA. For example, the contract requires that the "player": Attend each training camp; play scheduled games; report at the time and place fixed by the Rockets in good physical condition; give his best services and loyalty to the Rockets; observe and comply with all [*157] requirements of the Rockets respecting conduct of its team and its players; play only for the Rockets or its assignees; keep in good physical condition throughout each season; agree to give immediate notice of any injury suffered by him; submit to a medical examination and treatment by a physician designated by the Rockets; and report to any other club to whom his contract has been assigned.

The contract also requires that the "player": Be neatly and fully attired in public and conduct himself according to the highest standards on and off the court; refrain from any conduct that is detrimental to the best interests of the Rockets or of the association; not engage in sports endangering his health or safety; allow the Rockets or the association to take his picture at such times as the Rockets or

24: LEAVELL V CM

association may designate; make himself [**37] available for interviews by representatives of the media conducted at reasonable times; agree to participate in all other reasonable promotional activities of the Rockets and the association; and conform his personal conduct to standards of good citizenship, good moral character, and good sportsmanship.

Under the contract, the Rockets had the right to impose fines, sanctions, and other disciplinary measures on the "player" for violating the requirements of the Rockets respecting conduct of its team and players. The contract also provides that the association could impose fines, sanctions, and other disciplinary measures.

The terms of the Uniform Player Contract exhibit an intent to give the Rockets a degree of control over the activities of an individual "player" that transcends the control most employers have over their employees. However, as written, the December 11, 1984, player contract, designated Allen Frazier Leavell, Inc., as the "player" rather than petitioner. The 1984 Uniform Player Contract made no specific reference to petitioner as an individual. The Rockets recognized this. While the Rockets were willing to obtain petitioner's services by executing a contract with [**38] his corporation, the Rockets were not willing to jeopardize the rights that they would have otherwise obtained by contracting with an individual player. This problem was solved by requiring petitioner to individually execute a written agreement with the Rockets, which was titled "Personal Guarantee By Player". In this agreement, petitioner promised that he would personally perform [*158] the services required of the "player" in accordance with the terms and conditions of the December 11, 1984, player contract. The consideration for petitioner's personal agreement to be bound to the terms of the NBA Uniform Player Contract was the Rockets' promise to pay compensation for his basketball services to corporation. Without petitioner's personal agreement, which was also executed on December 11, 1984, the Rockets would not have signed the Uniform Player Contract in question. With the agreement, the Rockets were in the same position with respect to their rights to control petitioner's activities as if he had personally signed the player contract. [18] Given these facts, the personal service corporation's rights to control the manner and means by which petitioner performed the basketball [**39] and related activities required by the player contract were at best illusory.

18 It is unclear from the record whether the Rockets were aware of, or even inquired about, the terms of the agreement between petitioner and his corporation. Had they inquired, they would have known that there was no written contract giving Allen

24: LEAVELL V CM

> Frazier Leavell, Inc., rights to petitioner's services. It is doubtful that the Rockets would have relied on an unwritten agreement, the terms of which may have existed only in petitioner's mind. However, by requiring petitioner's personal written agreement that he would individually provide the services and meet the obligation required of the "player", pursuant to the Dec. 11, 1984, Uniform Player Contract, these potential problems were obviated.

Petitioner argues that his point guard position placed him in a leadership position where he could control decisions about his and his teammates' playing tactics. However, the discretion inherent in petitioner's position as a skilled professional basketball [**40] player is not sufficient to remove him from employee status. It is well recognized that the extent of control necessary for a professional to qualify as an employee is less than that necessary for a nonprofessional. Professional & Executive Leasing, Inc. v. Commissioner, 862 F.2d 751 (9th Cir. 1988), affg. 89 T.C. 225 (1987). The type of discretion that petitioner had as a player is not sufficient to negate the overall control of the Rockets, who retained the right to direct petitioner's activities as to where, when, and how he was to perform services. The Rockets' coach had the right to control player activity during training camp, practice sessions, and games. If the Rockets were dissatisfied with petitioner's response to directives, they had the power to reduce his playing time, fine him, suspend him, or ultimately remove him from the team. [19]

> 19 The employer-employee relationship between the Rockets and petitioner is further evidenced by the fact that the Rockets, in association with the NBA of which it was a member, provided petitioner and other Rockets basketball players the facilities for training camps, practices, games, and paid the players' transportation, housing, and meal costs while players were attending away games. Likewise, the 2-year duration of the 1984 Uniform Player Contract is consistent with our finding that an employer-employee relationship existed between the Rockets and petitioner. See supra note 16.

[**41] [*159] Where, as in this case, an individual taxpayer attempts to provide his services through a personal service corporation, the determination of whether income derived from such services should be attributed to the individual taxpayer or his personal service corporation depends on who is the actual employer of the individual taxpayer. This determination must be based on all the facts and circumstances. Based on all the facts and circumstances in this case, we hold that

24: LEAVELL V CM

petitioner was the employee of the Rockets. It follows that the compensation paid by the Rockets in return for petitioner's services is attributable to petitioner. Decision will be entered under Rule 155.

CHABOT, PARKER, COHEN, GERBER, PARR, HALPERN, and BEGHE, JJ., agree with this majority opinion.

CHIECHI, J., concurs in the result only. APPENDIX

NATIONAL BASKETBALL ASSOCIATION UNIFORM PLAYER CONTRACT

(Rookie or Veteran--Two or More Seasons)

THIS AGREEMENT made this 11 day of December 1984 by and between the Houston Rockets (hereinafter called the "Club"), a member of the National Basketball Association (hereinafter called the "Association") and Allen Frazier Leavell, Inc. [**42] whose address is shown below (hereinafter called the "Player").

WITNESSETH:

In consideration of the mutual promises hereinafter contained, the parties hereto promise and agree as follows:

1. The Club hereby employs the Player as a skilled basketball player for a term of two year(s) from the 1st day of September 1984. The Player's employment during each year covered by this contract shall include [*160] attendance at each training camp, playing the games scheduled for the Club's team during each schedule season of the Association, playing all exhibition games scheduled by the Club during and prior to each schedule season, playing (if invited to participate) in each of the Association's All-Star Games and attending every event (including, but not limited to, the All-Star Game luncheon and/or banquet) conducted in association with such All-Star Games, and playing the playoff games subsequent to each schedule season. Players other than rookies will not be required to attend training camp earlier than twenty-eight days prior to the first game of each of the Club's schedule seasons. Rookies may be required to attend training camp at an earlier date. Exhibition games shall not [**43] be played on the three days prior to the opening of the Club's regular season schedule, nor on the day prior to a regularly scheduled game, nor on the day prior to and the day following the All-Star Game. Exhibition games prior to each schedule season shall not exceed eight (including intra-squad games for which admission is charged) and exhibition games during each regularly scheduled season shall not exceed three.

24: LEAVELL V CM

2. The Club agrees to pay the Player for rendering services described herein the sum of see addendum per year, (less all amounts required to be withheld from salary by Federal, State and local authorities and exclusive of any amount which the Player shall be entitled to receive from the Player Playoff Pool) in twelve equal semi-monthly payments beginning with the first of said payments on November 1st of each season above described and continuing with such payments on the first and fifteenth of each month until said sum is paid in full; provided, however, if the Club does not qualify for the playoffs, the payments for the year involved which would otherwise be due subsequent to the conclusion of the schedule season shall become due and payable immediately after the [**44] conclusion of the schedule season.

3. The Club agrees to pay all proper and necessary expenses of the Player, including the reasonable board and lodging expenses of the Player while playing for the Club "on the road" and during training camp if the Player is not then living at home. The Player, while "on the road" (and at training camp only if the Club does not pay for meals directly), shall be paid a meal expense allowance as set forth in the Agreement currently in effect between the National Basketball Association and National Basketball Players Association. No deductions from such meal expense allowance shall be made for meals served on an airplane. While the Player is at training camp (and if the Club does not pay for meals directly), the meal expense allowance shall be paid in weekly installments commencing with the first week of training camp. For the purposes of this paragraph, the Player shall be considered to be "on the road" from the time the Club leaves its home city until the time the Club arrives back at its home city. In addition, the Club agrees to pay $ 50.00 per week to the Player for the four weeks prior to the first game of each of the Club's schedule seasons that [**45] the Player is either in attendance at training camp or engaged in playing the exhibition schedule.

4. The Player agrees to observe and comply with all requirements of the Club respecting conduct of its team and its players, at all times whether [*161] on or off the playing floor. The Club may, from time to time during the continuance of this contract, establish reasonable rules for the government of its players "at home" and "on the road," and such rules shall be part of this contract as fully as if herein written and shall be binding upon the Player. For any violation of such rules or for any conduct impairing the faithful and thorough discharge of the duties incumbent upon the Player, the Club may impose reasonable fines upon the Player and deduct the amount thereof from any money due or to become due to the Player during the season in which such violation and/or conduct occurred. The Club may also suspend the Player for violation of any rules so established, and, upon such suspension, the compensation payable to the Player under this

24: LEAVELL V CM

contract may be reduced in the manner provided in the Agreement currently in effect between the National Basketball Association and National Basketball [**46] Players Association. When the Player is fined or suspended, he shall be given notice in writing, stating the amount of the fine or the duration of the suspension and the reason therefor.

5. The Player agrees (a) to report at the time and place fixed by the Club in good physical condition; (b) to keep himself throughout each season in good physical condition; (c) to give his best services, as well as his loyalty to the Club, and to play basketball only for the Club and its assignees; (d) to be neatly and fully attired in public and always to conduct himself on and off the court according to the highest standards of honesty, morality, fair play and sportsmanship; and (e) not to do anything which is detrimental to the best interests of the Club or of the Association.

6. (a) If the Player, in the judgment of the Club's physician, is not in good physical condition at the date of his first scheduled game for the Club, or if, at the beginning of or during any season, he fails to remain in good physical condition (unless such condition results directly from any injury sustained by the Player as a direct result of participating in any basketball practice or game played for the Club during [**47] such season), so as to render the Player, in the judgment of the Club's physician, unfit to play skilled basketball, the Club shall have the right to suspend such Player until such time as, in the judgment of the Club's physician, the Player is in sufficiently good physical condition to play skilled basketball. In the event of such suspension, the annual sum payable to the Player for each season during such suspension shall be reduced in the same proportion as the length of the period during which, in the judgment of the Club's physician, the Player is unfit to play skilled basketball, bears to the length of such season.

(b) If the Player is injured as a direct result of participating in any basketball practice or game played for the Club, the Club will pay the Player's reasonable hospitalization and medical expenses (including doctor's bills), provided that the hospital and doctor are selected by the Club, and provided further that the Club shall be obligated to pay only those expenses incurred as a result of continuous medical treatment caused solely by and relating directly to the injury sustained by the Player. If, in the judgment of the Club's physician, the Player's injuries [**48] resulted directly from playing for the Club and render him unfit to play skilled basketball, then, so long as such unfitness continues, but in no event after the Player [*162] has received his full salary for the season in which the injury was sustained, the Club shall pay to the Player the compensation prescribed in paragraph 2 of this contract for such season. The Club's obligations hereunder shall

24: LEAVELL V CM

be reduced by any workmen's compensation benefits (which, to the extent permitted by law, the Player hereby assigns to the Club) and any insurance provided for by the Club whether paid or payable to the Player, and the Player hereby releases the Club from any and every other obligation or liability arising out of any such injuries.

(c) The Player hereby releases and waives every claim he may have against the Association and every member of the Association, and against every director, officer, stockholder, trustee, partner, and employee of the Association and/or any member of the Association (excluding persons employed as players by any such member), arising out of or in connection with any fighting or other form of violent and/or unsportsmanlike conduct occurring (on or adjacent to [**49] the playing floor or any facility used for practices or games) during the course of any practice and/or any exhibition, championship season, and/or play-off game.

7. The Player agrees to give the Club's coach, or to the Club's physician, immediate notice of any injury suffered by him, including the time, place, cause and nature of such injury.

8. Should the Player suffer an injury as provided in the preceding section, he will submit himself to a medical examination and treatment by a physician designated by the Club. Such examination when made at the request of the Club shall be at its expense, unless made necessary by some act or conduct of the Player contrary to the terms of this contract.

9. The Player represents and agrees that he has extraordinary and unique skill and ability as a basketball player, that the services to be rendered by him hereunder cannot be replaced or the loss thereof adequately compensated for in money damages, and that any breach by the Player of this contract will cause irreparable injury to the Club and to its assignees. Therefore, it is agreed that in the event it is alleged by the Club that the Player is playing, attempting or threatening to play, or [**50] negotiating for the purpose of playing, during the term of this contract, for any other person, firm, corporation or organization, the Club and its assignees (in addition to any other remedies that may be available to them judicially or by way of arbitration) shall have the right to obtain from any court or arbitrator having jurisdiction, such equitable relief as may be appropriate, including a decree enjoining the Player from any further such breach of this contract, and enjoining the Player from playing basketball for any other person, firm, corporation or organization during the term of this contract. In any suit, action or arbitration proceeding brought to obtain such relief, the Player does hereby waive his right, if any, to trial by jury, and does hereby waive his right, if any, to interpose any

24: LEAVELL V CM

counterclaim or set-off for any cause whatever.

10. The Club shall have the right to sell, exchange, assign or transfer this contract to any other professional basketball Club and the Player agrees to accept such sale, exchange, assignment or transfer and to faithfully perform and carry out this contract with the same force and effect as if it had been entered into by the Player with [**51] the assignee Club instead [*163] of with this Club. The Player further agrees that, should the Club contemplate the sale, exchange, assignment or transfer of this contract to another professional basketball Club or Clubs, the Club's physician may furnish to the physicians and officials of such other Club or Clubs all relevant medical information relating to the Player.

11. In the event that the Player's contract is sold, exchanged, assigned or transferred to any other professional basketball Club, all reasonable expenses incurred by the Player in moving himself and his family from the home city of the Club to the home city of the Club to which such sale, exchange, assignment or transfer is made, as a result thereof, shall be paid by the assignee Club. Such assignee Club hereby agrees that its acceptance of the assignment of this contract constitutes agreement on its part to make such payment.

12. In the event that the Player's contract is assigned to another Club the Player shall forthwith be notified orally or by a notice in writing, delivered to the Player personally or delivered or mailed to his last known address, and the Player shall report to the assignee Club within forty-eight [**52] hours after said notice has been received or within such longer time for reporting as may be specified in said notice. If the Player does not report to the Club to which his contract has been assigned within the aforesaid time, the Player may be suspended by such Club and he shall lose the sums which would otherwise be payable to him as long as the suspension lasts.

13. The Club will not pay and the Player will not accept any bonus or anything of value for winning any particular Association game or series of games or for attaining a certain position by the Club's team in the standing of the league operated by the Association as of a certain date, other than the final standing of the team.

14. This contract shall be valid and binding upon the Club and the Player immediately upon its execution. The Club agrees to file a copy of this contract with the Commissioner of the Association prior to the first game of the schedule season or within forty-eight (48) hours of its execution, whichever is later; provided, however, the Club agrees that if the contract is executed prior to the start of the

24: LEAVELL V CM

schedule season and if the Player so requests, it will file a copy of this contract with the [**53] Commissioner of the Association within thirty (30) days of its execution, but not later than the date hereinabove specified. If pursuant to the Constitution and By-Laws of the Association, the Commissioner disapproves this contract within ten (10) days after the filing thereof in his office, this contract shall thereupon terminate and be of no further force or effect and the Club and the Player shall thereupon be relieved of their respective rights and liabilities thereunder.

15. The Player and the Club acknowledge that they have read and are familiar with Section 35 of the Constitution of the Association, a copy of which, as in effect on the date of this Agreement, is attached hereto. Such section provides that the Commissioner and the Board of Governors of the Association are empowered to impose fines upon the Player and/or upon the Club for causes and in the manner provided in such section. The Player and the Club, each for himself and itself, promises promptly to pay [*164] to the said Association each and every fine imposed upon him or it in accordance with the provisions of said section and not permit any such fine to be paid on his or its behalf by anyone other than the [**54] person or Club fined. The Player authorizes the Club to deduct from his salary payments any fines imposed on or assessed against him.

16. Notwithstanding any provisions of the Constitution or of the By-Laws of the Association, it is agreed that if the Commissioner of the Association shall, in his sole judgment, find that the Player has bet, or has offered or attempted to bet, money or anything of value on the outcome of any game participated in by any Club which is a member of the Association, the Commissioner shall have the power in his sole discretion to suspend the Player indefinitely or to expel him as a player for any member of the Association and the Commissioner's finding and decision shall be final, binding, conclusive and unappealable. The Player hereby releases the Commissioner and waives every claim he may have against the Commissioner and/or the Association, and against every member of the Association, and against every director, officer, stockholder, trustee and partner of every member of the Association, for damages and for all claims and demands whatsoever arising out of or in connection with the decision of the Commissioner.

17. The Player and the Club acknowledge [**55] and agree that the Player's participation in other sports may impair or destroy his ability and skill as a basketball player. The Player and the Club recognize and agree that the Player's participation in basketball out of season may result in injury to him. Accordingly, the Player agrees that he will not engage in sports endangering his health or safety (including, but not limited to, professional boxing or wrestling, motorcycling,

24: LEAVELL V CM

moped-riding, auto racing, sky-diving, and hang-gliding); and that, except with the written consent of the Club, he will not engage in any game or exhibition of basketball, football, baseball, hockey, lacrosse, or other athletic sport, under penalty of such fine and suspension as may be imposed by the Club and/or the Commissioner of the Association. Nothing contained herein shall be intended to require the Player to obtain the written consent of the Club in order to enable the Player to participate in, as an amateur, the sport of golf, tennis, handball, swimming, hiking, softball or volleyball.

18. The Player agrees to allow the Club or the Association to take pictures of the Player, alone or together with others, for still photographs, motion pictures [**56] or television, at such times as the Club or the Association may designate, and no matter by whom taken may be used in any manner desired by either of them for publicity or promotional purposes. The rights in any such pictures taken by the Club or by the Association shall belong to the Club or the Association, as their interests may appear. The Player agrees that, during each playing season, he will not make public appearances, participate in radio or television programs or permit his picture to be taken or write or sponsor newspaper or magazine articles or sponsor commercial products without the written consent of the Club, which shall not be withheld except in the reasonable interests of the Club or professional basketball. Upon request, the Player shall consent to and make himself available for interviews by representatives of the media conducted at [*165] reasonable times. In addition to the foregoing, the Player agrees to participate, upon request, in all other reasonable promotional activities of the Club and the Association.

19. The Player agrees that he will not, during the term of this contract, directly or indirectly entice, induce, persuade or attempt to entice, induce [**57] or persuade any player or coach who is under contract to any member of the Association to enter into negotiations for or relating to his services as a basketball player or coach, nor shall he negotiate for or contract for such services, except with the prior written consent of such member of the Association. Breach of this paragraph, in addition to the remedies available to the Club, shall be punishable by fine to be imposed by the Commissioner of the Association and to be payable to the Association out of any compensation due or to become due to the Player hereunder or out of any other moneys payable to him as a basketball player. The Player agrees that the amount of such fine may be withheld by the Club and paid over to the Association.

20. (a) In the event of an alleged default by the Club in the payments to the Player provided for by this contract, or in the event of an alleged failure by the

24: LEAVELL V CM

Club to perform any other material obligation agreed to be performed by the Club hereunder, the Player shall notify both the Club and the Association in writing of the facts constituting such alleged default or alleged failure. If neither the Club nor the Association shall cause such alleged [**58] default or alleged failure to be remedied within five (5) days after receipt of such written notice, the National Basketball Players Association shall, on behalf of the Player, have the right to request that the dispute concerning such alleged default or alleged failure be referred immediately to the Impartial Arbitrator in accordance with Article XXI, Section 2(h), of the Agreement currently in effect between the National Basketball Association and National Basketball Players Association. If, as a result of such arbitration, an award issues in favor of the Player, and if neither the Club nor the Association complies with such award within ten (10) days after the service thereof, the Player shall have the right, by a further written notice to the Club and the Association, to terminate this contract.

(b) The Club may terminate this contract upon written notice to the Player (but only after complying with the waiver procedure provided for in subparagraph (f) of this paragraph (20) if the Player shall do any of the following:

(1) at any time, fail, refuse or neglect to conform his personal conduct to standards of good citizenship, good moral character and good sportsmanship, to keep [**59] himself in first class physical condition or to obey the Club's training rules; or

(2) at any time, fail, in the sole opinion of the Club's management, to exhibit sufficient skill or competitive ability to qualify to continue as a member of the Club's team (provided, however, that if this contract is terminated by the Club, in accordance with the provisions of this subparagraph, during the period from the fifty-sixth day after the first game of any schedule season of the Association through the end of such schedule season, the Player shall be entitled to receive his full salary for said season); or

[*166] (3) at any time, fail, refuse or neglect to render his services hereunder or in any other manner materially breach this contract.

(c) If this contract is terminated by the Club by reason of the Player's failure to render his services hereunder due to disability caused by an injury to the Player resulting directly from his playing for the Club and rendering him unfit to play skilled basketball, and notice of such injury is given by the Player as provided herein, the Player shall be entitled to receive his full salary for the season in which the injury was sustained, less all workmen's [**60] compensation benefits (which,

24: LEAVELL V CM

to the extent permitted by law, the Player hereby assigns to the Club) and any insurance provided for by the Club paid or payable to the Player by reason of said injury.

(d) If this contract is terminated by the Club during the period designated by the Club for attendance at training camp, payment by the Club of the Player's board, lodging and expense allowance during such period to the date of termination and of the reasonable travelling expenses of the Player to his home city and the expert training and coaching provided by the Club to the Player during the training season shall be full payment to the Player.

(e) If this contract is terminated by the Club during any playing season, except in the case provided for in subparagraph (c) of this paragraph 20, the Player shall be entitled to receive as full payment hereunder a sum of money which, when added to the salary which he has already received during such season, will represent the same proportionate amount of the annual sum set forth in paragraph 2 hereof as the number of days of such season then past bears to the total number of days of such schedule season, plus the reasonable travelling expenses [**61] of the Player to his home.

(f) If the Club proposes to terminate this contract in accordance with subparagraph (b) of this paragraph 20, the applicable waiver procedure shall be as follows:

(1) The Club shall request the Association Commissioner to request waivers from all other Clubs. Such waiver request must state that it is for the purpose of terminating this contract and it may not be withdrawn.

(2) Upon receipt of the waiver request, any other Club may claim assignment of this contract at such waiver price as may be fixed by the Association, the priority of claims to be determined in accordance with the Association's Constitution or By-Laws.

(3) If this contract is so claimed, the Club agrees that it shall, upon the assignment of this contract to the claiming Club, notify the Player of such assignment as provided in paragraph 12 hereof, and the Player agrees he shall report to the assignee Club as provided in said paragraph 12.

(4) If the contract is not claimed, the Club shall promptly deliver written notice of termination to the Player at the expiration of the waiver period.

(5) To the extent not inconsistent with the foregoing provisions of this subpara-

24: LEAVELL V CM

graph (f) the waiver [**62] procedures set forth in the Constitution and By-Laws of the Association, a copy of which, as in effect on the date of this agreement, is attached hereto, shall govern.

(g) Upon any termination of this contract by the Player, all obligations of the Club to pay compensation shall cease on the date of termination, [*167] except the obligation of the Club to pay the Player's compensation to said date.

21. In the event of any dispute arising between the Player and the Club relating to any matter arising under this contract, or concerning the performance or interpretation thereof (except for a dispute arising under paragraph 9 hereof), such dispute shall be resolved in accordance with the Grievance and Arbitration Procedure set forth in the Agreement currently in effect between the National Basketball Association and the National Basketball Players Association.

22. Nothing contained in this contract or in any provision of the Constitution or By-Laws of the Association shall be construed to constitute the Player a member of the Association or to confer upon him any of the rights or privileges of a member thereof.

Addendum

Salary

1984-85 $ 132,000

Bonus (Limited To $ 18,000 [**63] Total)

If Rockets win 30 games, Player earns $ 1,000 and $ 1,000 for each win beyond 30 for the 1984-85 season.

If Player averages more than ten minutes per game for the 1984-85 season, player earns $ 5,000.

If Player is among the top three on the Club in average assists for the 1984-85 season, player earns $ 5,000.

If the Player is among the top three on the club in average steals for the 1984-85 season, Player earns $ 5,000.

Any bonus earned will be paid upon completion of the 1985 NBA playoffs.

Salary

24: LEAVELL V CM

1985-86 $ 200,000

23. This contract contains the entire agreement between the parties and there are no oral or written inducements, promises or agreements except as contained herein.

EXAMINE THIS CONTRACT CAREFULLY BEFORE SIGNING IT

IN WITNESS WHEREOF the Player has hereunto signed his name and the Club has caused this contract to be executed by this duly authorized officer.

Witnesses:

/s/ Ray Patterson

/s/ James A. Foley

By Ray Patterson

Title: President and General Manger

[*168] /s/ Lance Jay Luchnick

Attorney At Law

/s/ Allen Leavell

Allen Leavell Player

Player's Address 6735 Gentle Bend, Houston, Tx. 77069

RECEIVED & RECORDED

[**64] DEC 13, 1984

/s/ David J. Stern

COMMISSIONER

EXCERPT FROM CONSTITUTION OF THE ASSOCIATION MISCONDUCT OF OFFICIALS AND OTHERS

35. (a) The provisions of this Section shall govern all members, and officers, managers, coaches, players and other employees of a member and all officials and other employees of the Association, all hereinafter referred to as "persons." Each

24: LEAVELL V CM

member shall provide and require in every contract with any of its officers, managers, coaches, players or other employees that they shall be bound and governed by the provisions of this Section. Each member, at the direction of the Board of Governors or the Commissioner, as the case may be, shall take such action as the Board or the Commissioner may direct in order to effectuate the purposes of this Section.

(b) The Commissioner shall direct the dismissal and perpetual disqualification from any further association with the Association or any of its members, of any person found by the Commissioner after a hearing to have been guilty of offering, agreeing, conspiring, aiding or attempting to cause any game of basketball to result otherwise than on its merits.

(c) Any person who gives, makes, issues, authorizes or endorses [**65] any statement having, or designed to have, an effect prejudicial or detrimental to the best interests of basketball or of the Association or of a member or its team, shall be liable to a fine not exceeding $ 1,000, to be imposed by the Board of Governors. The member whose officer, manager, coach, player or other employee has been so fined shall pay the amount of the fine should such person fail to do so within ten (10) days of its imposition.

(d) If in the opinion of the Commissioner any other act or conduct of a person at or during a pre-season, championship, playoff or exhibition game has been prejudicial to or against the best interests of the Association or the game of basketball, the Commissioner shall impose upon such person a fine not exceeding $ 1,000 in the case of a member, officer, manager or coach of a member, or $ 10,000 in the case of a player or other employee, or may order for a time the suspension of any such person from any connection or duties with pre-season, championship, playoff or exhibition games, or he may order both such fine and suspension.

(e) The Commissioner shall have the power to suspend for a definite or indefinite period, or to impose a fine not [**66] exceeding $ 1,000, or inflict both such suspension and fine upon any person who, in his opinion, shall have been guilty of conduct prejudicial or detrimental to the Association.

[*169] (f) The Commissioner shall have the power to levy a fine of $ 1,000 upon any Governor or Alternate Governor who, in the opinion of the Commissioner, has been guilty of making statements to the press damaging to the Association.

(g) Any person who, directly or indirectly, entices, induces, persuades or attempts to entice, induce, or persuade any player, coach, trainer, general manager or any other person who is under contract to any other member of the Association to

24: LEAVELL V CM

enter into negotiations for or relating to his services or negotiates or contracts for such services shall, on being charged with such tampering, be given an opportunity to answer such charges after due notice and the Commissioner shall have the power to decide whether or not the charges have been sustained; in the event his decision is that the charges have been sustained, then the Commissioner shall have the power to suspend such person for a definite or indefinite period, or to impose a fine not exceeding $ 5,000, or inflict both such [**67] suspension and fine upon any such person.

(h) Any person who, directly or indirectly, wagers money or anything of value on the outcome of any game played by a team in the league operated by the Association shall, on being charged with such wagering, be given an opportunity to answer such charges after due notice, and the decision of the Commissioner shall be final, binding and conclusive and unappealable. The penalty for such offense shall be within the absolute and sole discretion of the Commissioner and may include a fine, suspension, expulsion and/or perpetual disqualification from further association with the Association or any of its members.

(i) Except for a penalty imposed under subparagraph (h) of this paragraph 35, the decisions and acts of the Commissioner pursuant to paragraph 35 shall be appealable to the Board of Governors who shall determine such appeals in accordance with such rules and regulations as may be adopted by the Board in its absolute and sole discretion.

CONCUR BY: SWIFT

CONCUR

SWIFT, J., concurring in the result only: Upon further consideration and with the benefit of the opinion of the U.S. Court of Appeals for the Eighth Circuit in Sargent v. Commissioner, 929 F.2d 1252 (8th Cir. 1991), [**68] revg. 93 T.C. 572 (1989), I believe the majority opinion incorrectly relies too heavily on employee-independent contractor principles in analyzing the relationships of petitioner and his personal service corporation (PSC) with the Rockets. I would decide the issue before us on the basis of the two-pronged control or contractual analysis of Johnson v. Commissioner, 78 T.C. 882 (1982), affd. without published opinion 734 F.2d 20 (9th Cir. 1984), that traditionally has been used in analyzing the issue of the assignment of income as between a PSC and its individual owners. Under that analysis and based on certain undisputed [*170] and particularly pertinent facts in this case, I believe that a conclusion would be required herein that petitioner individually, and not petitioner's PSC, is to be charged with the income

24: LEAVELL V CM

relating to petitioner's services as a basketball player for the Houston Rockets.

Employee-Independent Contractor Analysis

After expressly finding that petitioner entered into an exclusive employment contract with his PSC for his basketball services (see majority op. p. 142) and [**69] that petitioner's PSC entered into a contract to provide basketball services to the Rockets (majority op. p. 142), the majority's analysis focuses on the "control" that is exercised by the Rockets and by the Rockets' coach over petitioner as a basketball player, and the majority concludes that petitioner was an "employee" of the Rockets with regard to such services and therefore that the income received from the Rockets should be charged or assigned to petitioner individually, not to petitioner's PSC. This analysis is directly contrary to and inconsistent with the majority's findings that petitioner had an employment contract with his PSC for his basketball services and that petitioner's PSC contracted to provide basketball services to the Rockets. Moreover, the majority opinion overlooks the fact that the team or coach's control that is exercised over players on competitive sports teams is inherent in team sports. Such control has little, if anything, to do with whether the player is an employee of, or an independent contractor with, the team. Such control simply reflects the way team sports are played.

Whether one considers a Little League baseball team, a high school basketball [**70] or wrestling team, a college football team, or a professional basketball, baseball, football, hockey, or soccer team, one must acknowledge that with each team sport, with each team, with each coach, and with each player, in order for the team to win and to be competitive, the team and the coach control many aspects of the game and of the individual player's participation in each game and on the team. Such control, in the context of competitive team sports, is simply the way the game is played by everyone--male and female, volunteer and professional, independent contractor and employee. The team simply plays better when [*171] the players are coached, when the players play as a team, and when the coach has control over most aspects of the game and of the individual player's participation on the team.

Upon further consideration of participation in team sports in the above light, it is evident that the control that is exercised by teams and by coaches over individual players on the teams has little to do with whether a particular individual player is an employee or an independent contractor of the team (and it certainly tells us little to nothing about whether the player is an employee [**71] of a PSC). In each situation, the game is played essentially the same. The coach's control is essentially the same. The nature of and degree of control that the team and coach exercise

24: LEAVELL V CM

are not affected by whether the player treats himself or herself as a direct employee of the team or as an employee of his or her PSC to which the employee is attempting to attribute the income received from the team.

It should be noted that the parties herein, with regard to petitioner's relationship with the Rockets, do not make an employee-independent contractor argument or analysis in their briefs, and they do not here ask us to determine whether petitioner was an employee or independent contractor of the Rockets. We are asked here simply to apply traditional assignment-of-income principles to the facts before us, to evaluate the bona fide nature of petitioner's alleged contract with his PSC (not just the existence of some amorphous oral contract with no terms), and to evaluate whether the written contract with the Rockets for petitioner's basketball services was, in substance and reality, a contract with petitioner, not with petitioner's PSC.

Assignment of Income

Ever since the Court of [**72] Appeals for the Tenth Circuit's decision in United States v. Empey, 406 F.2d 157 (10th Cir. 1969), it has been clear that even though PSC's may be generally recognized as viable corporations for Federal income tax purposes under Moline Properties, Inc. v. Commissioner, 319 U.S. 436 (1943), Federal income tax adjustments may still be appropriate with regard to particular income received for particular services of the individual owners of the PSC's. [*172] See, e.g., Keller v. Commissioner, 77 T.C. 1014 (1981), affd. 723 F.2d 58 (10th Cir. 1983), in which the taxpayer's PSC was recognized as a legitimate corporation and some income received by the PSC was taxed to the PSC, but certain other income received by the PSC was taxed to the individual owner of the PSC.

Under the case authority, the fact that a PSC is a viable corporation and has a legitimate business purpose will not preclude the application of the assignment of income doctrine or adjustments under section 482 with respect to particular income received by the PSC where the contractual rights of the PSC [**73] vis-a-vis the service recipient with regard to the particular income in question are not established by valid contracts--first, between the service provider and the PSC; and second, between the PSC and the service recipient. See Johnson v. Commissioner, 78 T.C. at 890.

As we explained in Johnson v. Commissioner, supra at 891, a case involving facts similar to the facts of this case:

Given the inherent impossibility of logical application of a per se actual earner test, a more refined inquiry has arisen in the form of who controls the earning of

24: LEAVELL V CM

the income. An examination of the case law from Lucas v. Earl hence reveals two necessary elements before the * * * [PSC], rather than its * * * [service provider], may be considered the controller of the income. First, the * * * [service provider] must be * * * an employee of the * * * [PSC] whom the * * * [PSC] has the right to direct or control in some meaningful sense. Second, there must exist between the * * * [PSC] and the * * * [service recipient] a contract or similar indicium recognizing the * * * [PSC's] controlling position. [Citations and fn. refs. omitted.]

In Sargent v. Commissioner, 929 F.2d at 1256-1257, [**74] the above statement of this traditional test was approved and quoted verbatim by the Court of Appeals for the Eighth Circuit, and the Court of Appeals explained further--

the Tax Court * * * [in Johnson] ultimately held the contracts to be dispositive of the issue of control:

* * * *

Ultimately, * * * [the taxpayer] was required to pay individual income tax on the entire amount paid to his PSC, but only because his PSC had no contractual arrangement with the * * * [service recipient]. Said the Tax Court regarding the second prong of the "control" test: "[c]rucial is the fact that there was no contract or agreement between the * * * [service recipient] and [the PSC]." We are not faced with such a dilemma in this [*173] case. Not only did * * * [the service provider] have a contractual arrangement with their respective PSC's, thereby passing the first prong of the analysis, each PSC also had a contractual relationship with the * * * [service recipient]. Consistent with its analysis in the past, the Tax Court in Johnson concluded that the existence of bona fide contracts between the parties satisfied the requisite elements of control. * * * [Citation omitted; emphasis [**75] added.]

In Sargent v. Commissioner, supra, our opinion at 93 T.C. 572 (1989) was reversed by the Court of Appeals for the Eighth Circuit, but mainly because the Eighth Circuit rejected the team control test that we had enunciated in our opinion. Because the Eighth Circuit concluded that the facts of Sargent established the existence of the necessary bona fide contracts between the service providers and the PSC's and between the PSC's and the service recipients, the income was treated by the Eighth Circuit as earned by the PSC's.

The facts of this case are more similar to the facts of Johnson v. Commissioner, supra, and, in my opinion, this case should be controlled by the two-pronged control or bona fide contract test set forth in Johnson v. Commissioner, supra.

24: LEAVELL V CM

In this case, petitioner did not have a written contract with his PSC, and petitioner has not established any of the specific terms and conditions of a bona fide oral contract between petitioner and his PSC.

A written contract did exist with the Rockets, but in that written contract certain corporate formalities were not adhered [**76] to and significant irregularities appear in that petitioner, not his PSC, signed the contract as the player and contracting party. On the first page of the 1984 Uniform Player Contract with the Rockets (1984 Contract), petitioner's individual given first name, his given middle name, and his last name (namely, "Allen Frazier Leavell") are typed in as the "Player" and as a party to the contract. The word "Inc." is handwritten next to petitioner's full given name without any initials or date indicating when the word "Inc." was added to the document. Also, when the word "Inc." was added in handwriting, petitioner's given middle name was not deleted from the contract.

On the signature line on the last page of the 1984 Contract with the Rockets, only petitioner's individual name appears as the "Player" and as a party to the contract. There is no indication on the signature line that petitioner was signing [*174] the 1984 Contract as an officer or representative of his PSC. Nowhere in the 1984 Contract does the correct name of petitioner's PSC (namely, Allen Leavell, Inc.) appear.

In connection with the 1984 Contract, the Rockets required that petitioner individually execute a personal [**77] guarantee in which petitioner personally and individually agreed to play professional basketball for the Rockets. Under the terms of the personal guarantee, petitioner agreed to be personally bound by all of the terms and conditions set forth in the 1984 Contract, and petitioner agreed to perform the professional basketball services described in the 1984 Contract.

Earlier, in 1983, with respect to petitioner's professional basketball services for the Rockets during the 1983-84 basketball season, a written contract (1983 Contract) with the Rockets was entered into reflecting terms similar to the terms of the 1984 Contract. On the first page of the 1983 Contract, petitioner's PSC is named as the "Player" and as a party to the contract. On the signature line of the 1983 Contract, however, only petitioner's individual name appears as the "Player" and as a party to the contract. There is no indication on the signature line that petitioner was signing the 1983 Contract as an officer or representative of his PSC.

Most, if not all, of the specific terms and the specific language of the 1984 Contract with the Rockets implicitly speak in terms of petitioner individually as

24: LEAVELL V CM

the "Player" [**78] governed by the contract. For example, only petitioner, individually, not his PSC, could possibly play "10 minutes per game" or be "one of the top three players in assists or steals".

Additionally, the Rockets did not rely on the contract with petitioner's PSC but required petitioner to sign a personal guarantee, thereby indicating the Rocket's reliance not on the 1984 Contract, but rather reliance on the personal guarantee and on petitioner individually for performance under the contract.

The majority opinion defers to the trial judge's finding that an oral contract existed between petitioner and his PSC. The mere existence of a contract, however, is in my opinion insufficient in and of itself to establish the bona fide nature of the contract. Petitioner must prove that the contract contained essential terms that establish the bona fide nature of the contract. Those terms, if they existed, are missing from the record in this case.

[*175] In summary, my suggested analysis in this case in favor of respondent is consistent with the decided cases in this area, and it is based on the cumulative effect of the following three points: (1) The record is inadequate to determine the substance [**79] and terms of any bona fide oral contract between petitioner and petitioner's PSC; (2) the 1984 Contract with the Rockets contained irregularities inconsistent with petitioner's position in this case that he had a bona fide contract with his PSC that controlled the performance of his basketball services for the Rockets; and (3) the Rockets required petitioner individually to provide a personal guarantee.

I emphasize that the contractual irregularities and deficiencies discussed and highlighted in this side opinion are not disputed. They are acknowledged in the majority opinion, and they should, in my opinion, control the outcome of this case. They lead to the conclusion that petitioner, not his PSC, is to be charged with the income received from the Rockets.

Section 269A

In 1982, Congress enacted section 269A, applicable to years beginning after December 31, 1982, in response to court decisions involving the relationship between the assignment of income doctrine and the use of closely held PSC's. Congress intended that section 269A overturn the decisions reached in cases like Keller v. Commissioner, 77 T.C. 1014 (1981), affd. 723 F.2d 58 (10th Cir. 1983), [**80] where an individual service provider owner of a PSC attempts to attribute income to the PSC that was in substance earned by the individual service provider. H. Conf. Rept. 97-760, at 633-634 (1982), 1982-2 C.B. 600, 679-680.

24: LEAVELL V CM

Generally, section 269A allows respondent to reallocate income from a PSC to a service-provider owner if substantially all of the services are performed for one other entity, and if the principal purpose for forming the PSC or the principal use of the PSC is to avoid or evade Federal income tax. It is significant that in enacting section 269A Congress did not inject into that remedial statute the employee-independent contractor analysis and factors that the majority utilizes in its analysis (i.e., the employee-versus-independent-contractor status of the individual service provider to the service recipient is simply not a factor).

[*176] The applicability and scope of section 269A has not yet been addressed in any published opinion. In this case, respondent, without adequate explanation, has conceded that the facts before us are not within the scope of section 269A. I suggest that in future similar situations respondent not shy away [**81] from utilizing the statutory provisions Congress has provided to address adjustments involving the assignment of income between PSC's and individual owners of the PSC's.

DISSENT BY: LARO

DISSENT

LARO, J., dissenting: The majority clings tightly to the principles underlying the "team-sports doctrine" developed in Sargent v. Commissioner, 93 T.C. 572 (1989), revd. 929 F.2d 1252 (8th Cir. 1991). [1] With this adherence, I cannot agree and must respectfully dissent.

> 1 I use the term "team-sports doctrine" to refer to the rationale of Sargent v. Commissioner, 93 T.C. 572 (1989), revd. 929 F.2d 1252 (8th Cir. 1991), that effectively precludes a "team member" from incorporating his or her personal services. Although the majority opinion states that "Nowhere in Sargent did we state or imply that the mere description of the service recipient as a 'team' would be determinative", majority op. p. 153, the practical effect of this Court's majority opinion in Sargent v. Commissioner, supra is that the personal services furnished by a team-sports member to his or her personal service corporation will not be recognized for Federal income tax purposes.

[**82] The judicially created team-sports doctrine is an unprecedented alternative test first applied in Sargent v. Commissioner, supra. This doctrine negated the first prong of the traditional two-prong control test which had evolved from the assignment of income rule enunciated in Lucas v. Earl, 281 U.S. 111, 115 (1930).

24: LEAVELL V CM

2 The majority claims a disavowal of the team-sports doctrine, but espouses a chameleonic "manner and means" test under which a team athlete will be precluded from incorporating his or her services. Although the majority acknowledges that "the mere use of the word 'team' to describe the organization that is the recipient of personal [*177] services is not determinative of employer status", majority op. p. 152, I am unable to envision a situation when a member of a "team" could incorporate his or her services under the majority's manner and means test. 3 The manner and means test is merely the Sargent team-sports doctrine reintroduced and redesigned under yet another name. I ask myself "What's in a name?" and I conclude "that which we call a rose By any other name would smell as sweet". Shake-speare, Romeo and Juliet, act II, [**83] sc. ii, 43.

> 2 As stated in the majority opinion: "Sargent was the first case involving a personal service corporation in which * * * [the Court] applied the assignment of income doctrine by reference to the common law test for determining whether an employer-employee relationship existed between the service recipient and the individual service provider." Majority op. p 150; but see infra note 12. Although the majority opinion purports to reapply this common law test to the facts at bar, it does not explain the need to abandon the traditional analysis for assignment of income cases. By failing to do so, the majority opinion does not justify its need to depart from the traditional methodology. Moreover, the majority opinion fails to address adequately a critical part of the reasoning of the Court of Appeals in Sargent v. Commissioner, supra, finding error in the fact that this Court did not apply such a common law test to the "team member" in Pflug v. Commissioner, T.C. Memo. 1989-615. The majority opinion chooses to refute the Court of Appeals' reasoning concerning our inconsistent application in Pflug v. Commissioner, supra, in a brief footnote. See majority op. p. 154 note 14.

[**84]

> 3 The majority has also not listed such an example.

The typical personal service corporation (PSC) scenario involves three players: A PSC, its shareholder/service provider, and a service recipient. As explained below, the focus of the traditional assignment of income methodology is on the relationships between the service provider and his or her PSC, on the one hand, and the PSC and the service recipient, on the other. 4 The team-sports doctrine changes

24: LEAVELL V CM

this focus. The team-sports doctrine concentrates primarily on the relationship between the service provider and the service recipient. The manner and means test does likewise. Indeed, the manner and means test forces the Court to examine meticulously the relationship between a service recipient and service provider, and determine whether the service recipient "controls" the service provider notwithstanding a bona fide employment contract that was executed between the service [*178] provider and his or her PSC. In the case of a member of a team sport, such as petitioner, he or she will never meet the majority's manner and means test due to, [**85] for example: (1) The perceived control that a coach has over the team's members, (2) the need for team members to blend their talents and perform as a team in order to win, and (3) the inherent impossibility for each member of the team to schedule independently when, where, and how he or she will furnish his or her services to the team.

> 4 The Congress responded to a perceived abuse in this area by enacting sec. 269A. Sec. 269A generally allows the Commissioner to allocate items between a PSC and its employee/shareholders in order to reflect clearly the income of the employee/shareholders or the PSC, if the "principal purpose" for the PSC is the avoidance or evasion of Federal income tax. Respondent did not determine or argue that sec. 269A applies to the instant case. In fact, she has disavowed its application by making the following stipulations:
>
> 22. The corporation, Allen Leavell, Inc., was formed for the primary purpose of creating flexibility for Allen Leavell to act as a free agent or claim the benefits of free agency in the event the Houston Rockets failed to release him from obligations imposed by the Uniform Player Contract.
>
> 23. Although certain tax benefits may have resulted from the incorporation of Allen Leavell, Inc. by Allen Leavell, the corporation was not formed for the principal purpose of evading or avoiding federal income taxes by securing the benefits of deductions, credits, or other allowances which would not otherwise be available.
>
> 24. Accordingly, based upon the facts of this case, the parties agree and Respondent concedes that no allocation of income, deductions, or credits is to be made under the specific authority of I.R.C. section 269A.

24: LEAVELL V CM

[Emphasis added.]

> Given that respondent has, in effect, stipulated that the tool Congress has given to the Government to deal with perceived abuses by PSC's is not applicable and that the income in question is not to be reallocated under that section, the majority opinion's use of the "manner and means" test is nothing more than a solution in search of a problem.

[**86] The Court developed the team-sports doctrine in Sargent v. Commissioner, supra at 580, based on the Court's belief that the nature of team sports "involves a high level of control over player activity by coaches and managers". Id. at 580. The majority opinion states that it is not applying this doctrine to the facts at hand. Instead, the majority pronounces, a service provider (and not his or her PSC) is the earner of income if the facts and circumstances show that "the service recipient has the right to control the manner and means by which the services are performed." Majority op. pp. 149, 154-155. In making its pronouncement, the majority appears to recognize that it is inappropriate to deny the right to incorporate to an individual merely because he or she is a member of a team. At the same time, however, the majority adopts a manner and means test that leads to the same result. The majority's attempt to dignify its result by utilizing this facts and circumstances test is not persuasive. The rules that apply to assignment of income cases involving a PSC and its sole shareholder/service provider have been firmly embedded [**87] in our jurisprudence throughout the last 65 years.

In Justice Oliver Wendell Holmes' seminal opinion in Lucas v. Earl, 281 U.S. 111 (1930), the Supreme Court enunciated the bedrock principle that income is taxed to him or her who earns it. Assignments of income, "however skillfully devised", cannot escape Federal income taxation by anticipatory arrangements. Id. at 115; see also United States v. Basye, 410 U.S. 441, 449-451 (1973); Commissioner v. Culbertson, 337 U.S. 733, 739-740 (1949). Pursuant to the Court's directive, courts continue to dissect skillfully devised arrangements to determine the true earner of income. The instant case, involving a professional basketball player and his wholly owned personal service corporation, requires this Court to do just that. In so doing, we must: (1) Consider Justice [*179] Holmes' opinion in Lucas v. Earl, supra, and its progeny, and (2) reconsider the core of our opinion in Sargent v. Commissioner, supra.

In Lucas v. Earl, supra, a husband and wife [**88] agreed to be joint tenants of all the property acquired by them during their marriage. The husband later earned salary and fees from personal service contracts to which his wife was not a

24: LEAVELL V CM

party. The husband allocated 50 percent of this income to his wife pursuant to their agreement. Respondent disregarded their agreement and determined that the husband was taxable on 100 percent of his personal service income. Id. at 113-114. In upholding respondent's determination, the Supreme Court stated:

There is no doubt that * * * [a predecessor to section 61] could tax salaries to those who earned them and provide that the tax could not be escaped by antici-patory arrangements and contracts however skillfully devised to prevent the salary when paid from vesting even for a second in the man who earned it. That seems to us the import of the statute before us and we think that no distinction can be taken according to the motives leading to the arrangement by which the fruits are attributed to a different tree from that on which they grew. [Lucas v. Earl, supra at 114-115.]

This assignment of income doctrine, however, does not exist [**89] in a vacuum. The doctrine coexists with other, equally well-settled rules of tax law. For exam-ple, in Moline Properties, Inc. v. Commissioner, 319 U.S. 436, 438-439 (1943), the Supreme Court stated that a wholly owned corporation is a separate taxable entity that can operate only through its employees, and an individual can mini-mize his or her taxes through a corporate form of business. As long as the corpo-ration is involved in a legitimate business activity, the Court stated, any tax advantages properly flowing from incorporation are free from attack by the Government. [5] As the Court stated:

The doctrine of corporate entity fills a useful purpose in business life. Whether the purpose be to gain an advantage under the law of the state of incorporation or to avoid or to comply with the demands of creditors or [*180] to serve the cre-ator's personal or undisclosed convenience, so long as that purpose is the equiva-lent of business activity or is followed by the carrying on of business by the cor-poration, the corporation remains a separate taxable entity. * * * [Moline Properties, Inc. v. Commissioner, supra at 438-439; [**90] fn. refs. omitted.]

> 5 The Supreme Court observed, however, that there are recog-nized exceptions to treating a corporation as a separate taxable entity. For example, the Court stated: "the corporate form may be disregarded where it is a sham or unreal. In such situations the form is a bald and mischievous fiction." Moline Properties, Inc. v. Commissioner, 319 U.S. 436, 439 (1943). As documented by the facts at hand, the instant case is not one that warrants disre-gard for the corporate form.

24: LEAVELL V CM

With the tension between Lucas v. Earl, supra, and Moline Properties, Inc. v. Commissioner, supra, in mind, this Court pronounced: "The policy favoring the recognition of corporations as entities independent of their shareholders requires that we not ignore the corporate form so long as the corporation actually conducts business." [6] Keller v. Commissioner, 77 T.C. 1014, 1031 (1981), affd. 723 F.2d 58 (10th Cir. 1983). [**91] The majority disregards this pronouncement. Indeed, the taxpayer today is similar to the taxpayer in Keller v. Commissioner, supra. In Keller v. Commissioner, supra, respondent challenged a wholly owned professional corporation formed by a pathologist to hold his partnership interest in a medical partnership. Contemporaneously with forming this corporation, the pathologist agreed to render his services to the corporation in exchange for the corporation's paying him certain annual compensation. Id. at 1016-1017. Respondent argued then, as she similarly argues today, that the pathologist was taxable on 100 percent of the income received by the professional corporation under the doctrines of lack of business purpose and substance over form, and because the pathologist was the "true earner" of the income. Respondent argued that the pathologist's formation of the professional corporation accompanied by his execution of the employment contract constituted an anticipatory assignment of income to the corporation. Id. at 1030.

> 6 In the instant case, respondent is asking the Court to ignore corporation to the extent that it marketed petitioner's professional basketball services.

[**92] This Court rejected respondent's arguments. The Court recognized the existence of the pathologist's professional corporation and refused to reallocate the income from the corporation to the service-provider/pathologist under the assignment of income doctrine. The Court observed that an employer/employee relationship existed in the case, stating that "We find that an employment relationship was created in this case by the employment agreement and that it was [*181] maintained by the parties to the agreement after the execution". [7] Id. at 1032.

> 7 The Congress responded to the fact pattern of Keller v. Commissioner, 77 T.C. 1014, 1031 (1981), affd. 723 F.2d 58 (10th Cir. 1983), by enacting sec. 269A, applicable to taxable years beginning after Dec. 31, 1982. See supra note 4. According to the legislative history, "The conferees intend that the provisions * * * [of sec. 269A] overturn the results reached in cases like Keller v. Commissioner, 77 T.C. 1014 (1981), where the corporation served no meaningful business purpose other than to

secure tax benefits which would not otherwise be available." H. Rept. 97-760, at 633-634 (1982), 1982-2 C.B. 600, 679-680. Because respondent conceded that no allocation is to be made under sec. 269A, the Court should apply the analysis that we applied in Keller v. Commissioner, supra and reach a result that is consistent thereto. The majority, however, does not. It develops a new analysis to apply to the fact pattern of Keller v. Commissioner, supra, and reaches a result that is contrary to our opinion there. In so doing, the majority has obviated the need for respondent to utilize the precise tool that the Congress gave her to deal with fact patterns similar to Keller v. Commissioner, supra, such as the facts at hand.

[**93] Our approach in Keller v. Commissioner, supra with respect to the assignment of income issue was followed in Haag v. Commissioner, 88 T.C. 604, 610-614 (1987), affd. without published opinion 855 F.2d 855 (8th Cir. 1988); Bagley v. Commissioner, 85 T.C. 663, 674-676 (1985), affd. 806 F.2d 169 (8th Cir. 1986); Johnson v. Commissioner, 78 T.C. 882, 889-892 (1982), affd. without published opinion 734 F.2d 20 (9th Cir. 1984); Pacella v. Commissioner, 78 T.C. 604, 622 (1982); and Pflug v. Commissioner, T.C. Memo. 1989-615. In each of these cases, the Court held that income was not reallocable from a PSC to the service-provider under the assignment of income doctrine if the service-provider met both prongs of a two-prong control test evolving from case law beginning with Lucas v. Earl, 281 U.S. at 115. [8] Johnson v. Commissioner, supra at 891; see also sec. 31.3121(d)-1(c)(2), [**94] Employment Tax Regs. Under this two-prong test, a [*182] PSC controls the service-provider, and, hence, earns the income, if: (1) The service-provider is an employee of the PSC, and the PSC has the right to direct and control him or her in a meaningful sense, [9] see, e.g., Vnuk v. Commissioner, 621 F.2d 1318, 1320-1321 (8th Cir. 1980), affg. T.C. Memo. 1979-164; Bagley v. Commissioner, supra at 675-676; and (2) the PSC and the service-recipient have a contract or similar indicium recognizing the controlling position of the PSC, see, e.g., Pacella v. Commissioner, supra at 622; see also Haag v. Commissioner, supra at 612-614 (second prong met despite absence of written or formal contract between PSC and service-recipient; employment agreement existed between PSC and service-provider, and the service-recipient recognized the PSC as the entity through which the service-provider performed his services); Johnson v. Commissioner, supra at 893 (PSC was not the controller of the service-provider; as stated [**95] by the Court: "Crucial is the fact that there was no contract or agreement between the * * * [service-recipient] and * * * [the PSC]"). In connection with this two-prong test, Professors Bittker and Eustice

24: LEAVELL V CM

have stated that

Although the contours of this bifurcated control over the income test remain to be developed by the courts, a contract between a personal service corporation and its shareholder-employee should ordinarily be effective unless it (1) fails to supersede a prior contract between the shareholder-employee and the customers to whom the services are rendered, (2) is disregarded in practice, or (3) is ineffective under local law because the corporation cannot legally practice in the area. [Bittker & Eustice, Federal Income Taxation of Corporations and Shareholders, par 2.07[2], at 2-26 (5th ed. 1987); fn. ref. omitted.]

> 8 While recognizing that the assignment of income doctrine may apply in the corporate context, the Court has observed that this control test is better than the true earner test articulated in Lucas v. Earl, 281 U.S. 111, 115 (1930), because a corporation is an inanimate person that can earn service income only through the performance of its employees and agents. See, e.g., Bagley v. Commissioner, 85 T.C. 663, 675 (1985), affd. 806 F.2d 169 (8th Cir. 1986); Haag v. Commissioner, 88 T.C. 604, 610-611 (1987), affd. without published opinion 855 F.2d 855 (8th Cir. 1988); see also Vercio v. Commissioner, 73 T.C. 1246, 1254-1255 (1980). The control test generally asks the question: "Who controls the earning of the income, the individual or his or her corporation?" Johnson v. Commissioner, 78 T.C. 882, 891 (1982), affd. without published opinion 734 F.2d 20 (9th Cir. 1984); Bagley v. Commissioner, supra at 675. The majority does not ask or answer this question. By failing to do so, the majority ignores the importance of the following precedent in Schneer v. Commissioner, 97 T.C. 643, 659-660 (1991) (quoting Johnson v. Commissioner, supra at 890):

> "Recognition must be given to corporations as taxable entities which, to a great extent, rely upon the personal services of their employees to produce corporate income. When a corporate employee performs labors which give rise to income, it solves little merely to identify the actual laborer." * * * an employee of a personal service corporation * * * is outside the holding of Lucas v. Earl, supra, to some degree because of the "entity concept." The business entity is cast as the earner of the income, obviating the need to analyze whether there has been an assignment of income.

24: LEAVELL V CM

[**96]

> 9 The right to control an employee is usually evidenced by an employment contract between the PSC and the service-provider. See, e.g., Haag v. Commissioner, supra at 612 (employment agreement gave the PSC control over the service-provider's medical practice although the service-provider could unilaterally rescind, modify, or ignore the agreement), affd. without published opinion 855 F.2d 855 (8th Cir. 1988). As observed by the Court of Appeals for the Eighth Circuit, there exists "ample Tax Court precedent which upholds the sanctity of contractual relations between taxpayers and their respective personal service corporations." Sargent v. Commissioner, 929 F.2d 1252, 1258 (8th Cir. 1991), revg. 93 T.C. 572 (1989).

As she did in Sargent v. Commissioner, 93 T.C. 572 (1989), revd. 929 F.2d 1252 (8th Cir. 1991), respondent urges us to reject this two-prong test and apply the team-sports doctrine that she advocated in Sargent [**97] . [10] Currently viewing this issue in the light of a different record, and with the benefit of the [*183] opinion of the Court of Appeals for the Eighth Circuit, we should decline respondent's invitation to abandon the traditional assignment of income analysis. Instead, we should decide the Sargent v. Commissioner, supra, issue according to the traditional analysis, generally developed by the Supreme Court and this Court, and the contract theory enunciated by the Court of Appeals for the Eighth Circuit in Sargent v. Commissioner, 929 F.2d 1252 (8th Cir. 1991). We should not depart from this analysis because: (1) Lucas v. Earl, supra, and its progeny, provides a solid framework on which to decide the issue herein, (2) contrary tests, such as the teamsports doctrine and the manner and means test, are not adequate barometers for resolving a claim of an assignment of income because they disregard any valid contractual relationship existing between the employer and employee, and (3) it is inconsistent to apply a contrary method to an athlete merely because he or she is a member of a judicially defined team.

> 10 Respondent had announced the team-sports doctrine as her litigating position in G.C.M. 39553 (Sept. 3, 1986).

[**98] In Sargent v. Commissioner, supra, each taxpayer was a professional hockey player who formed a wholly owned PSC to negotiate with his professional hockey team, the club. [11] Each taxpayer entered into an employment agreement with his PSC whereby the taxpayer agreed that he would exclusively perform services for the PSC as a professional hockey player and consultant. On the same

24: LEAVELL V CM

day, each PSC entered into an agreement with the club whereby the PSC primarily agreed to furnish to the club the services of its employee/taxpayer as a hockey player and consultant; in return, the club agreed to pay the PSC specified remuneration. Each taxpayer, his PSC, and the club also entered into an agreement whereby: (1) The PSC represented to the club that the PSC had the [*184] right to cause its employee to perform services on its behalf, and (2) the PSC would cause the employee to perform the agreed-upon services to the club in order to fulfill the PSC's obligations under the agreement. [12]

> 11 Prior to the Tax Reform Act of 1986 (TRA), Pub. L. 99-514, 100 Stat. 2085, the Code provided numerous incentives for a professional to incorporate his or her services. For example, a service-provider could take modest salaries from his PSC and, in effect, divert income from his or her personal services to his or her PSC; before the TRA, the maximum marginal rate of tax for corporations was lower than the maximum marginal rate of tax for individuals. Similarly, the individual could adopt a fiscal year for the PSC which ended on the last day of the first month of his or her individual taxable year. With proper tax planning, the individual could then defer the recognition of the personal service income earned in one year until the next year by drawing the majority of his or her salary in the first month after the end of his or her taxable year. The TRA minimized many of these incentives. See, e.g., secs. 1, 11 (maximum corporate rate of tax higher than maximum individual rate of tax); sec. 441(i) (taxable year of a PSC generally must be the calendar year); see also sec. 11(b)(2) (certain PSC's are taxed at a flat rate of 35 percent, rather than at the graduated rates of tax in sec. 11(a) that are otherwise applicable to corporations); supra note 6.

[**99]

> 12 As is true in the case at hand, each taxpayer also personally guaranteed his PSC's obligations to the service-recipient. Sargent v. Commissioner, 93 T.C. 572 (1989). The Court in Sargent v. Commissioner, supra, found no relevance in this personal guarantee. The majority does. In my mind, the majority places too much emphasis on this fact. The personal guarantee of a 100-percent shareholder is commonly required in the business world. In this regard, the majority does not indicate how their analysis would apply to this everyday occurrence.

24: LEAVELL V CM

Following the execution of these agreements, each taxpayer played hockey for the club pursuant to his exclusive agreement with his PSC, and the club remitted payments for each taxpayer's services directly to his PSC. Each PSC, in turn, paid a portion of the payments to the taxpayer and contributed another portion of the payments to the PSC's pension plan. Each PSC withheld Federal income taxes and withheld and paid employment taxes in connection with the payments that it made to its employee/taxpayer. Sargent v. Commissioner, 93 T.C. at 573-577. [**100]

The Court held that each taxpayer was taxable on the entire amount paid to his PSC by the club. In so holding, the Court stated that the facts presented "a classic situation for the application of the assignment of income doctrine articulated in Lucas v. Earl, 281 U.S. 111 (1930), and its progeny," and turned aside our traditional analysis for deciding assignment of income cases, reasoning that "the nature of team sports is a critical element which must be taken into account in determining the existence of an employer/employee relationship in accordance with common law principles". [13] Sargent v. Commissioner, 93 T.C. at 579-581, 583. Based on this "critical element", the Court proceeded to hold that each taxpayer was controlled by his team, the club, rather than his PSC. The Court held that each taxpayer was an employee of the club, rather than his PSC, and was taxable on the amounts paid by the club to his PSC for his services. Id. at 583.

> 13 In abandoning our traditional analysis, the Court stated that the Court had never addressed whether an employer/employee relationship existed in any of our prior assignment of income opinions. Sargent v. Commissioner, 93 T.C. at 582. As subsequently noted by the Court of Appeals for the Eighth Circuit, however, "Each time the legitimacy of the employee's relationship with the * * * [PSC] was raised [in our prior assignment of income cases], the Tax Court pointed to the existence of a contractual relationship between the * * * [PSC] and the employee/service-provider as the rationale for upholding the legal significance of the PSC." Sargent v. Commissioner, 929 F.2d at 1258.

[**101] [*185] The Court of Appeals for the Eighth Circuit disagreed. The appellate court firmly rejected the team-sports doctrine and focused on the contractual relationship between each taxpayer and his PSC. Sargent v. Commissioner, 929 F.2d at 1258. In holding that the amounts were taxable to the PSC's, the appellate court determined that section 31.3121(d)-1(c)(2), Employment Tax Regs., and this Court's prior opinions, directed that the PSC's (and not the club) were the

24: LEAVELL V CM

employers of the taxpayers because both prongs of the two-prong test were met; namely:

(1) Each taxpayer was an employee of his PSC whom the PSC had the right to direct or control in some meaningful way; and

(2) a contract or similar indicium recognizing the PSC's controlling position existed between each PSC and the club.

Respondent contends that the Court of Appeals for the Eighth Circuit erroneously reversed our decision in Sargent v. Commissioner, supra. Respondent argues in her brief that "the Eighth Circuit employed a superficial form over substance analysis relying on the mere existence of the taxpayers' contracts with their respective * * * [PSC's], rather than the control [**102] imposed directly on the taxpayers by the team's coaching staff and management." (Emphasis added.) The majority agrees. Majority op. p. 154. Both are mistaken. The PSC's right to control its employee/taxpayer in Sargent v. Commissioner, supra, was evidenced by more than the "mere existence" of the employment contract. The contractual relationships at issue there met the two-prong control test mentioned above. [14] The majority's holding to the contrary fails to appreciate the well-settled principle that a wholly owned corporation is an entity separate and apart from its shareholder. [*186] See, e.g., Moline Properties, Inc. v. Commissioner, 319 U.S. 436 (1943). The majority's disregard for this well-settled principle is clearly seen from its following statement: "we believe that Judge Arnold's dissent in Sargent captured the essence of that case when he wrote: 'The idea that the coach issued orders to Sargent and Christoff in their capacity as corporate officers, which orders they then relayed to themselves as corporate employees, is fanciful.'" Majority op. p. 155. As a point of fact, this "fanciful" scenario is present (and, with the exception [**103] of today, respected) in any solely owned corporation setting where the sole shareholder is also an officer and employee of the corporation. The fact that an individual shareholder may serve simultaneously in the role of officer and employee of his or her wholly owned corporation is indisputable and flows naturally from the fact that he or she may form such a corporation.

> [14] I do not mean to suggest that the "mere existence" of an employment contract may or may not be enough to satisfy the two-prong control test. The Court need not resolve that issue today. The record in Sargent v. Commissioner, supra, as well as the record at bar, evidences an employer/employee relationship between the PSC and the service-provider through more than an employment contract. With respect to Sargent v. Commissioner,

24: LEAVELL V CM

93 T.C. at 573-577, I note: (1) Following the receipt of legal advice, each taxpayer formed his PSC for a legitimate business purpose that involved "selling" his services to the club as an employee of the PSC, (2) the club entered into an agreement whereby each PSC represented to the club that the PSC had the right to cause its employee to perform services on its behalf, (3) the club remitted payments for each taxpayer's services directly to their PSC's, (4) each PSC withheld Federal income taxes, and withheld and paid employment taxes, in connection with the payment of service income to the taxpayers, (5) the PSC's filed the necessary employer/employee payroll tax returns with the Commissioner, and (6) the club recognized and respected the employment contracts between each taxpayer and his PSC.

[**104] The majority states that "the most important factor" for deciding the issue at hand is the "right to control the manner and means by which the individual service provider renders the services for which compensation is being paid." Majority op. p. 155. I disagree. The fact that the majority is mistaken is seen from our opinions outside of Sargent v. Commissioner, supra. For example, the facts of the instant case are similar to the facts of Johnson v. Commissioner, 78 T.C. 882 (1982), affd. without published opinion 734 F.2d 20 (9th Cir. 1984). In Johnson the taxpayer (Johnson) was a basketball player with the San Francisco Warriors (Warriors) of the National Basketball Association (NBA). In 1974, Johnson signed a contract with an unrelated corporation (PMSA) that: (1) Gave PMSA the right to Johnson's services in professional sports for 6 years starting on August 16, 1974, (2) gave PMSA the right to control Johnson's services in professional sports, and (3) obligated PMSA to pay Johnson $ 1,500 a month. Johnson also signed a Uniform Player Contract with the Warriors that obligated him to play basketball for the Warriors [**105] for the 1974-75 and 1975-76 basketball seasons. Id. at 884. In the following year, 1975, Johnson assigned his rights under the 1974 Uniform Player Contract to a second unrelated corporation (EST). The Warriors remitted the contract payments for Johnson's services directly to EST following that assignment. In deciding the assignment of income issue there, the Court did not discuss the majority's means and methods test. The [*187] Court simply applied the two-prong test. With respect to the first prong, the Court looked solely to the contracts to determine whether it was met:

we accept arguendo that the * * * [PMSA-Johnson] agreement was a valid contract which required the payments with respect to * * * [Johnson's] performance as a basketball player ultimately to be made to PMSA or EST. * * * We also accept arguendo that the * * * [PMSA-Johnson] agreement gave PMSA a right of

24: LEAVELL V CM

control over * * * [Johnson's] services * * *. Thus, the first element is satisfied. * * * [Johnson v. Commissioner, supra at 891-892.] [15]

> 15 The Court ultimately held against Johnson because the Warriors did not have an agreement with either PMSA or EST that addressed the taxpayer's basketball services. Accord Johnson v. United States, 698 F.2d 372 (9th Cir. 1982). In the instant case, by contrast, petitioner's basketball services were discussed in both his contract with corporation and the Rockets' contract with corporation.

[**106] Likewise, in Pflug v. Commissioner, T.C. Memo. 1989-615, a case involving a taxpayer/actress, the Court passed on whether the taxpayer was an employee of a PSC or an independent contractor. [16] As we had done in Johnson v. Commissioner, supra, the Court looked exclusively to the two-prong control test and concluded that the taxpayer was the PSC's employee. The Court relied solely on the contract between the taxpayer and the PSC and held that the PSC had the right to control the taxpayer by virtue of its employment contract with her. As later observed by the Court of Appeals for the Eighth Circuit in Sargent v. Commissioner, 929 F.2d at 1257:

This Court is perplexed to find that those same contractual arrangements which were dispositive of the issue of "control" in Pflug were summarily discarded in the case before us. By the same token, those same "team" factors which were dispositive of the issue of control in the case before us were not even discussed in Pflug.

Was not Joanne Pflug a part of a team every bit as "controlled" as Sargent and Christoff? Like a hockey team in which different [**107] players assume different roles to insure success, the members of Pflug's team included the cast, writers, directors, and producers all working toward the common goal [*188] of producing a successful TV series. More importantly, just as a hockey player has a generalized set of plays tailored to fit his talents and the talents of his teammates, so, too, Ms. Pflug's "plays" included movements carefully choreographed to mesh with other cast members, a script prepared for her to follow, cue cards to insure that little or no deviation from the designed "play" occurred, and numerous retakes to guarantee that ultimate control vested in the hands of the studio, not Ms. Pflug's PSC. Nevertheless, the Tax Court concluded that Ms. Pflug was an employee of her PSC.

There can be little question that Ms. Pflug was part of a team under more strin-

24: LEAVELL V CM

gent production controls than those placed on either Sargent or Christoff by the Club. But, as the Tax Court concluded, "* * * by virtue of the contract [Pflug] entered with Charwool [the PSC], Charwool had the requisite right to control [Pflug]." * * *

Appellants' contractual arrangements, which were every bit as bona fide as those entered into by Ms. [**108] Pflug, should and do provide the requisite control for Appellants to be considered employees of their respective PSCs. [Fn. ref. and citation omitted.]

> 16 In Pflug v. Commissioner, T.C. Memo. 1989-615, the taxpay-
> er contracted with her husband's wholly owned PSC to perform
> her acting services exclusively as its employee. Subsequently, the
> taxpayer and her husband separated, and, in June 1982, the tax-
> payer severed her relationship with the PSC. From 1975 until
> June 1982, all contracts for the taxpayer's acting services were
> executed between the PSC, as the taxpayer's employer, and the
> service-recipients (producers). The producers paid the PSC all
> amounts for the taxpayer's services and did not pay or withhold
> any employment taxes with regard to these amounts; the PSC, in
> turn, paid a salary to the taxpayer and paid employment taxes
> with respect to the salary. The PSC included on its Federal
> income tax returns the amounts paid to it by the producers and
> deducted its payments to the taxpayer as wage expense.

[**109] Accordingly, reverting to the traditional approach and applying the two-prong control test to the case at hand, I would hold that both prongs were met. With regard to the first prong, petitioner was corporation's employee, and corporation had the right to (and in fact did) control him in a meaningful sense. Corporation was a valid corporation formed under the laws of Texas for legitimate business purposes; i.e., to serve as petitioner's employer for his basketball services, personal appearances, and endorsement opportunities. [17] Corporation also continuously operated in a business-like manner, e.g., corporation followed corporate formalities, had its own checking account, filed tax returns, incurred liabilities, had a payroll, and entered into contracts. Although petitioner may have formed corporation, in part, with an eye towards minimizing taxation, "one may so arrange his affairs that his taxes shall be as low as possible; he is not bound to choose that pattern which will best pay the Treasury; there is not even a patriotic duty to increase one's taxes." Helvering v. Gregory, 69 F.2d 809, 810 (2d Cir. 1934), affd. 293 U.S. 465 (1934). [**110]

24: LEAVELL V CM

17 Respondent has not disputed corporation's viability to the extent that corporation was petitioner's employer for purposes other than to market his basketball services. In this regard, the record does not indicate that corporation controlled petitioner's personal services with regard to his basketball services in any less of a significant manner than it controlled his personal services with regard to his personal appearances and endorsements. Concluding that corporation is not a viable entity with respect to petitioner's basketball services, but not with respect to his personal appearances and endorsements, is a distinction without a difference and is arbitrary.

[*189] With regard to petitioner's relationship with corporation, petitioner was corporation's employee. Petitioner agreed to provide his exclusive basketball services to third parties in his capacity as an employee of corporation, and corporation had the right to "sell" petitioner's services to any team during the time period specified in the 1984 Uniform [**111] Player Contract. Corporation also had the right to designate the professional basketball team for which petitioner would play basketball and had the right to dictate the time and place of petitioner's personal appearances and endorsement opportunities. Although petitioner did not introduce into evidence a written employment contract between himself and corporation, I, as the trier of fact, found the trial witness' testimony on the existence of such an employment agreement to be credible and undisputed by respondent. The following facts also exemplify the existence of an employment agreement between corporation and petitioner: (1) Corporation was specifically formed to serve as petitioner's employer for his basketball services, personal appearances, and endorsement opportunities; (2) Mr. Luchnick negotiated the 1984 Uniformed Player Contract, and did so in his capacity as one of corporation's officers; (3) Mr. Patterson signed the 1984 Uniform Player Contract on behalf of the Rockets, and did so with the understanding that the Rockets were obtaining petitioner's basketball services in his capacity as an employee of corporation; (4) the Rockets dealt with corporation and respected [**112] both its corporate form and its employer/employee relationship with petitioner; (5) corporation issued petitioner a 1985 Form W-2 to inform him that it had paid him wages during the 1985 calendar year (corporation would have issued petitioner a 1985 Form 1099-MISC if corporation had wanted to inform petitioner that it had paid him nonemployee compensation during that year); and (6) petitioner reported his compensation from corporation as wage income.

That petitioner was an employee of corporation is further seen from the NBA and the Rockets' recognition of corporation as petitioner's employer. The record is

24: LEAVELL V CM

barren of any suggestion or implication that petitioner, corporation, or the Rockets ignored the employment agreement under which corporation employed petitioner. When a taxpayer, such as petitioner, has exercised considerable bargaining power in arm's-length [*190] negotiations over the manner in which he or she will provide his or her services to a recipient, the Court should weigh heavily the parties' belief in the type of employment relationship that they created. Penn v. Howe-Baker Engrs., Inc., 898 F.2d 1096, 1103 n.9 (5th Cir. 1990) (parties' [**113] intent is a "significant factor" when weighing the common law factors that distinguish an employee from an independent contractor). [18] The majority has not done so. [19]

> [18] The majority holds that petitioner is a "professional" as that term is used in Professional & Executive Leasing Co. v. Commissioner, 862 F.2d 751 (9th Cir. 1988), affg. 89 T.C. 225 (1987). The majority, therefore, concludes that petitioner is subject to a lower standard in determining whether he should be considered an employee of the Rockets. Notwithstanding my disagreement with the majority's test in the first place, I believe that the majority has misapplied the term "professional" as it was used in Professional & Executive Leasing Co. v. Commissioner, supra. The term "professional" as used in Professional & Executive Leasing Co. applied to individuals who were engaged in a licensed profession, such as doctors and attorneys. In our case, petitioner is a basketball player who is called a professional in order to distinguish him from an amateur.

> [19] With respect to petitioner's arrangement as an employee of corporation, the legitimacy of such an arrangement in the taxable year in issue is also discerned from the fact that the NBA prohibited corporate employers of NBA players after that year. Such a prohibition by the NBA would have been unnecessary had the NBA considered these corporate employers to be shams.

[**114] In connection with the second prong of the two-part test, the PSC (corporation) and the service-recipient (Rockets) had a contract or similar indicium recognizing the controlling position of corporation. The 1984 Uniform Player Contract evidenced the relationship between corporation and the Rockets and was reached following arm's-length negotiations between Mr. Patterson and Mr. Luchnick. In negotiating the 1984 Uniform Player Contract, Mr. Patterson was acting as an officer of the Rockets, and Mr. Luchnick was acting as an officer of corporation. By virtue of the 1984 Uniform Player Contract, the Rockets recog-

24: LEAVELL V CM

nized and appreciated that petitioner was an employee of corporation, and respected the employer/employee relationship existing between corporation and petitioner. The Rockets also issued corporation a 1985 Form 1099-MISC, reporting the amount of compensation that the Rockets paid to corporation during the 1985 calendar year, and did not pay or withhold payroll or income taxes on this compensation. Corporation, in turn, issued petitioner a 1985 Form W-2 reporting the amount of compensation that it had paid to him during that calendar year.

In conclusion, I would hold that [**115] the $ 204,333 is not includable in petitioner's gross income because both prongs of the two-prong control test were met. Because the majority chooses to reach a contrary result by adopting and applying [*191] a result-oriented manner and means test, I respectfully dissent.

HAMBLEN, JACOBS, and WELLS, JJ., agree with this dissent.